Empire of
the People

AMERICAN POLITICAL THOUGHT

Wilson Carey McWilliams and Lance Banning

Founding Editors

Empire of the People

Settler Colonialism and the Foundations of Modern Democratic Thought

Adam Dahl

University Press of Kansas

Published by the University Press of Kansas (Lawrence, Kansas 66045), which was organized by the Kansas Board of Regents and is operated and funded by Emporia State University, Fort Hays State University, Kansas State University, Pittsburg State University, the University of Kansas, and Wichita State University

Published by the University Press of Kansas (Lawrence, Kansas 66045), which was organized by the Kansas Board of Regents and is operated and funded by Emporia State University, Fort Hays State University, Kansas State University, Pittsburg State University, the University of Kansas, and Wichita State University

Library of Congress Cataloging-in-Publication Data

Names: Dahl, Adam, author.
Title: Empire of the people : settler colonialism and the foundations of modern democratic thought / Adam Dahl.
Description: Lawrence : University Press of Kansas, [2018] | Series: American political thought | Includes bibliographical references and index.
Identifiers: LCCN 2017054864
ISBN 9780700626069 (cloth : alk. paper)
ISBN 9780700626076 (pbk. : alk. paper)
ISBN 9780700626083 (ebook)
Subjects: LCSH: United States—Territorial expansion—Political aspects. |Land settlement—Political aspects—United States—History. | Indians of |North America—Colonization. | Democracy—United States—History. Manifest Destiny.
Classification: LCC E179.5 .D125 2018 | DDC 973.1—dc23.
LC record available at https://lccn.loc.gov/2017054864.

British Library Cataloguing-in-Publication Data is available.

One can speak, then, of the fall of an empire at that moment when, though all of the paraphernalia of power remain intact and visible and seem to function, neither the citizen-subject within the gates nor the indescribable hordes outside it believe in the morality or the reality of the kingdom anymore—when no one, any longer, anywhere, aspires to the empire's standards.

—James Baldwin, "The House of Bondage" (1980)

CONTENTS

ACKNOWLEDGMENTS

Like most books by first-time authors, this one also began in graduate school and thus owes an enormous debt to my mentors there. First and foremost, Joan Tronto and Joe Soss deserve thanks. Joan patiently followed the project at every step, and she has been supportive even when I wasn't entirely clear about exactly what I was doing. As an assistant professor stumbling through my new life on the tenure-track, I was graciously helped by Joan in navigating the publication process. Joe saw my research interests twist and turn in numerous directions over the past number of years, and at times he could better express what I was up to than I myself could. He continues to be a valued friend and mentor from whom I continue to learn. Liz Beaumont provided crucial guidance and help at key moments, and she encouraged me to keep going even when I thought I hit a dead end. Dara Strolovitch always pushed me on difficult questions and issues, and the book is undoubtedly stronger because of it. Antonio Vazquez-Arroyo was continually enthusiastic about the project, and his teaching on how to do ideological history has significantly shaped my own intellectual approach. He still serves as an inspiring model of friendship, mentorship, and intellectual engagement.

Charmaine Chua, Garnet Kindervater, and Zein Murib all read numerous chapter drafts. In addition to being good friends, they were always willing to let me bounce ideas off them even when they had their own things to work on. David Temin has read more drafts than I can remember and has helped me in everything from honing the argument to finessing the title. Azer Binnet, Ashley English, David Forrest, Caleb Goltz, Matt Hindman, Chase Hobbs-Morgan, Darrah McCracken, Eli Myerhoff, Bryan Nakayama, Libby Sharrow, Chris Stone, and Sergio Valverde all offered comments on earlier drafts at some point. Joe Lowndes, Nancy Luxon, Paulina Ochoa Espejo, Sean Parson, Jennifer Pitts, Aziz Rana, Rogers Smith, Sharon Stanley, and Justin Wert offered helpful comments on chapter drafts at later stages of the project. Several other colleagues and scholars have also lent me their ears and offered helpful advice and encouragement along the way: Barbara Arneil, Sean Beienburg, Kevin Bruyneel, Edmund Fong, Paul Frymer, Daragh Grant, Karuna Mantena, Charles Mills, Jeanne Morefield, Robert Nichols,

Mark Rifkin, Nick Smith, Lisa Wedeen, Elizabeth Wingrove, and Robinson Woodward-Burns.

The writing of this book would have been impossible without crucial financial support from the Mellon Foundation and the American Council of Learned Societies, which provided me with a fellowship that allowed me to write free from teaching responsibilities and conduct archival research in Chicago and New York. Staff at the New York Historical Society, the New York Public Library, and the Newberry Library also provided assistance during my visits.

Several other institutions have also provided crucial support in the writing of this book. My colleagues at the University of the South helped protect my time as a young faculty member. My new colleagues at the University of Massachusetts, Amherst have been thoroughly supportive, intellectually and practically.

Kim Hogeland at the University Press of Kansas was enthusiastic about the project early on and judiciously saw it through to publication. She garnered three reviews that proved to be extremely helpful. Kennan Ferguson, Alexander Hirsch, and one anonymous reviewer all offered critical but constructive comments that undoubtedly made the book stronger. An earlier version of chapter 6 appeared as "Nullifying Settler Democracy: William Apess and the Paradox of Settler Sovereignty," Polity, 48 (April 2016): 279–304. Parts of Chapters 1 and 2 appeared as "Commercial Conquest: Empire and Property in the Early U.S. Republic," American Political Thought, 5 (Summer 2016): 421–445. Thanks to the journals for allowing me to reprint them.

My family has been most important in helping me stay sane throughout the long process of writing and editing. My parents, Pam and Nelson, were always supportive and eager to hear about my progress on the book. My brothers, Nate and Tyler, couldn't have cared less what I was working on, but spending time with them over the summers helped ease the stress of writing. Gouda, Mali, and Harmon would like to think they helped, but the most I can say is that they provided much-needed distractions when the pressures of writing became immense. Most importantly, I would like to thank Laura Attanasio for her grace, patience, and intellect. Between picking up the slack around the house when I was too "busy" to help and listening to me ramble on about nineteenth-century American politics and culture, she has been a wonderful and insightful partner in life and living.

Empire of
the People

Introduction

The Settler Colonial Foundations of Modern Democratic Thought

"We seek not the empire of the sword—not the empire of the Inquisition—not the empire of despotism; but the empire of the people—the empire of the rights of man."
— Daniel Ullmann, The Course of Empire (1856)

Rethinking "Colonial America"

American democracy owes its origins to the *colonial settlement* of North America by European colonists. Since the birth of the republic, observers have emphasized how American democratic thought and identity arose out of the distinct pattern by which English settlers colonized the new world. *Empire of the People* shows how dominant interpretive and historical currents of modern democratic theory have neglected the other side of this equation: the constitutive role of *colonial dispossession* in shaping democratic values and ideals.[1] By placing the development of American political thought and culture in the context of nineteenth-century settler colonialism, this book reveals how practices and ideologies of indigenous dispossession have laid the theoretical foundations of American democracy. Discussions of colonial America seldom take place in the context of broader debates about the legacies of European colonialism. As the literary critic Michael Warner states, "Very few sentences about colonial America would be significantly altered if the word 'colonial' were simply replaced by the word 'early.'"[2] If colonialism and empire entail the imposition of political rule and dependency status on colonized subjects, then American development is anticolonial to the extent that it was born out of revolt against empire. Yet by placing American democratic thought in the context of settler colonialism—a distinct form of colonialism aimed at the expropriation of native land rather than the exploitation of native labor—its colonial tendencies come into more direct focus.

Colonial settlement and colonial dispossession are two sides of the same coin. On the one hand, colonial settlement refers to the movement of people to a new political space in order to create a new socio-political order. "Settlement" and the related terms "colony" and "plantation" thus refer to the process by which settlers plant a colonial base that marks the origins of that society and establishes further dynamics of social, political, and cultural development. Rooted in the thinking of English theorists Sir Thomas More and Richard Hakluyt, English colonizers understood colonial settlement in agricultural terms as the planting of a seed from which self-perpetuating political communities would flourish. In its familiar etymology, the term "colonus" connotes both inhabitation and cultivation, combining processes of agriculture and settlement of foreign territories into a single process.[3] On the other hand, *colonial dispossession* entails the displacement of preexisting social and political forms to constitute a new political community. The spatial movement of settlers from metropolitan centers to colonial peripheries most often entails the dispossession of indigenous communities by divorcing them from their territorial and cultural foundations.

Despite the dual character of colonization, dominant narratives of American democracy rely on a bifurcated understanding that emphasizes the formative role of colonial settlement while neglecting colonial dispossession. Nowhere is this more evident than in one of the urtexts of American democratic identity, J. Hector St. John de Crèvecœur's *Letters from an American Farmer* (1782). In this seminal text of American political theory, Crèvecœur emphasizes the role of agricultural settlement in shaping key principles of democratic thought—pluralism, the rule of law, social equality, and popular sovereignty. For Crèvecœur, the novelty of American identity derives from the natural conditions of new world geography that prevent the formation of feudal institutions. Bound together by the common project of settlement, regardless of ethnic and religious differences, Americans are a "race of cultivators." In highlighting the centrality of land and nature in shaping this new American identity, Crèvecœur asks, "What should we American farmers be without the distinct possession of that soil?"[4] Although he emphasizes the process of colonial settlement, Crèvecœur disavows the centrality of colonial dispossession to the construction of democratic thought and culture.

In characterizing the process of colonizing the island of Nantucket, Crèvecœur wrote, "This happy settlement was not founded on intrusion, forcible entries, or blood. . . . Neither political nor religious broils, neither disputes with the natives, nor any other contentions, have in the least agitated or disturbed its detached society. Yet the first founders knew nothing either of Lycurgus or Solon, for this settlement has not been the work of eminent men or powerful legislators." When it comes to explaining "the political state of the natives," he noted that they "were not extirpated by fraud, violence, or injustice as hath been the case in so many provinces" but were naturally "hastening towards a total annihilation."[5] While he briefly acknowledges the colonial violence involved in other settlements, Crèvecœur masks the constitutive effects of colonial conquest on American democratic identity. In taking Nantucket as a microcosm for the settlement of the nation, Crèvecœur asserted that, in contrast to Europe, here "everything is modern, peaceful, and benign. Here we have had no war to desolate our fields."[6] Rather than a political process involving war and conquest, Crèvecœur presents settlement as a natural process. By colonizing the land, settlers become the corporeal incarnation of nature, subsuming the democratic characteristics of the landscape into the organic body politic. The basic features of American democratic peoplehood thus emerge from the land.

In treating the American founding as a natural process of colonial settlement rather than an act of "powerful legislators," Crèvecœur short-circuited what William Connolly calls "the paradox of political founding." Found most forcefully in Book II of Jean-Jacques Rousseau's *Social Contract*, the paradox of political founding illustrates the problems by which a people become a political people capable of ruling themselves: "For an emerging people to be capable of appreciating the sound maxims of politics and to follow the fundamental rules of statecraft, the effect would have to become the cause . . . men would be, prior to the advent of laws, what they ought to become by means of laws." For Rousseau, the "true constitution" of republics is "not engraved on marble or bronze, but in the hearts of citizens."[7] Yet citizens cannot develop the proper habits, customs, and opinions of republican self-rule without first having a system of good laws. To dissolve the chicken-or-egg type paradox, Rousseau introduced the figure of the legislator, who uses extra-legal means to establish the foundation of law. For Connolly, this points to a larger problem besetting all democratic governments—the fact that any political order is founded on extra-legal violence that stands outside of democratic legitimacy.[8]

In a manner emblematic of American political thought more generally, Crèvecœur's account of colonial settlement dissolved the paradox by disavowing colonial dispossession. This book traces the conceptual and theoretical lineages of this disavowal throughout the course of American democratic theory in the eighteenth and nineteenth centuries. In a material sense, colonial dispossession involves the construction of a new society on top of expropriated land. Conceptually, it entails the construction of a spatial imaginary that empties the territorial ground of democracy of its prior inhabitants by disavowing the presence of indigenous orders. I treat colonial dispossession less as a policy or institution than as a theoretical mechanism that allows settlers to ideologically obscure the foundational violence of colonial conquest. Colonial dispossession is a form of what Walter Benjamin calls "founding violence" or "law-making violence," a process by which the elimination of native life-forms enables the constitution of new legal, cultural, and political norms.[9] Such foundational violence establishes the basis of democratic sovereignty. As James Tully writes of settler colonial dispossession, "the ground of the [colonial] relation is the appropriation of the land, resources, and jurisdiction of the indigenous peoples, not only for the sake of resettlement and exploitation . . . but for the territorial foundation of the dominant [i.e., democratic] society itself."[10]

Thus, to uphold the legitimacy of American settler democracy, settler political thought must disavow the origins of democracy in colonial dispossession and in turn erase the political and historical presence of native peoples. It is important to clarify, however, that by focusing on the foundational disavowal of native dispossession, I do not mean a "politics of forgetting" or a form of "national amnesia."[11] Disavowal in ordinary language is a "refusal to acknowledge" and in psychoanalytic terms is "the refusal to recognize the reality of traumatic perception."[12] Disavowal is not simply a passive ignorance of native life-forms in the historical archive of colonial violence. It is an active refusal to historically and ethically grapple with the presence and political claims of indigenous peoples as well as the colonial violence that paved the way for the emergence of modern American democracy. While amnesia and forgetting are passive and might be noted merely by registering the silences in a text, disavowal implies the active and interpretive production of indigenous absence. In settler democratic thought, the absence of native conquest is not assumed or forgotten; it is discursively produced.[13] Consequently, the traces of disavowed colonial violence remain in historical and textual memory.

Focusing on the theoretical disavowal of colonial dispossession in democratic thought sheds new light on the familiar problem of the relationship between race and democracy. To explain the persistence of slavery in colonial Virginia and its centrality to emergent notions of political liberty, Edmund Morgan famously argued that slavery and freedom in the American political imagination, rather than being mutually exclusive, developed in relation to one another. In so doing, Morgan resisted the temptation to flip the script by casting slavery and oppression as dominant trends in colonial thought and advances in liberty and equality as the exception. In Morgan's account, racial slavery was not antithetical to American liberty, but laid the conceptual and economic foundation of freedom for white settlers. In a conceptual sense, American colonists developed their notions of freedom not despite but because of slavery by contrasting their own status as freemen with that of their slaves. In a material sense, individual freedom rested on the economic independence afforded by the profits from slave labor. At the political and collective level, then, the vast economic growth produced by slave labor enabled the emergence of a free American state and citizenry. The central problem for American colonists prior to the Revolution was the "struggle for a separate and equal station among the nations of the earth."[14] Slavery constituted freedom at both an individual and collective level, allowing colonists to develop their notions of political and individual liberty.

According to Morgan, slavery and liberty existed not in an oppositional or even identical relationship to one another, but in a web of contradictions, giving rise to what he calls "the American paradox of slavery and freedom, intertwined and interdependent, the rights of Englishmen supported on the wrongs of Africans."[15] While Morgan made these claims through analysis of literature in colonial Virginia, his emphasis was on slavery rather than indigenous dispossession. *Empire of the People* recasts the paradox of race to focus not just on the relationship between slavery and freedom, but also on the relationship between democracy and dispossession. Dispossession was not an unfortunate by-product of modern democracy, nor was settler colonial ideology an entirely separate political tradition from democratic thought. The two surged alongside each other and reinforced each other in their historical development. This pushes historically oriented scholars of race and politics in a different direction to bring questions of land and indigeneity back into the fold in studies of American political thought. Institutions and ideologies of conquest and colonization, as well as those of slavery and racial exclusion, were closely linked to the development of democratic ideals and institutions.

For all Morgan did to advance our understanding of the complex relationship between race and democracy, he neglected crucial dynamics of colonial America. By adhering to a periodization of "colonial America" as pre-republican and pre-independence, Morgan ignored the colonial dynamics of America that persisted not only into the republican period but also into the present. I thus propose to shift the meaning of "colonial America" to a theoretical register away from an exclusively historical register that casts the qualifier "colonial" in terms of temporal periodization. In its theoretical register, the idea of "colonial America" centers on the constitutive role of settler colonialism in shaping American democratic thought. Understood in this way, "colonial America" names not a phase of American intellectual and political development, but the settler colonial foundations of American democracy that continue to structure the basic features of modern democratic thought and politics.

The critical indigenous theorist Jodi Byrd helpfully highlights why political theorists have not sufficiently appreciated the centrality of settler colonialism to the making of modern democracy. Indigenous politics tend to get framed through a politics of race and racialization. As Byrd writes, "When the remediation of the colonization of American Indians is framed through discourses of racialization that can be redressed by further inclusion into the nation-state, there is significant failure to grapple with the fact that such discourses further reinscribe the original colonial injury."[16] By framing processes of colonization in terms of a politics of exclusion (the solution to which inclusion into the constitutional, multicultural state) rather than a politics of dispossession and sovereignty (the solution to which is the reclamation of indigenous governance), discourses of racialization in turn reinforce structures of settler sovereignty through the incorporation of indigenous peoples into the imperial state as the remedy for conquest. In a related way, treating the problem of colonization in terms of "internal colonialism" tends to cast indigenous peoples as "minorities within" settler states rather than as conquered and dispossessed populations. The idea of internal colonialism thus feeds "the construction of the United States as a multicultural nation that is struggling with the legacies of racism rather than as a colonialist power engaged in territorial expansion since its beginning."[17]

If we are to properly understand the settler colonial foundations of American democratic thought, we need alternative frameworks of analysis that capture the history of native communities in the United States as a process of colonization and dispossession. Recovering and contesting these historical elisions is essential because the enduring legacies of colonial dispossession and their disavowal counteract native claims to self-governance in the present.[18]

Democracy and Empire

Despite the fact that modern democratic thought is coexistent with and deeply implicated in empire from its inception, the writing of imperial and colonial histories of modern democracy has only just begun. Perhaps one of the most enduring conceptual frameworks in these efforts has been that of "liberal imperialism."[19] Although historians are still debating its complex and contested legacy, the core of liberal imperialism is a defense of European expansion on the basis of the unfitness of non-European subjects for liberal government. Its claim to embrace a "universal constituency" notwithstanding, liberalism employs a variety of exclusion clauses to justify the continued exploitation of colonial subjects and intervention in non-European societies. By privileging anthropological capacities rooted in Enlightenment culture, liberal imperialism exempts colonized societies from the promise of liberal ideals. As a result, colonized societies are relegated to the "waiting room of history" where they are subject to regimes of enlightened despotism before they can rule themselves through liberal principles.[20]

While scholars of imperial history and modern political thought have analyzed ideologies of liberal imperialism at the heart of the British and French empires, much less attention has been given to how ideologies and practices of settler expansion figured into the formation of American democratic theory. Despite a growing literature exploring how key concepts of European political thought were articulated in response to the politics of imperial expansion, the role of empire in American thought is severely understudied.[21] Rooted in new currents of scholarship, this book examines the ideological and cultural development of American democracy in the context of settler colonialism. Specifically, it examines the process by which democratic conceptions of freedom, popular sovereignty, consent, and equality emerged through practices and ideologies of settler colonization. In doing so, I develop the concept of *democratic empire* as a distinct ideological formation from liberal imperialism.

Despite their historical and theoretical sophistication, discussions of liberal imperialism fail to capture the distinct imperial and colonial dynamics of the nineteenth-century United States for two primary reasons.[22] First, they neglect the central role of popular sovereignty and constituent power in fostering settler colonial processes of expansion. Second, they center on the strategies of exclusion that liberal imperialists employed to justify the exploitation and extraction of indigenous labor and resources rather than the expropriation of indigenous land. Frameworks of liberal imperialism thus misconstrue American ideologies and practices of colonization by mapping onto American development a set of concepts and categories that were developed in different geographic and historical contexts. Because of this, the ideology of democratic empire provides a more appropriate interpretive framework for analyzing the relationship between democracy and empire in settler colonial contexts.

The key differences between the two ideological formations can be further understood by considering the case of John Stuart Mill. Often taken as the representative figure of liberal imperialism, Mill famously wrote, "Despotism is a legitimate mode of government in dealing with barbarians, provided the end be their improvement, and the means justified by actually effecting that end. Liberty, as a principle, has no application to any state of things anterior to the time when mankind have become capable of being improved."[23] In his effort to discern the proper scope of individual liberty, Mill provided a powerful justification of British colonial rule. While the imperial metropolis was to be governed through liberal principles of representative government, Mill condemned colonial subjects in India to the arbitrary rule of British administrators. Yet despite his positive views about the democratization of British society, Mill insulated the rule of the British colonies in India from popular control. Indeed, he was irate when Parliament abolished the East India Company after the Sepoy Rebellion of 1857 and imposed direct rule on the colonies. For Mill, colonial expansion was the domain of intellectual elites who possessed special talents for leading colonial subjects down the path of civilization. Precisely because of, rather than despite, its liberal elements, Mill's was a decidedly antidemocratic imperialism that excluded the democratic masses from having any role in carrying out British imperial ambitions.[24]

Such a position might seem irrelevant in the larger scheme of things, but it is precisely in opposition to this aspect of liberal imperialism that the ideology of democratic empire comes into clear focus. Lacking a robust conception of popular sovereignty, an emphasis on liberal imperialism alone cannot explain how American expansionists constructed popular constituencies that demanded territorial expansion and then enlisted those constituencies in the process of empire-building. Although liberal imperialism justifies colonial rule through the positive ethical benefits that it confers to the colonized, it makes no pretense to democratic rule in the acquisition of new territory. In the ideology of democratic empire, conversely, democratic self-rule is not simply the *end* of imperial expansion but is also its primary *means*. Rather than a centralized state or colonial administration, democratic empire casts "the people" in their sovereign capacity for self-government as the primary agent of colonial expansion.[25] My central argument is that settler-colonial discourses constructed the "sovereign people" as an imperial constituency who demanded territorial expansion as a necessary correlate of democratic equality and self-rule. American democracy emerged through a conceptualization of space and time in which the vitality of democratic society rested on the disavowal of colonial dispossession.

Among imperial historians, democratic empire refers to "empires where all classes in the home territories share in the project of rule."[26] The idea has perhaps been most forcefully advanced by the early twentieth-century sociologist Franklin Giddings, who wrote, "The world has been accustomed to think of democracy and empire as antagonistic phenomena. It has assumed that democracy could be established only on the ruins of empire, and that the establishment of empire necessarily meant the overthrow of liberty by a triumphant reign of absolutism." Yet, Giddings argued, the modern era is "witnessing the simultaneous development of both democracy and empire," resulting in the formation of "democratic empire." Throughout the nineteenth century, Giddings observed how the two most powerful nations on earth—Britain and the United States—became more democratic in their internal organization while expanding their boundaries through the acquisition of new territorial possessions. The basic principle of democratic empire is that as a nation establishes itself as "the nucleus of an empire" it can successively annex new territories and continue to be democratic. By reconciling colonial expansion with egalitarian principles, democratic empires govern acquired territories democratically while maintaining a strong imperial government.[27]

Although this basic understanding captures many key features, it tends to view the impulse for democratic expansion within a theoretical framework of democratic responsiveness, in which democratic empires expand because they are beholden to the demands of "the people" for land, liberty, and equality. That is, colonial expansion occurs because democratic-imperial states are responsive to the desires of popular constituencies for more territory and the political and ethical benefits it affords. This understanding of democratic empire, however, rests on a static notion of "the people" as a bounded entity. Democratic theorists have recently argued that the idea of the people that underwrites modern theories of popular sovereignty is not an objective referent, an aggregation of individuals, or a culturally bounded entity, but is rather a political process in its own right that involves a dialectical interaction between citizens and institutions.[28]

In lamenting the "stigma of empire" that democracy bears, Sheldon Wolin has provocatively shown how the shifting dynamics of American empire have both redrawn the boundaries of popular sovereignty and transformed the meaning of democratic citizenship. Wolin writes, "Virtually from the beginnings of the nation the making of the American citizen was influenced, even shaped by, the making of American imperium."[29] In the twentieth and twenty-first centuries Wolin was particularly concerned with how the rise of American superpower has resulted in a passive and demobilized democratic citizenry. But in the context of nineteenth-century territorial expansion, the process of expanding political space engendered a new kind of active and highly mobile democratic citizen.

Frameworks of democratic responsiveness thus fail to capture how the process of settler expansion figured into the creation of democratic citizens and democratic publics. In the process of constructing the sovereign people as an imperial constituency, ideologies of democratic empire embraced the constituent power of the people as the authorizing force of territorial expansion. The idea of democratic empire does not simply point to how the people provided the engine of settler expansion but rather to the dynamics by which settler colonialism itself constituted democratic peoplehood. If claims to represent the people or speak on the people's behalf in fact construct the people as a popular constituency, as Jason Frank has shown, then efforts to enlist the people in the process of empire building constituted the American people as an imperial constituency. That is, attempts to justify democratic expansion by invoking the demands of popular movements for land and liberty do not reflect a predetermined constituency. They draw the boundaries of popular sovereignty as such. Notions of democratic empire that view settler expansion as the product of popular demands for land and liberty are limited because they treat the people as a bounded entity whose political demands get translated into state policy rather than as the product of settler colonial dispossession.

Race, Space, and Settler Colonialism

In the first and most basic sense, settler colonialism entails the outward migration of settlers from a metropolitan center to establish colonial outposts on the periphery of empire. Settler regimes expand through the replication of metropolitan cultures and institutions in new territory. Settlers seek to make that space familiar by importing their own customs and social relations. Although they are replications of metropolitan societies, settler colonies necessarily exist as distinct and separate communities. Settler colonialism thus proceeds through the removal of a fragment of the metropolitan population who abandon the old order to constitute a new and separate political society, giving rise to "founding cultures" and "new world imaginaries" that both continue and break with metropolitan cultures.[30] In creating new societies in a new political space, settler colonists must deal with preexisting orders and identities that occupy and inhabit that space. To mask the vital role of conquest in establishing the territorial foundation of settler society, settler colonial ideologies systematically obscure land appropriation and native dispossession. In this way, settler ideology embraces racial logics that operate through space rather than culture or biology.

Two factors distinguish settler colonial ideology from other forms of colonial and imperial ideology. First, settlers share a common racial identity with citizens of the mother country. Accordingly, settlers count as civilized subjects who migrate with their rights and liberties intact when they colonize new spaces. Second, in settler colonial thought, settlers have fully developed their capacities for self-rule and thus achieved the status of political maturity prior to settlement. Thus, distinct from colonial subjects who lacked a common racial identity and capacities for self-rule, settlers obtain inherent claims to democratic rule vis-à-vis imperial governments.[31] What is important in settler colonial ideology, then, is that it talks about race less through body politics than through the politics of land and space. This shifts attention away from exclusive emphasis on anthropological conceptions of race as a cultural or physiological attribute of individuals to spatial representations of land as a cultural, historical, and political attribute of indigenous peoplehood. In settler colonial ideology, conceptualizations of land and space imply conceptualizations of race.

Mill himself reflected this spatial (rather than cultural or biological) understanding of race when he distinguished between two different types of colonies in the British Empire. While some colonies "are composed of people of similar civilization to the ruling country; capable of, and ripe for, representative government" (e.g., settler colonies in Canada and Australia), others "are still at a great distance from that state" (e.g., India).[32] Mill is making here what is now a widely recognized distinction between "settler colonies" and "occupation" or "exploitation colonies."[33] If exploitation colonies rely on either the extraction of valuable resources or the exploitation of indigenous labor, settler colonies are characterized by the expropriation of indigenous land. Through the "mass transfer" of European populations across space, settler colonization implies the "demographic takeover" of indigenous land.[34] Nevertheless, while Mill took great pains to construct civilizational hierarchies—what Uday Mehta calls "strategies of exclusion"—that barred colonized subjects in India from entrance into the universal constituency of liberalism, he cast land in settler colonies as empty and naturally belonging to white settlers.[35] In settler colonialism, structures of colonial domination follow spatial logics of native disavowal rather than biological-exclusivist or cultural-developmentalist logics.

Distinct from the exploitation colonialism of the late nineteenth-century French and British Empires in India and Africa, in which the relationship between colony and imperial metropolis was signified by the exploitation of indigenous labor, settler colonialism works through the elimination of the native and the expropriation of indigenous land. Also, distinct from mass migrations in which migrants return to the home country, settlers come to stay. As such, settler "invasion is a structure and not an event."[36] Settler colonialism names more than an event or process concerning the creation of a new society; it characterizes the structure of a society founded on conquest and the elimination of native modes of life. Settlers are, in the words of Lorenzo Veracini, "founders of political orders who carry their sovereignty with them."[37] In settler regimes, colonial expansion operates through the constituent power of settlers to establish their sovereignty on top of expropriated land. As a form of constituent power, settler colonialism entails the foundational violence of conquest in which the elimination of old orders and identities enables the consolidation of a new political order.

Liberal imperialism and democratic empire thus rely on distinct strategies of colonial domination. If liberal-imperial strategies of exclusion/domination focus on justifying the continued exploitation of indigenous labor and the rule of colonial administration, the strategies of exclusion/domination in democratic empire are oriented toward rationalizing indigenous dispossession and land appropriation. In its focus on land appropriation, settler strategies revolve around what Patrick Wolfe calls the "logic of native elimination" in which a "new colonial society" is erected "upon an expropriated land base."[38] Although they greatly vary, ideological rationalizations of such processes center on strategies of colonial disavowal where settlers refuse to acknowledge the indigenous presence by casting land as "empty" or uncultivated, what in legal discourse is known as *terra nullius* (land belonging to no one). Other means of colonial disavowal involve narratives of the "vanishing Indian" in which settlers justified territorial expropriation by casting indigenous communities as retrograde and decaying societies, thereby loosening their sovereign claims over the land.[39] Nevertheless, all such strategies rest on the assertion of European superiority over the native political forms, and they all encourage the disappearance of native societies to make way for a newer, more purportedly advanced form of society. Ideologies of democratic empire rely upon strategies of exclusion that define the boundaries of popular sovereignty through the disavowal and elimination of indigenous sovereignty as having any legitimate claim to new world territory.

Although "native elimination" is a harsh term that evokes images of physical genocide, indigenous dispossession need not necessarily proceed through physical extermination. Often, mechanisms of forced removal and assimilation offer more ideologically consistent modes of native elimination. In a certain sense, indigenous assimilation was opposed to racially exclusivist thinking because it acknowledged the mental and physical capacities of Indians to acculturate to white civilization. Nevertheless, policies of assimilation embraced the assumption that native modes of life were inferior to European forms of social and political organization. Assimilation thus appeared to white settlers as a means of offering the "gift" of civilization to Indians rather than as a form of elimination. In any case, the practical effect of assimilationist policies was the extirpation of indigenous land claims. In the case of native peoples, "democracy's intolerance of difference has operated through inclusion as much as through exclusion. Some differences are absorbed rather than excluded."[40]

Ideological History

By tracing the complex relationship between democratic thought and settler colonialism, this book offers not an intellectual history of democracy and colonialism but rather an ideological history. In the fashion of Cambridge School techniques of discourse analysis developed by Quentin Skinner and others, the intellectual history of political discourse puts primary focus on the linguistic regularities and shared vocabularies that provide the context for the emergence of political concepts and ideas. The meaning of a text or idea is not uncovered through a close reading aimed at retrieving moral axioms about human nature or universal truths about political order; it requires situating a text in its historical context. Drawing on speech act theory, such interpretive techniques emphasize the public legibility of political argument. Because political discourses are united by broad regularities in the vocabularies political actors use to influence politics, intellectual historians can uncover the intention of an author by examining the linguistic contexts that govern the formation of political arguments. Through contextualization, intellectual historians can illuminate the linguistic conventions that help us understand what an author was doing with a particular political language.[41]

Although my approach to ideological history adopts many of these interpretive techniques, it also moves beyond these approaches to emphasize the social and material contexts of political ideology. Instead of focusing solely on discursive and linguistic contexts, Ellen Meiksins Wood argues for attention to the "deep structural contexts and long-term social transformations" that shape political thought.[42] In its exclusive focus on political languages peculiar to specific historical moments, Skinnerian approaches risk detaching consideration of the social conditions and economic processes from the discursive structures and linguistic contexts that shape political debate. This, in turn, restricts the range of historical contexts that account for the historical specificity of a given political discourse. Attention to how political ideas develop in relation to large-scale historical and social processes widens the range of contextual factors relevant to the formation of political ideologies.

A broader sense of what counts as relevant historical context is necessary if we are to pay attention to how material processes of settler colonization laid the foundation of democratic society in the United States. A more synthetic understanding requires attention to the institutional processes of *settler colonization* (as a material set of practices and policies of land appropriation) that shaped the conceptual development of democratic ideas, as well as the ideologies and discourses of *settler colonialism* (as a theoretical and ideological tradition of political thinking) that lend justification to those institutional practices. The two should not be broken down into a dichotomous binary-like base and superstructure but should be seen as two moments of an integrated totality. To have a truly dynamic understanding of politics and culture, political development must be understood as "a continuous interaction between ideology and the material forces of history."[43] Accounting for a broader range of historical contexts that shape ideological traditions requires attention to how both material and ideological aspects mediate each other in a dialectical fashion.

Within this contextual understanding of ideological history, the concept of ideology operates on two levels of analysis. At the simpler and programmatic level, ideological history involves tracing the conceptual lineages and discursive effects of "legitimizing constructs" that rationalize power relations and the construction of colonial hierarchies. In this sense, ideology is not simply dogma or doctrine, but rather "the system of beliefs, values, fears, prejudices, reflexes, and commitments—in sum, the social consciousness—of a social group, be it a class, a party, or a section."[44] At a deeper level, ideologies are not simply instrumental constructs used to justify power and domination but actually structure consciousness and group identity.[45] In focusing on the role of ideology in constituting popular constituencies as imperial constituencies, I attend to what Priscilla Wald calls "official stories," authorizing narratives that "constitute Americans."[46] Rather than isolated currents of political thought, settler colonial narratives shaped the ongoing redefinition of democratic peoplehood and democratic thought.

Although I focus on the ideological development of democratic empire in the US context, I have no intention of presenting the American experience with settler colonialism as exceptional or unique. One can find parallels with this ideological configuration by placing democratic empire in transnational and comparative perspective. Perhaps the most obvious point of comparison is the British Empire of the nineteenth century, not in the exploitation colonies of Africa and Southeast Asia but in the settler colonies of Canada, Australia, South Africa, and New Zealand. The experience of the rebellions of Lower and Upper Canada, partially to thwart repetition of the American rebellion, led British colonial architects to integrate democratic principles and imperial frameworks of rule in the Durham report of 1838 (Chapter 1). The outcome significantly mirrored the American framework of combining territorial expansion with democratic self-rule in settler colonies. Beyond Anglo settler states, one sees profound parallels in French Algeria. Alexis de Tocqueville, for instance, looked to American ideologies and practices of colonization in his own efforts to construct a settler colonial state in North Africa. Although he ultimately concluded the differences were too great to fully replicate the American model of colonization, the cross-national circulation of settler ideology helps illuminate the American case (Chapter 3).

In this way, I also move beyond comparative frameworks toward a transnational perspective. If comparative perspectives emphasize the similarities and differences between US colonial history and other settler states by treating them as discrete and insular units of analysis, transnational history highlights the cross-national circulation of colonial practices and ideologies. From this perspective, the United States is not one among many units of analysis but has played a central role in developing settler colonial technologies of power. "Inserted into the history of colonialism," Mahmood Mamdani states, "America appears less as exceptional and more as a pioneer in the history and technology of settler colonialism. All the defining institutions of settler colonialism were produced as so many technologies of native control in North America." For instance, the South African system of native "reserves," which carved out separate homelands for each indigenous ethnic group and provided the basis for apartheid, was based on the US reservation system used to confine indigenous peoples to spaces outside of the commercial channels of settler expansion.[47] Throughout the nineteenth and twentieth centuries, European colonizers looked to the United States for examples of how to govern native peoples in colonial outposts. Architects of settler rule in Australia drew on the racialist ideas of US theorists to reconcile democracy with colonial domination in the antipodes.[48] Through attention to these networks of "overlapping territories" and "intertwined histories," I illustrate how transnational flows of settler colonial ideology influenced modern democratic thought.[49]

Chapter Overview

What I seek to establish throughout the book is that native dispossession and settler colonialism did not simply shape American institutional and social development, but that they infused into and constituted the basic conceptual logics of democratic theory. My focus on the logics of native elimination and indigenous absence shows how practices and ideologies of colonization have been foundational not just for democratic institutions and constitutional law but more precisely for central theoretical constructions of American democratic theory. In this regard, my account also differs from much of the literature on conquest and frontier violence in focusing less on the liberal, individualist ethos of self-reliance than on conceptions of popular sovereignty, social equality, federalism, and democratic peoplehood.

Emphasizing democratic dispossession in this way sheds significant light on empire and colonialism not simply as a political project but as dynamics that were foundational to the construction of modern democratic thought.

The book proceeds through three phases. The first phase charts the ideological origins of democratic empire by examining the relationship between federalism and empire in colonial and early republican thought. Chapter 1 focuses on debates about the proper balance between colonial authority and imperial sovereignty during the Imperial Crisis. It further establishes that the conflict between colonial settlers and metropolitan authorities was largely a debate over the proper terms and conditions of imperial organization. The fundamental point that settlers made in these arguments was that barriers to settler colonization subjected the colonies to the metropolitan center in a way that cast them as colonial dependencies. In response, settlers articulated an alternative vision of imperial expansion in which the constituent parts of empire were equal rather than dependent entities. The chapter then argues that the Northwest Ordinance of 1787 institutionalized a new world conception of empire that privileged the equality of quasi-sovereign settler communities over notions of empire organized around the governance of colonial dependencies. Despite the central principles of equality at the center of this new notion of empire, the ordinance allowed for the further dispossession of indigenous communities as a necessary feature of republican expansionism.

The second chapter argues that the practice of colonization in settler constitutionalism represented a distinct form of constituent power wherein the self-constitution of settler democracy coheres around regimes of indigenous disavowal and native expropriation. Evident in a range of micro-constitutional practices such as the Vermont Constitution, the Watauga Compact, the Cumberland Compact, and the Constitution of the State of Franklin, democratic notions of popular consent and constituent sovereignty were vitally linked to spatial notions of North American land as vacant and unpeopled. This distinct understanding of settler democracy raised significant difficulties as American constitutionalists attempted to build an expansive though stable republic. To the extent that colonization entailed the right of settlers to dissolve the bonds of imperial order and constitute new political orders, it threatened to contain American expansion within preestablished territorial boundaries. By seeking separation and independence from territorial empire, settler practices of colonization potentially subverted American efforts at continental expansion. The Northwest Ordinance tacitly dealt with this problem by conceiving of the right of settlers to self-constitute republican order in colonized lands as the driving force of settler colonial expansion. In this regard, the Northwest Ordinance engendered a *colonization-constitution dialectic* in which the constituent power of settlers to create self-governing polities on the frontier was integrated into the colonial apparatus of the American Constitution.

The second phase examines the ideological development of democratic empire from the Jacksonian period through the end of the Civil War. Chapter 3 traces how new conceptions of democracy expressed in Tocqueville's *Democracy in America* acquired their conceptual coherence in relation to the politics of settler expansion and land appropriation. At the center of Tocqueville's thought was a socio-cultural conception of democracy that located the foundations of the democratic polity in culture and society rather than the formal constitution. In this socio-cultural concept of democracy, settler expansion guarded against the resurgence of feudal land title in the Americas by ensuring the primacy of social equality in the context of an expanding and industrializing political economy. For Tocqueville, American democracy was defined by the double absence of feudalism and indigenous sovereignties. Insofar as American democracy conceptually emerged in reference to ideologies of indigenous disavowal, settler colonialism provided the foundation of democratic society. Regimes of settler colonialism and indigenous dispossession constituted the territorial basis of American democracy by shaping the values, habits, and customs that defined the boundaries and character of democratic peoplehood.

Chapter 4 expands this analysis to the writings of Ralph Waldo Emerson and John O'Sullivan against the backdrop of the US conquest of Mexico. While O'Sullivan presented a conventional socio-economic argument in favor of colonial expansion in which the acquisition of new land ensured the landed independence of democratic settlers, Emerson recast this argument in the terms of transcendental and romantic philosophy. In O'Sullivan's theory of colonization, settler expansion ensured the continued social equality of settlers and in turn laid the social basis for a democratic polity founded on the sovereignty of the people. Emerson amended this familiar argument by casting the cultivation and colonization of land as necessary not just for social development but also for the moral development of citizens. Thus, colonization stabilized the democratic polity not simply by maintaining an economic balance between social classes but by creating the moral ethos of democratic citizenship.

Chapter 5 examines similar themes in the political thought of Abraham Lincoln, Galusha Grow, and Walt Whitman. In the free-soil politics of the 1850s, the expansion of slavery represented a feudal threat to democratic equality. In response, free-soil democrats rearticulated democratic empire as a form of free labor empire that privileged egalitarian expansion over the oligarchic empire of slavery. These theorists emphasized the moral benefits of free labor that suited settlers for democratic citizenship. Similar to Emerson, Whitman revised these moral and economic arguments into a poetic theory of democracy. For Whitman, the true foundation of democracy was in its cultural rather than constitutional form. Central to the creation of democratic culture was the formation of democratic literature that imparted democratic virtues to citizens and cemented the moral bonds that united individuals and states in a grander federal union. As this chapter explains, free-soil expansion and native dispossession provided the linguistic raw material for the creation of democratic culture. To develop a uniquely "native" American vernacular that demarcated democratic literature from its European precedents, Whitman integrated indigenous languages and cultural traditions. Yet when he described the western landscape, his poetic vision of North America emptied the continent of its indigenous presence.

While the previous two sections focus on official narratives and legitimizing constructs of settler ideology, the last section mines resources within American democratic thought that might aid in a larger project of decolonizing democratic theory. Toward this end, Chapter 6 examines the concept of "Indian nullification" in the political writings of the Pequot Indian William Apess by situating his defense of indigenous sovereignty in the context of debates about the legitimacy of nullification in US constitutionalism. It illustrates how Indian nullification operates not as a feature of constitutional design asserting minority rights over the tyranny of the majority, but rather as a rhetorical form of political contestation exposing the foundational violence of American settler democracy. Apess shows how democratic equality and self-rule rest on settler colonialism and indigenous dispossession, highlighting the "paradox of settler sovereignty" that provides the basis for American democracy. Indian nullification is not a simple demand that the boundaries of liberal citizenship be expanded to include Indians. It is a way of narrating the forms of settler conquest that establish the material and conceptual foundation of democratic equality for white settlers. Apess thus illuminates the possibilities within democratic theory for unsettling the colonial foundations of modern democracy.

Although several other Native American political theorists might provide a compelling counterpoint to settler ideologies of democratic empire, Apess exemplifies the foundational critique that this book explores. The inclusion of Apess is therefore not meant to be exhaustive of his thought or as a full representation of Native American political thinking, but as a means of tying the counter-narrative offered in this book to indigenous critiques of settler colonialism. To further contextualize Apess in relation to broader currents of Native American political thought, I briefly contrast his legal and political thought with that of other native thinkers such as Tecumseh, Black Hawk, and Elias Boudinot throughout the book. Nevertheless, while my primary concern in *Empire of the People* is to trace the contours of indigenous disavowal and epistemological elimination in American democratic theory, it is beyond the scope of this book to entirely fill in those absences. While this is a productive avenue for future scholarship, my account of Apess's thought is suggestive of one possible route for deeper engagement with Native American political thought in its historical contexts.[50]

If the primary task of this book is to deconstruct exceptionalist narratives of American democracy by highlighting the entwinement of democracy and dispossession, the afterword closes with a reconstructive effort to sketch the outlines of a decolonial theory of democracy. Specifically, it highlights two features of the decolonial theory of democracy: (1) a nonsovereign conception of democracy that relinquishes the aspiration to collective self-mastery and (2) a transmodern conception of democracy that attends to the productive influence of indigenous traditions on the modern democratic tradition. Through a conceptual and historical reconstruction of the relationship between settler expansion and American democracy, I call for a decolonial theory of democracy that de-normalizes settler political thought as the unsurpassable horizon of democratic politics.

PART ONE

Federalism and Empire

1 From Colonial Dependence to Imperial Equality

"What is a new state formed in the Western deserts of America, if it be not a new colony?"
—*Edward Gibbon Wakefield*, England and America (1833)

"To secure a conquest, it was always necessary to plant a colony, and territories, thus occupied and settled, were rightly considered, as mere extensions, or processes of empire."
—*Samuel Johnson*, Taxation No Tyranny (1775)

In recent years, political theorists have sought to retrieve federalism as an alternative mode of international organization that departs from both nation-state and global-state models. Although it is a neglected dimension of her overall thought, Hannah Arendt offered an original and compelling argument for replacing nation-state institutions, which she saw as inherently tending toward imperialism, with federal institutions of shared sovereignty.[1] Federalism was desirable for Arendt because it diffused aspirations for national sovereignty and individual autonomy, both of which contradicted her view about the plurality of politics and nonsovereign freedom. In prioritizing shared sovereignty over national autonomy, federalism posed an alternative to the model of nation-state sovereignty premised upon the assumption of a unitary sovereign that neglected the human condition of plurality among men, because it represented the ideal of multiple, overlapping sites of power. In developing these arguments, Arendt applauded the model of nonsovereign federation in the political thinking of the American founders, whom she admired for their "consistent abolition of sovereignty within the body politic of the republic."[2] This and the next chapter complicate this theoretical retrieval by uncovering the settler colonial foundations of American federalism.

Arendt went to great pains to distinguish "imperialism" based on the nation-state model from what she simply called "empire." In *The Origins of Totalitarianism*, she wrote, "Imperialism is not empire building and expansion is not conquest. . . . In contrast to true imperial structures, where the institutions of the mother country are in various ways integrated into the empire, it is characteristic of imperialism that national institutions remain separate from the colonial administration."[3] Arendt's contrast perfectly resembles the distinction between settler colonial expansion where colonial institutions are combined with metropolitan institutions in a single imperial framework and exploitation colonialism where colonies are governed through administrative structures of colonial dependency. By attributing an "imperial" status to European states, Arendt exceptionalized US federalist expansion as anti-imperial insofar as it rejected the principle of colonial dependency. Yet only by ignoring settler colonialism as a form of imperial expansion could she assert that "the colonialism and imperialism of European nations . . . [was] the one great crime in which America was never involved."[4]

For Arendt, James Madison's "federal principle of uniting separate and independently constituted bodies" prepared the constituent units of empire for a "constant enlargement whose principle was neither expansion nor conquest but the further combination of powers."[5] In making these claims, Arendt obscured the colonial violence that laid the basis of American federalism by disavowing the presence of indigenous peoples in North America. The federal principle arose in the early stages of colonial history in models such as the Mayflower Compact, the charter of the Virginia Company, and the Fundamental Orders of Connecticut. When "the settlers of the New World" constructed their federal arrangements, they did so in a "state of nature," an "uncharted" and "untrod wilderness, unlimited by any boundary."[6] In order to institutionalize the federal principle, settlers imagined an empty wilderness that was devoid of both prior indigenous political orders and foundational colonial violence.

Despite her attempt to cast federalist expansion as an alternative to imperial conquest, Arendt reinforced settler ideologies that erased indigenous political orders from the political landscape. What Arendt ultimately ignored, and what this chapter seeks to establish, is that American federalism did not represent an alternative to colonial empire but rather an alternative mode of colonial expansion that operates through what I call, borrowing from Anders Stephanson, "the principle of federative replication," which consists of two key dimensions that are explored in this and the next chapter, respectively.[7] The first dimension of federative replication—*the principle of imperial equality*—involves a new world conception of empire that privileged the equality of the constituent units of empire (i.e., settler colonial states) over notions of empire organized around relations of colonial dependence. In the second—what I call *the coloniality of constituent power*—colonization operates as a form of constituent power through the sovereign capacity of settlers *qua* founders to establish new political societies on top of expropriated land.

Turning to the first dimension of federative replication, this chapter argues that the Northwest Ordinance of 1787 institutionalized a form of empire without colonial dependence. In their attempts to break free from the authority of the imperial metropolis, American settlers developed imperial self-conceptions that privileged localized self-rule and equality between the constituent units of empire as the hallmark of a new democratic model of empire.[8] Federalism thus emerged as a way of reconciling imperial frameworks of expansion with democratic-republican ideals of self-rule at the local level. By privileging the equality of settler states in relation to the imperial state, federalism provided a means of reconciling conflicts between the imperial authority of the metropolis and the settler sovereignty of colonies. Rather than an alternative to empire, federalism allowed settlers to combine imperial sovereignty with popular sovereignty in a single framework of territorial expansion. The Northwest Ordinance is rarely considered to be an important text for political theory. This is puzzling because while the Declaration of Independence and the Constitution both figure as among the most important texts in the history of political thought, the Northwest Ordinance perhaps did more to build a settler colonial empire of continental proportions. By treating the ordinance as the preeminent text in American settler thought, I show how settler colonialism established the foundations of democratic sovereignty in the United States.

In developing this larger claim, I begin by exploring how colonial thinkers during the Imperial Crisis developed new conceptions of empire in opposition to emerging frameworks of colonial dependency. The central contribution of colonial writers such as Benjamin Franklin, Richard Bland, and Thomas Jefferson was not to oppose the legitimacy of empire writ large but to conceive of a framework of federal imperialism that granted the status of imperial equality to the constituent units of empire. The second section illustrates how these conceptions of empire were institutionalized in the land ordinances of the 1780s, most notably the Northwest Ordinance of 1787. By placing settler colonies on an "equal footing" with the original states of the union, the Northwest Ordinance utilized the principle of federative replication to compel a process of colonial expansion that rejected principles of colonial dependency in favor of imperial equality. The last section situates the politics of American settler colonialism in a transnational context by attending to the circulation of settler colonial ideologies in the global imperial order. Specifically, I turn to the British theorist Edward Gibbon Wakefield's use of the Northwest Ordinance to develop his theory of systematic colonization. Central to Wakefield's theory was his contention that settler colonies must be put on a plane of equality with metropolitan governments so as to prevent them from sliding into a status of colonial dependency.

Settler Conceptions of Empire in British North America

Amid escalating global conflict over control of North America in the 1750s, British colonists began to confront questions about imperial organization that addressed the balance between the provincial sovereignty of settler colonists and the imperial sovereignty of metropolitan authorities. In these debates, settlers saw the American colonies not simply as dependent appendages of the British Empire, but as a source of imperial power. One sees this colonial mindset forcefully at work in Benjamin Franklin's "Observations Concerning the Increase of Mankind" (1751), which articulated a vision of an expanding agrarian republic based on a simple empirical observation that proved to be strikingly accurate: the population of colonial America would continue to double every twenty-five years, ushering in a future in which "the greatest Number of Englishmen will be on this Side the Water." The central implication was that the abundance of open land would lead to a drastic increase in population in North America, which further propelled vast economic growth through the expansion of British markets. In Franklin's view, this would lead to a great "Accession of Power" to the British Empire. Such assertions significantly challenged dominant conceptions of empire wherein the colonial periphery served the core both politically and economically. Franklin reversed this formula and instead asserted that further colonization of the new world would establish America as a central pillar of Britain's global empire.[9]

Underlying Franklin's argument was the idea that the expansion of colonial dominion ensured political stability and the durability of settler institutions. John Adams made the point explicit in his well-known interpretation of James Harrington's The Commonwealth of Oceana (1656). The only viable means of preserving "the balance of power on the side of equal liberty and public virtue" was to divide the land into small quantities so that the multitude may be in possession of landed estates. In doing so, the multitude will be brought into the balance of power and will be more likely to partake in the "care of the liberty, virtue, and interest" of the republic.[10] For Adams, the viability of a mixed republic rested on landed independence to keep a landless class of dependents from forming, who would seek to transform the structures of the prevailing order. Political stability and the security of individual liberty implied territorial expansion to make sure there was, in Franklin's words, "room enough" for the easy subsistence of the agrarian citizenry. Franklin praised the statesman that "acquires new Territory, if he finds it vacant, or removes Natives to give his own People Room."[11] In Franklin's vision, the widespread distribution of cheap land prevented social instability and political discontent in the metropolis, which in turn required the conceptual and physical removal of natives to provide political space for the expanding populace.

By the Seven Years' War, due to the role of the colonies in the ascendance of British commerce, colonists began to see themselves not simply as equal partners in the imperial enterprise, but as the very foundation of British power. Franklin wrote in 1760, "I have long been of opinion that the foundations of future grandeur and stability of the British Empire lie in America."[12] John Adams gave further voice to this sentiment. When empires decline, "the empire of the world" transfers to another location further west. Based on Franklin's calculations about its expanding population, Adams speculated that North America would become the last "great seat of empire." But if the seat of empire was in the process of translation, then the current seat of empire was in decline. North America would not only step in to take its place, it would altogether suspend the historical succession of empires, inaugurating what Bishop Berkeley considered the fifth and closing act of the great human drama.[13]

These assertions about the rise of American global power drew on a medieval historical trope inflected with a modern twist. The doctrine of translatio imperii held that the center of power and culture in the world was continually traveling westward. As one empire fell, the seat of global rule transferred to another state further west, a dominant power that carried history along the path of progress. Originating in the Orient and progressing through Greek, Roman, and European civilizations, the transfer of imperial rule would find its final resting place in the Pacific Rim of the Americas, returning the seat of empire to its ancient origins and bringing the entire world within its domain. In the modern political imagination, America was a space removed from the laws of history—the "land of the future," as Hegel called it—a space unaffected by the past sedimentations of ancient empires. North America was the frontier of modernity, the site of a future political form that would transcend the depredations of the past.[14] The poet Joel Barlow gave voice to this view on the eve of the Constitutional Convention, imagining a world anxiously awaiting a new global order: "Till that new empire, rising in the west / Shall sheathe the sword, the liberal main ascend / And, join'd . . . the scale of power suspend / Bid arts arise, and vengeful factions cease / And commerce lead to universal peace."[15]

Standing in the way of Franklin's vision of settler expansion were the French and Indians, who thwarted the expansion of settlers. To secure his imperial vision, he tried to enact his ideas into law and policy in the Albany Plan of 1754, which sought to concentrate power in a colonial agency tasked with securing new lands and protecting settlers. The plan stated that a "union of the colonies is absolutely necessary" for the "mutual defense and security" of colonial liberty. Securing liberty meant eliminating the obstacles to settler expansion that were stalling the economic progress afforded by the abundance of land. Significantly presaging the federal structure of the US Constitution, the plan called for Parliament to establish "one general government" under which each colony may be subsumed while still maintaining the liberties guaranteed by its present constitution. While the Albany Congress rejected the plan, it reflected an emerging understanding of federal institutions as a means of combining settler sovereignty and imperial sovereignty in a single legal framework.[16]

While Franklin and others continually argued for the centrality of colonial unity, a powerful discourse circulating among imperial administrators also began to call for the strict separation of the colonies and increased centralization in colonial governance. Foremost among these administrators was Thomas Pownall, the governor of the Massachusetts Bay Colony during the Seven Years' War. Pownall's conception of a "civil empire" reinforced the image of Britain as an enlightened force for progress in the world. In the modern era, Pownall held that extensive trade relations and relations of equality exhibited in the settlement of the Americas were in ascendance over ancient empires in which "the power of the sword was the predominant spirit of the world." New forms of power arising from these global relations would replace relations of war, coercion, and force as the primary means of expansion: "the spirit of commerce will become that predominant power."[17] This change in the meaning of empire enabled the emergence of new imperial visions in which the brutalities of empire—conquest and domination—could be avoided and replaced with freedom, equality, and consent.

Contrasted with Franklin's vision of settler colonial empire, Pownall articulated a relatively conventional view of empire based on the core-periphery model in which profits and people circulated back and forth between metropolis and colony. What Pownall added to this model, however, is the stipulation that while profits were to flow back to the center, the interests and rights of colonists must be affirmed. To preempt colonial revolt, Pownall advised that the colonies should be considered not as "mere appendages of the realm" but as equal though dependent partners in the "commercial dominion of Great Britain."[18] To adjudicate competing claims for legislative authority between the colonial assemblies and Parliament, Pownall called for a "Line of Demarcation" that separated the spheres of internal and external authority. His originality here was in establishing a middle ground between Tory proponents of undivided sovereignty such as William Blackstone and colonists like Franklin, who argued for a form of divided sovereignty stemming from multiple sources of imperial authority. While the colonies retained internal (i.e., settler) sovereignty, the metropolitan government had absolute (i.e., imperial) sovereignty over external matters of empire such as war, treaties, and commerce.[19] Commerce was doubly important not simply because it bound the colonies to the metropolis, but also because it kept them "disconnected and independent of each other." If the colonies were united only by commerce, which always flowed through the "common center" of empire, they were left with "no other principle of intercommunication" than that mediated by Britain.[20]

If Pownall's model of empire relied on the dependence of the colonies on the metropolitan center, Franklin's model reflected a federalist conception of empire in which the constituent units of empire were not subordinated to a metropolitan center. One also sees this notion of empire at work in the writings of Stephen Hopkins, governor of the Rhode Island colony. Hopkins agreed with Pownall that the external rule of empire superseded the internal rule of the colonies in matters of its proper domain. But he disagreed on what the proper balance of this power should be. For Hopkins, the "supreme and overruling authority" of Parliament does not trump colonial rights and sovereignty, which must be equal to those of metropolitan citizens. An "imperial state" such as Great Britain "consists of many separate governments each of which hath peculiar privileges," in which no superior part is entitled to make laws for lesser parts without their consent. Hopkins's imperial vision dispersed power among multiple centers, which maintained the proper balance between imperial authority and colonial liberty.[21] In this view, the federalist principle provided a means of constituting an empire that reconciled the settler sovereignty of the colonial assemblies with the power and strength of an imperial state.[22]

Pownall's fears and reservations about imperial administration directly stemmed from the dilemmas of colonial rule arising from British victory in the Seven Years' War. Pownall held settler expansion and self-government to be the "indefeasible and unalterable right" of the colonists.[23] After the war, however, Britain began to significantly curtail the right of expansion and consequently the right of self-government with the Royal Proclamation of 1763, which instituted by royal prerogative an imaginary line running down the Appalachians beyond which it was illegal to settle or speculate in lands.[24] Despite the rise of ideas about free commerce, the proclamation operated on mercantilist logics of containment motivated by several concerns such as the desire of imperial administrators to retain exclusive control of western trade routes and the imperatives of maintaining order on the frontier after the war. Due to mounting indigenous resistance in Pontiac's War in 1763, limiting western lands to the near-exclusive use of indigenous tribes and tightly regulated trade was a more feasible policy than outright expansion, which faced forceful native resistance.[25]

British policy violated settler conceptions of liberty in several ways. By reserving western lands for indigenous tribes, the line effectively wrote indigenous land rights into law by executive fiat, rejecting the primary ideological basis of settler colonization—i.e., the disavowal of native sovereignty. Because colonists perceived Indians as mostly wandering tribes, the proclamation squandered the virgin land of the new world and defied the Lockean "common sense" that upheld the natural right of English colonists to add their labor to uncultivated "waste land." The policy also clashed with settler notions of freedom of exchange and social equality. The mercantilist control of western trade routes required heavily garrisoned forts along the frontier. To fund colonial defense, British officials implemented a stamp tax that required all colonists to fund colonial security.[26] The policy maddened colonists whose notions of liberty upheld the dream of property holding and the escape from feudal society. In their own minds, they were being forced to pay for the restriction of their own freedom without their consent, and, absent cheap land, their own confinement to a lower social rank. Modern liberty in the American context thus had an expansionist tendency that embraced the spatial mobility of settlers as a necessary correlate of social mobility.

At the center of these debates about the relationship between imperial sovereignty and settler sovereignty was the question of how the colonies were settled. In asserting the right of royal prerogative over the colonies, the Tory Samuel Johnson explained, "For the satisfaction of this inquiry, it is necessary to consider, how a colony is constituted; what are the terms of migration, as dictated by nature, or settled by compact; and what social or political rights the man loses or acquires, that leaves his country to establish himself in a distant plantation."[27] In answering this question—"how a colony is constituted"—and in similarly defending the royal prerogative, Blackstone distinguished between two kinds of colonies: "Plantations or colonies, in distant countries, are either such where the lands are claimed by right of occupancy only, by finding them desert and uncultivated, and peopling them from the mother-country; or where, when already cultivated, they have been either gained by conquest, or ceded to us by treaties." Blackstone was clear that "our American plantations are principally of this latter sort, being obtained in the last century either by right of conquest and driving out the natives (with what natural justice I shall not at present inquire), or by treaties." Because the North American colonies were founded on conquest and subsequent treaties, they were "distinct, though dependent dominions" unaffected by the English constitution.[28] The authority of the royal prerogative in the colonies thus derived from the avowal of native conquest.

The obverse of Blackstone's argument was that the presence of English liberties in the colonies depended upon the absence of colonial dispossession and native conquest.[29] In order to assert settler sovereignty over imperial sovereignty, settlers systematically disavowed native conquest. If the colonies were not conquered entities, then there was no legitimate basis upon which to assign the status of colonial dependency. The historian Craig Yirush explains that in engaging these questions, settler theorists connected colonial self-rule to frameworks of settler colonialism through two key arguments. First, in transplanting themselves from England to America, they argued that they carried their rights and sovereignty to newly settled territories by entitlement. Central here was the idea of the common law, which settlers used to justify their claims that migration had not undermined their inherent rights as Englishmen. Settlers viewed English rights as derivative of England's ancient constitution and a birthright that they were entitled to regardless of their place of residency.[30] Second, they articulated a "labor theory of empire," in which the energy expended in settling new territory guaranteed not just a right to property but also political rights on par with subjects who remained in England. Because they undertook the risk and labor of planting the colonies, settlers asserted that they were of value to the metropolis. Through a process of contractual colonization, they demanded settler sovereignty in exchange for colonizing new lands and creating permanent settlements.[31]

These two arguments found forceful expression in the writings of Richard Bland, a member of the Virginia House of Burgess and delegate to the First Continental Congress, who in *The Colonel Dismounted* (1764) developed a federal vision of empire that reserved for the colonies a zone of internal autonomy not subject to royal prerogative. Bland distinguished between the "external government" of the empire and the "internal government of the colony."[32] While the latter was the domain of settler sovereignty and concerned matters specific to colonial affairs, the former was the domain of Parliament and imperial sovereignty. In this decentralized, federalist vision of empire, the separation of two zones of authority in settler colonial empire best ensured the protection of settler rights of self-government. For Bland, the internal autonomy of the colonies stemmed from the fact that the inherent rights of colonists could not be abrogated or alienated merely by crossing the Atlantic. In asserting colonial rights, Bland argued that "we cannot lose the right of Englishmen by our removal to this continent." Rather than a legal system geographically particular to the mother country, the common law, "being the common consent of the people from time immemorial and the birthright of every Englishman, does follow him wherever he goes, and consequently must be the general law by which the colony is to be governed."[33] The necessary though unarticulated assumption of this vision of federal empire was that settlers have abstract rights of self-government that inhered in them as a body of people and not in the specificity of geographic context. When settlers emigrate to create a new colony, those rights automatically serve as the basis of the new colonial government.[34]

Bland also used the labor theory of empire to counter claims that the colonies were founded on conquest. For Bland, jurists like Blackstone erroneously equated English settlers with conquered populations. Francis Bacon, agreeing with Blackstone, expressed the logical conclusion of this idea, which barred colonists from rights of self-government by virtue of the conquest of native populations: "A country gained by conquest hath no right to be governed by English laws." In opposition, Bland argued, "If we are the descendants of Englishmen, who by their consent and at the expense of their own blood and treasure undertook to settle this new region for the benefit and aggrandizement of the parent kingdom, the native privileges enjoyed by our progenitors must be derived to us from them, as they could not be forfeited by their migration to America."[35] Bland buttressed this argument in An Inquiry into the Rights of the British Colonies (1766), where he wrote, "The Colonies in North America . . . were founded by Englishmen; who . . . established themselves, without any Expense to the Nation, in this uncultivated and almost uninhabited Country."[36] By representing North American land as terra nullius, Bland disputed Blackstone's claim that the colonies were founded on conquest. Bland thus asserted the legal validity of colonial rights and settler sovereignty through the erasure of native modes of governance and disavowal of colonial conquest.

Thomas Jefferson significantly expanded on Bland's defense of colonial liberty in A Summary View of the Rights of British America (1774), where he argued that the imposition of Norman feudal law in England and America had corrupted Anglo-Saxon rights and liberties enshrined in the English constitution. In Jefferson's view, feudal property law was virtually unknown in the early Saxon settlement of England: "Our Saxon ancestors held their lands, as they did their personal property, in absolute dominion, disencumbered with any superior." Under the Norman Conquest, William the Conqueror and the Norman lawyers imposed feudal land tenure on England by articulating a right of conquest that subjected all land to the absolute dominion of the Crown.[37] Through an imaginative historical revision, Jefferson placed the mythology of the Norman Yoke in service of settler claims for political rights against the royal prerogative.[38] He drew an explicit comparison between English settlers and ancient Saxons, who "left their native wilds in Northern Europe" to settle England under the auspices of the "universal law" of liberty. Similarly, "Settlements having thus been effected in the wilds of America, the emigrants thought proper to adopt that system of laws under which they had hitherto lived in the mother country." American territory is thus subject to the customary laws of the Anglo-Saxons instituted before the Norman Conquest rather than feudal law.[39] Rather than conquered and dependent colonies, the North American settlements were founded upon the English common law as an inherent sovereign right that settlers carried across the Atlantic.

Perhaps more than Bland, Jefferson also developed the labor theory of empire as a means of opposing the royal prerogative alongside the assertion that English settlers retained their rights and sovereignty in settling the new world. According to Jefferson, "America was conquered, and her settlements made, and firmly established, at the expense of individuals, and not of the British public. Their own blood was spilt in acquiring lands for their settlement, their own fortunes expended in making that settlement effectual; for themselves they fought, for themselves they conquered, and for themselves alone they have right to hold."[40] Like Lockean views of property, Jefferson also defended colonial property rights against feudal land title by pointing to the work and risk that settlers undertook to colonize new land.

British colonists thus claimed the rights of self-government not in opposition to empire, but rather *as* citizens of the British Empire. The Imperial Crisis was, in a basic sense, a disagreement over the "terms of empire."[41] Consistent with federal visions of empire, the basis of the colonial challenge to British rule was that the colonies of the empire should have an equal part in parliamentary rule. Rejecting their status as dependent subjects, colonists claimed the rights of republican liberty and self-rule as imperial citizens. As such, they did not reject the legitimacy of empire as a political form, but rather viewed it as consistent with prevailing notions of republican liberty and popular consent. Read in this light, the Revolution did not simply break the cords that bound colony to metropolis, leading to a new kind of anti-imperial republic. It represented the birth of what General Washington called an "infant empire" that would step onto the world stage to challenge its parentage for the seat of global rule.[42]

The Federal State as Settler State

In certain variants of eighteenth-century republicanism, liberty and empire could coexist, if at all, only uneasily. Edward Gibbon, for example, attributed one of the primary causes of Roman decline to the avarice of the nobles and the relentless pursuit of private gain through conquest and expansion. As private interest predominated over civic virtue, "public freedom" was lost in proportion to the "extent of conquest."[43] Settler ideology reversed this supposition by conceiving of colonial empire not in terms of corruption and the private pursuit of wealth and glory but as an essential feature of a stable republic. In this conception of imperial sovereignty, the territory of empire was the dominion of the governed rather than the exclusive domain of the monarchy or aristocracy. True to the spirit of the commonwealth vision it spawned from, this brand of settler republicanism promoted territorial expansion in pursuit of the public good.

With the end of the war in sight and British hold weakening over western territory, the thorny question arose of whether Virginia's title to the Ohio River Valley granted by its royal charter should be respected or if the land should be brought under the authority of the Continental Congress. Thomas Paine's pamphlet *Public Good: An Examination into the Claims of Virginia to the Vacant Western Territory* (1780) sought to answer this question by arguing that the subjection of western territory to the authority of the confederal government was necessary for the common economic prosperity of the new nation. Directly referring to his position in *Common Sense* (1776), Paine stated that the Northwest Territory should be a "national fund for the benefit of all" rather than a source of private profits. At once upholding popular rights to the land and erasing indigenous sovereignty, Paine asserted that the "vacant western territory of America" was the "common right of all." In defending this "common right" against the partial claims of the land companies, Paine argued, "A right, to be truly so, must be right within itself: yet many things have obtained the name of rights, which are originally founded in wrong. Of this kind are all rights by mere conquest, power or violence."[44] To acknowledge the presence of indigenous modes of governance and practices of indigenous dispossession would entail holding land obtained through conquest in a status of colonial dependency. The idea that indigenous peoples occupied no legitimate political position in the American political landscape crucially supported Paine's claim that the right of the people to the land was founded in justice and not conquest.

The problem of western land compounded when Maryland refused to sign the Articles of Confederation unless states with large land grants in their colonial charters relinquished their claims. To ease the anxieties of Maryland, Congress instituted many of Paine's ideas by outlining three principles to guide the disposal of public lands in the resolution of 1780. The first of these key principles was that "land shall be disposed of for the common benefit of the United States."[45] One of Paine's main ideas was that western land was the "common right" of all citizens. A crucial part of this was that authority over western lands should be granted to the Continental Congress rather than private corporations. Paine argued that successful colonization required that the confederation government be given positive powers to transform private land claims into public property. James Tully writes, "By locating sovereignty in the federal government, directly representing the people, Paine ensured that the Congress, and not Virginia or any other state, had jurisdiction over the western lands."[46] If the Revolution transferred imperial sovereignty from the Crown to "the people," then it also entailed the transfer of territorial sovereignty and thus title to western land to "the people." While he initially opposed Paine, James Madison, less than ten years later, similarly asserted that the west was a "national stock" of wealth that was essential to the public welfare of the new nation.[47] The idea of land as public property was crucial to the vitality of republican principles because it ensured that vast grants of land would not provide the basis of political power for a church or aristocracy.[48]

The second key principle of the 1780 land resolution was that western land should "be settled and formed into distinct republican states, which shall become members of the federal union."[49] The question was how this principle would be put into practice. In the land ordinance of 1784, passed by Congress for the purposes of settling the land of the Northwest Territory into distinct states, Thomas Jefferson outlined the process by which the territories of the northwest should become self-governing, republican states. When their population reached 20,000, territories obtained the right to petition Congress to establish permanent constitutions and become part of the Union. That Jefferson considered this to be a program of colonization is evident enough in his assertion that "our confederacy must be viewed as the nest, from which all America, North and South, is to be peopled."[50] Fixing his gaze on both the colonization of the Mississippi valley and South America, Jefferson saw the land ordinance as a means of transplanting republican communities to distant territories. Yet despite the expectation that newly settled colonies would become republican states, new settlements were governed by federally appointed colonial governors in much the same manner as many prewar British colonies until they reached a population of five thousand, at which point government transferred to a representative assembly with restricted suffrage.[51] James Monroe, who was largely responsible for translating Jefferson's original ordinances into the Northwest Ordinance of 1787, wrote that new territories were "in effect to be . . . colonial government[s] similar to that which prevailed in these states previous to the Revolution."[52] In this regard, new colonies were subject to a temporary status of colonial dependency where they underwent a period of imperial tutelage before they were transformed into self-governing republican states.[53]

The third and most important principle of the land ordinances was the idea that new republican states should "have the same rights of sovereignty, freedom and independence, as the other states."[54] This idea was explicit in Paine's defense of public authority over western land when we he wrote, "The United States now standing on the line of sovereignty, the vacant territory is their property collectively, but the persons by whom it may hereafter be peopled will also have an equal right with ourselves."[55] In June 1787, Congress passed the Northwest Ordinance, which replaced though retained the spirit of Jefferson's 1784 ordinance. Drawing on settler ideas of empire elaborated during the Imperial Crisis, the Ordinance institutionalized a framework of imperial federalism that rejected the core-periphery model of the British Empire and instead incorporated new territories into federal sovereignty as free and equal states rather than as dependent entities. In Jefferson's felicitous phrasing, which was also used in the 1784 ordinance, new republican states were to be admitted into the federal union "on an equal footing with the original states."[56] The innovation of the Ordinance for federalist thought was less in institutionalizing a system of shared sovereignty (which would be the Constitution's federalist legacy) than in outlining a model of colonization by which colonial entities would be integrated into empire without subordination to the metropolitan center. Imperial thought in early modern Europe treated territorial possessions obtained through conquest and colonization largely in terms of a center-periphery relation. The Northwest Ordinance, however, "promised an end to such second-class colonies."[57] In allowing new states to enter the union on equal footing with original states, it ensured that the colonization of distant territory would not result in settlers being stripped of their civic status. When settlers removed to settle new territories, they did not relinquish their sovereign rights but transported their sovereign power to found new democratic states on top of supposedly vacant land.

Reflecting back on the tumult of the 1770s, James Madison expressed this federal conception of empire as the driving force of independence: "The fundamental principle of the Revolution was that the Colonies were coordinate members with each other and with Great Britain, of an empire united by a common executive sovereign, but not united by any common legislative sovereign."[58] While the Constitution significantly diverted from such a formula in having both a common legislative and executive sovereign, what is important is the way equality among the "coordinate members" of an extended polity is taken as the defining feature of a new vision of empire. The language of empire here significantly reflects that of federalism. In both, the vigor of a powerful executive capable of directing territorial and economic expansion coexists alongside principles of popular sovereignty at the local level. Insofar as the constituent units of empire were co-equal and held checks over the executive sovereign, Madison heralded a new conception of empire that rejected colonial dependence as the organizing feature of an extended polity. Rather than an "alternative to empire,"[59] American federalism represented a way of organizing and constituting a settler-colonial empire based on popular sovereignty.

Despite forbidding patterns of colonial dependence, the Northwest Ordinance integrated into its framework of federal empire two modes of colonial violence: the expropriation of indigenous land and the expansion of slave labor. Upon a cursory glance, the legacy of the ordinance regarding slavery appears unambiguous. Article VI explicitly prohibited involuntary servitude in the Northwest Territory. But as legal historian Paul Finkelman has argued, the law was inherently ambivalent regarding slavery. While it formally prohibited slavery in Northwest Territory, it strengthened its presence in the nation. In addition to providing for the return of fugitive slaves to their owners, the ordinance tacitly carved out the territories south of the Ohio River for the expansion of slave labor.[60] One year after President Washington signed the law into effect under the authority of the new constitution, Congress passed the Southwest Ordinance in 1790, which organized the territories south of the Ohio River under the same framework as the 1787 law, only lacking the prohibition on slavery.[61] Far from being an abolitionist document, the Ordinance allowed the expansion of slavery within certain limits. More than the Constitution itself, it generated the central contradiction between an empire of slavery and an empire of liberty at the center of nineteenth-century political culture. To uphold its promises of federal and juridical equality, the Ordinance institutionalized two different processes of expansion in a single national framework: the expansion of free territories and of plantation society (see Chapter 6).

The position of Indian tribes in the framework of federal empire was similarly fraught with ambiguity. Taken at face value, the ordinance extended the principles of imperial equality to the state governments as well as to the Indian tribes occupying the western territories. Article III stipulated that Indian lands shall not be taken "without their consent" and that their "property, rights and liberty" shall not be infringed upon except in cases of just war.[62] Similar to colonial arguments during the Imperial Crisis, early republican expansionists masked the constitutive dynamics of conquest to uphold ideological visions of an empire of liberty. To achieve this end, Henry Knox, secretary of war under President Washington, formulated a "liberal system of justice" regarding Indian nations.[63] Knox articulated two different courses of action in dealing with indigenous polities making claims on the Northwest Territory: a policy of conquest, which involved the extermination of hostile tribes by physical force; and a policy of purchase and treaty that sought the consent of Indians in new territorial acquisitions. In place of military power, Knox sought the protection of Indians from white settlers by designating the federal government as the sole authority in the negotiation of treaties and purchases of land. In a 1789 report to Congress, he clearly echoed the spirit of the Northwest Ordinance: "The Indians being the prior occupants possess the right of the soil. It cannot be taken from them unless by their free consent." He thus eschewed the Lockean principle that uncultivated land constitutes a violation of natural law and warrants colonial settlement. Instead, he asserted the rights of Indians to their lands and viewed policies of consent as consistent with the "laws of nature."[64]

Knox's Indian policy sought expansion through consent rather than conquest in an effort to put the new nation on a solid base of legitimacy and forestall corruption and decline. Rejecting the "language of superiority and command," Knox held that it was "politic and just to treat the Indians more on a footing of equality" and to "convince them of the justice and humanity was well as the power of the United States."[65] He advised Congress that a policy aimed at influencing the tribes through the "benefits of civilized life" will "reflect permanent honor on the national character," which will add to the legitimacy of American claims on western territory against the Spanish and British empires. Citing its brutalities in Mexico and Peru, Knox warned that a policy of conquest would put the United States on the same level as Spain. If a peaceful policy of assimilation was not adopted, a "black cloud of injustice and inhumanity will impend over our national character."[66] Dispossession by conquest, Knox feared, would call the enlightened foundations of the new republic into question.

Despite the assumption of indigenous-settler equality in the Ordinance, the logic of native elimination crucially defined the framework of federative replication. Evident in one of Washington's personal letters toward the close of the war with Britain, the liberal system of justice forcefully enacted the erasure of indigenous cultures and land claims. Washington wrote,

> Policy and economy point very strongly to the expediency of being upon good terms with the Indians, and the propriety of purchasing their Lands in preference to attempting to drive them by force of arms out of their Country; which as we have already experienced is like driving the Wild Beasts of the Forest which will return as soon as the pursuit is at an end and fall perhaps on those that are left there; when the gradual extension of our Settlements will as certainly cause the Savage as the Wolf to retire; both being beasts of prey tho' they differ in shape.

In addition to relying on dehumanizing rhetoric, Washington's letter illustrates how the principles of purchase and consent in early US Indian policy fostered the elimination of the indigenous presence in the Northwest Territory. Rather than a policy of colonial conquest, the destruction of indigenous peoplehood proceeded through the "gradual extension of our Settlements."[67]

At the same time that Knox and Washington's liberal system of justice sought to build a model of US-indigenous relations premised on consent, contractual thinking retroactively authorized the prior modes of conquest that went into the present configuration of power in North America. The disavowal of conquest as a central force in the making of the early republic is forcefully evident in Washington's call for moderation and diplomacy in dealing with indigenous nations. In his attempt to make consent the overriding principle of US-indigenous relations, he asked Indians to "draw a veil over what is past."[68] Washington's advice illustrates how consensual principles at work in the treaty and purchase system in fact prevented Indians from making claims on US sovereignty based on past injustices. The liberal system of justice thus foreclosed the possibility of indigenous contestation of settler land claims by erasing the enduring legacy and present reality of colonial dispossession.

Magna Carta of the Colonies

The imperial and colonial dimensions of American federalism come into more direct focus by placing federalist thought and institutions in a transnational context. Perhaps the most obvious point of comparison is the

British Empire of the nineteenth century, not in the exploitation colonies of India but in the settler colonies of Canada, Australia, and New Zealand. One of the foremost theorists of British colonization in the nineteenth century was Edward Gibbon Wakefield, a political thinker and practical politician who became heavily involved in the colonization of South Australia and New Zealand in the 1830s. Along with other influential proponents of colonization such as Charles Buller, Wakefield helped found the National Colonization Society in 1830, which encouraged British officials to put his theory of settler colonization into practice.

Wakefield held that two key conditions make a colony. First, a colony depended on the existence of "waste land" that could be transformed into the private property of individuals through government policy. Second, the establishment of a colony involved "the migration of people; the removal of people to settle in a new place." Accordingly, Wakefield understood colonization not conventionally as the imposition of dependency status on foreign conquests but rather as "the removal of people from an old to a new country, and the settlement of people on the waste land of the new country."[69] To sustain the distinction between the "old" and "new" country, Wakefield disavowed the historical presence of indigenous peoples and modes of governance in new territorial spaces. He thus presented a distorted ideological picture of colonization that obscured the necessary colonial violence to make the "new country" in the first place.

In an anonymously published but influential work of political theory, *England and America: A Comparison of the Social and Political State of Both Nations* (1833), Wakefield first developed a theory of what he called "systematic colonization" through an explicit comparison of the social state of England with that of America.[70] The theory of systematic colonization is best understood as a series of propositions concerning the practice of colonization grouped under three key dimensions. The first dimension of colonization concerns the ultimate ends of colonization, which are three-fold. The first end of colonization from the perspective of the mother country is that colonization provided for "the extension of the market for the disposing of their surplus produce."[71] Although England had obtained an unprecedented degree of wealth through the production of industrial and agricultural commodities, the home country did not establish sufficient markets for the sale of these commodities. Surplus production, in addition to hindering economic growth, drove down wages and compounded problems of pauperism and unemployment. By creating new societies in distant colonies, the global expansion of commodity markets would relieve pressures put on domestic markets from surplus production.

The second end of colonization was that it provides "relief from excessive numbers."[72] Wakefield's theory of colonization rested on a specific characterization of the relationship between the colonies and the mother country. In the colonies, fertile land was in abundance while labor was scarce, while in the mother country there was an abundant population of laborers but land was scarce. The problem with this situation in the mother country was that a reserve army of surplus laborers further suppressed industrial wages and exacerbated the impoverished condition of workers, criminals, peasants, prostitutes, and paupers. A permanent underclass of underpaid and unemployed laborers created social contradictions in the metropolis and sharpened class conflict over the maldistribution of wealth and misery. Colonization offered a solution to these contradictions by providing a release for social pressures plaguing the metropolitan political economy.[73] It projected social contradictions away from metropolitan centers of commerce to colonial peripheries by replacing indigenous societies in colonial "waste lands" with surplus populations. Both of these two ends of colonization—relief from surplus populations and the expansion of markets—leads to the third end: "the enlargement of the field of employing capital and labor."[74] Far from a harm to be avoided that produces great costs to empire, colonization expands the productive potential of the imperial economy.

The second key dimension concerns the means of colonization, of which there are two: "the disposal of waste land" and "the removal of people" from the old to the new country.[75] Wakefield was clear that the second is ancillary to the first. How government distributed and disposed of colonial waste land ultimately determined the process by which people removed themselves from the mother country to settle the colony.[76] In Wakefield's system of colonization, the state must first claim possession of waste land by turning it into public property. Simply turning waste land into private property was not sufficient for constituting a program of systematic colonization. What mattered was how waste land was disposed. Wakefield preferred a method by which the home government sold land to colonists for a price. The objective was to prevent settlers from becoming independent subsistence farmers and instead force them into relations of wage labor. To do this, Wakefield advocated the sale of land to capitalists at a sufficient price that varied according to local conditions. A sufficient price must be high enough to prevent subsistence farming, which would create a glut of labor in the colonies, and low enough to encourage improvement of land by capitalists.[77]

In addition to free land grants to independent farmers, Wakefield also criticized the common practice of English expansion that involved disposing of colonial land through proprietary land grants given to wealthy families. Proprietary land grants were widely used in Upper and Lower Canada where the Crown disseminated land to loyalists, lords, and others who found favor with imperial officials and colonial governors. In Upper and Lower Canada, land (and thus power and prestige) were granted to a network of elites known as the Family Compact and the Chateau Clique, respectively, who in turn created a colonial aristocracy by transmitting land grants to subsequent generations.[78] Against these practices, Wakefield held that "for the good of all, the interference of government is . . . necessary to prevent a few individuals from seizing the waste land of a colony." To enter a colonial compact is to relinquish one's rights to appropriate uncultivated land, instead vesting those rights in a common governmental power that disposes of open land for the benefit of the whole community. The greatest good of the colony, Wakefield insisted, is "the progress of colonization," by which he means the transfer of labor and capital from the mother country to the colony.[79]

In theorizing the means of colonization, Wakefield drew on the example of the United States, which, with its sale of public lands in auction based on fixed prices, came closest to a "uniform system" of colonization. The United States launched a measured and rational campaign of colonization by asserting the domain of the federal government over all of the waste lands within its dominion.[80] The basis of this policy is Article IV of the Constitution, which gave Congress the "power to dispose of and make all needful rules and regulations respecting the territory or other property belonging to the United States."[81] Wakefield also referenced the land ordinance of 1784, which among many things instituted a public survey system to dispose of western land. In the American system of colonization, "the government of the United States has, generally, instead of giving away new land, sold it by auction to the highest bidder above a fixed minimum price."[82] Based on this institutional practice, Wakefield held that the United States was the only modern nation to adopt a policy of systematic colonization: "The North Americans are the most extensive colonizers (in the strict and proper sense of the word) that ever existed. They have plenty of waste land close to their increasing population."[83]

The third key dimension of the colonizing process concerned the government of the colonies. The primary problem of colonial government was that "if colonies were so many extensions of an old society, they would never submit to be governed from a distance. . . . A people entirely fit to manage themselves will never long submit to be managed by others, much less to be managed by an authority residing at a great distance from them."[84] Presaging by half a century Frederick Jackson Turner's frontier thesis, Wakefield speculated that settlers developed capacities for democratic self-government through the colonizing process itself. Drawing on the United States as an example, he asserted that colonization played a significant role in "rendering a people fit to enjoy self-government or democratic institutions."[85] The problem was that while democracy coincided with colonization, as extensions of empire, colonies were also subject to the rule of metropolitan authorities. For this reason, colonies must be ruled through democratic institutions of local self-government even as they are part of a broader imperial organization. Local self-government was desirable because it was both cheaper to the empire and more efficient to allow colonists to run their own affairs. Because colonists were invested in the prosperity and development of the colony, they were better suited to govern colonial affairs than a distant imperial administration that governed through principles of colonial dependency.

Wakefield's suggestions about the self-government of colonies found institutional expression in John George Lambton, Earl of Durham's *Report on the Affairs of British North America* (1838). After the explosion of armed revolts against the Family Compact and Chateau Clique in Upper and Lower Canada in 1837, British imperial officials dispatched Durham, along with Wakefield and Charles Buller serving in advisory roles, to Canada to study the situation and provide recommendations. In addition to the unification of Upper and Lower Canada under a single colonial assembly, the primary recommendation of Durham's report was to institute a policy of responsible government where Crown-appointed colonial governors would be accountable to the demands of the colonial assembly. J. S. Mill aptly explained the position of the Durham report: "It is now a fixed principle of the policy of Great Britain, professed in theory and faithfully adhered to in practice, that her colonies of European race, equally with the parent country, possess the fullest measure of internal self-government."[86] Unlike exploitation colonies in British India, where the focus was on extracting the value of indigenous labor and resources, Durham and Wakefield viewed settler colonies in New Zealand, Australia, and Canada as equals with the mother country, entitled to the same economic and political rights as metropolitan citizens. These principles of imperial equality and colonial self-government led one biographer of Wakefield to call the Durham report "the Magna Carta of the colonies" because it founded the "kingdom of responsible government."[87]

One of the main sources of information for the Durham report was John Arthur Roebuck, an agent to the British House of Commons appointed by the House of Assembly of Lower Canada. Durham solicited a paper on colonial government from Roebuck and heavily drew on his arguments in drafting his recommendations. In his paper, Roebuck developed an idea of federative empire that was explicitly modeled on the American example in which uncultivated and unpeopled lands became "constituent units of their mighty empire."[88] The main difficulty facing the British "colonial empire" was the task of "creating a new community in a wild, uncultivated region." While British colonization of the Americas (and, subsequently, its settler colonies in Canada, New Zealand, and Australia) followed no systematic plan, the United States provided a lesson in the "colonization of the immense unpeopled wastes" and the "change of the communities so formed, from colonies into that of sovereign states, and the reception of them into the great Federal Union, when they become integral portions of the great Empire, known to foreign powers as the United States of America."[89] Roebuck called the Northwest Ordinance an original "specimen of systematic colonization . . . because it is really the first instance on record of a government providing for the gradual creation of many independent nations by a carefully-considered and regular system; a system which we must imitate, if we desire to produce any great effect as a colonizing power."[90] In addition to providing an effective framework of colonization, the innovation of the Northwest Ordinance was in the way it integrated new colonies into a federal union on terms of imperial equality.

After the Durham report, the old commercial model of British Empire gave way to a "new idea of an empire of settlement" based on the principle of self-governing colonies. In this new conception of empire, British colonies, as bearers of English institutions and culture, were made equal partners with the English metropolis.[91] What is important for present purposes is that the British idea of an empire of settlement drew on precedents established by the Northwest Ordinance. By attending to the transnational dimensions of colonization, American expansion can be better understood as a settler colonial process that shares important features with other settler states in the British Empire.[92] Attention to the transnational diffusion of colonial ideology sheds significant light on the imperial dimensions of American democratic thought. Viewed through a transnational lens, the Northwest Ordinance might be better understood as Magna Carta of the Colonies than the Durham report itself.

Conclusion

Federalism is a defining feature of American political thought. In its basic conception, it seeks to define the proper balance between separate and independent states on the one hand and the national government on the other in an arrangement of shared sovereignty. For most political theorists, federalism is, in William Riker's words, an "alternative to empire."[93] In this familiar understanding, the British colonists of North America sought to replace imperial government, in which the colonies were dependent upon and subordinate to metropolitan authority, with democratic and federal governments marked by a relative degree of equality among separate and independent states. Rather than colonies, the American states retained some degree of sovereignty and autonomy even as they were incorporated into a broader federal union. If colonies were marked by their dependence upon metropolitan authorities, states in a federal system were equal with another.

But how accurate is this familiar portrait of American federalism? Or more precisely, what important dynamics of power and domination does it obscure? As the epigraph by Edward Gibbon Wakefield illustrates, the status of American states in the late eighteenth- and nineteenth-century Anglo political world was understood in explicitly colonial terms. Rather than an alternative to colonial empire, federalism provided a means of organizing and constituting a particular kind of settler colonial empire. In the political thinking of English settlers, the United States represented a new world conception of empire composed of equal and quasi-sovereign settler communities committed to a common project of landed expansion rather than dependent and subordinate colonies. Far from rejecting the legitimacy of empire outright, the revolutionaries and constitutional architects of the early republic planted the seeds of an independent empire that extended the dominion of European colonists. Although the model of settler expansion offered by the Northwest Ordinance rejected a hierarchical organization of empire where colonial sub-units are held in a status of subordination to metropolitan institutions, it nevertheless engendered profound degrees of colonial violence in sanctioning the elimination of indigenous sovereignties through a process of republican expansionism.

2 The Coloniality of Constituent Power

"By the mere act of removing, they [settlers] become legislators and statesmen; the legislators and statesmen of a new country too, created, as it were, by themselves."
—*Edward Gibbon Wakefield, England and America (1833)*

The idea of constituent power is one of the most enduring legacies of the American Revolution and American political thought more generally. Although it has deep roots in early modern and even medieval traditions of political thought, the concept of constituent power found its most forceful expression in the revolt of American settlers against British imperial rule. Hannah Arendt has asserted that one of the primary contributions of American political thought was in how the founders sought "to constitute an altogether different form of government, to bring about the formation of a new body politic, where the liberation from oppression aims . . . at the constitution of freedom."[1] For Arendt, the genius of the American revolutionary tradition was in founding a permanent political order based on popular consent, which provided legal stability in the absence of traditional forms of authority. At the same time, Arendt feared that expansion, conquest, and imperialism potentially undermined the stable foundations of republican rule in popular consent. Because republican government was founded on the doctrine of "genuine consent," its authority cannot be "stretched indefinitely" without destabilizing its foundations. Extending republican rule beyond its limits spurs an "inner contradiction between the nation's body politic and conquest" by eroding the permanence and durability of political institutions that, left unto themselves, "develop stabilizing forces which stand in the way of constant transformation and expansion."[2]

In further delineating the contributions of American revolutionary thought, Arendt wrote, "The colonization of North America and the republican government of the United States constitute perhaps the greatest, certainly the boldest, enterprise of European mankind."[3] Although Arendt acknowledged the connection between colonization and the revolutionary process by which the people constituted republican government, she concealed the settler colonial logics of constituent power by divorcing the realities of colonial dispossession from colonial settlement. Against these sanguine depictions of constituent power, this chapter uncovers what I call *the coloniality of constituent power* that operated as a central feature of settler political thought during the revolutionary period. If constituted power refers to institutionalized political power ensconced in settled constitutional forms and delegated powers such as elected assemblies, judicial bodies, or executive offices, constituent power is the power to begin, end, or modify those institutionally delegated powers. It entails the sovereign power of the people to constitute a new political order. As the preeminent source of political legitimacy in modernity, constituent power is necessarily superior to constituted power.[4] Read against the backdrop of the American and French revolutions, constituent power is "co-original and coeval" with "the birth of the modern doctrine of popular sovereignty," in which democracy comes to describe "popular foundings" and "collective acts of self-legislation."[5]

The coloniality of constituent power captures how modern forms of democratic power encapsulate logics of native elimination and indigenous disavowal.[6] As this chapter illustrates, claims to the constituent power of settlers to found new republics on expropriated land embraced two ideological justifications of native expropriation. First, settlers saw the frontier as a state of nature—vacant land that lacked indigenous modes of governance capable of making competing territorial claims against settler sovereignty. Second, colonial architects such as Thomas Jefferson treated indigenous peoples as occupying a savage state that would recede with the expansion of settlers westward. In both cases, democratic empire expands by replacing indigenous sovereignty with settler sovereignty through the conceptual erasure of native political forms. The coloniality of constituent power designates the second key dimension of the principle of federative replication—the sovereignty of settlers to found self-governing republics in the wilderness constituted the driving force of colonial expansion. In the framework of federative replication, colonization acts as a form of constituent power that provides the foundation of an imperial-democratic polity founded on the consent of the people.

Through a reading of the Vermont Constitution of 1777, the first section of this chapter argues that colonization represented a form of constituent power in a negative and positive sense, as the power to constitute a new order and as the power to suspend or dissolve old orders. In settler constitutional thought, colonization replaced the right to revolution as the dominant means of exercising constituent power. The second section examines the constitutional efforts of settlers to exercise their constituent sovereignty and found new republics along the Trans-Appalachian frontier in the 1770s and 1780s. These efforts posed a formidable challenge to the framework of democratic empire because settlers claimed popular sovereignty in opposition to the sovereignty of the tidewater states of America. To preempt the threat of separation and imperial disintegration, the Northwest Ordinance integrated the constituent power of settlers into the framework of federative replication. Finally, the last section turns to Jefferson's notion of the "empire of liberty," which captured this new democratic doctrine of colonial expansion in distilled ideological form. For Jefferson, the primary engine of colonial expansion was not the centralized state but the efforts of settler communities to plant their own sovereignty in distant land. This decentralized vision of federal expansion cast native peoples as occupying a savage social state that would wither away as settlers progressed westward.

Consent, Colonization, and Settler Constitutionalism

Settler colonialization is at root a process of dispossession by which settlers seek to appropriate native land not simply to expropriate native labor and resources but to build a permanent settlement and constitute a new society. Veracini perceptively captures the role of constituent power in settler colonial imaginaries: "While settlers see themselves as founders of political orders, they also interpret their collective efforts in terms of an inherent sovereign claim that travels with them and is ultimately, if not immediately, autonomous from the colonizing metropole."[7] The founding capacity of settlers to create new legal and political orders derives not just from their removal from the mother country but also from their desire to permanently settle new land. If constituent power is about "the production of constitutional norms"[8] that provide the constitutional organization of the state, then, as political founders, settlers wield a particular kind of constituent sovereignty that both erases old indigenous orders and produces new constitutional arrangements. Settler sovereignty is not simply the power of settler communities to rule themselves in a quasi-autonomous fashion.

It involves the power to eliminate other forms of sovereignty that might upset the claims settlers make on what they perceive as vacant land. This section outlines a distinct body of thought I call "settler constitutionalism" in which the colonization of land and native dispossession engender a form of constituent power, which in turn provides the basis for the production of legal norms of popular consent and popular sovereignty.

In his seminal work on American constitutionalism, Willi Paul Adams says of constituent power, "Americans invented not only the thing but also the name for it."[9] The Pennsylvania radical Thomas Young first used the term in debates over the statehood of Vermont. As a radical democrat, Young coined the term in 1777 to defend the right of the people of Vermont to construct their own constitution independent of the authority of other colonies that also made claims on the land. In doing so, Young made a distinction between the "supreme delegate power" and the "supreme constituent power." While the former designated the power of elected representatives who wielded delegated authority in settled constitutional forms, the latter represented the power of the people as the ultimate fountain of authority for the creation of constitutional norms. Young wrote of the settlers of Vermont: "They are the supreme constituent power, and of course their immediate Representatives are the supreme delegate power; and as soon as delegate power gets too far out of the hands of the constituent power, tyranny is in some degree established." Young then called on settlers to meet in townships to choose delegates for a constitutional convention. For Young, "the people at large [are] the true proprietors of governmental power."[10] Indeed, Young saw the exercise of constituent power by the people to found new constitutional orders as the very embodiment of the democratic doctrine of popular sovereignty.

The fact that the idea of constituent power in American political thought was first named and wielded in defense of settler sovereignty is not coincidental. The settlers of Vermont sought to constitute a new polity on land already claimed by existing states. Vermont was first created as a series of townships called the New Hampshire Grants in the mid-1700s. While the settlers of the New Hampshire Grants saw themselves as an autonomous jurisdiction, New York and New Hampshire made separate territorial claims on the land. Although the Crown settled the dispute in favor of New York in 1764, the Vermont settlers continued to see themselves as a distinct and separate colony. By the American Revolution, the colonial militia of Vermont played a crucial role in seizing Fort Ticonderoga from the British in 1775. Based on their participation in the War of Independence, Vermont settlers asserted claims to sovereign statehood. In July 1777 they declared their independence both from the state of New York and from the British Empire. To maintain colonial unity against Britain, Congress was forced to recognize New York's claim to the New Hampshire Grants.[11] After both Congress and New York refused to recognize Vermont as an autonomous state, the settlers proceeded to create a new constitution modeled on the radical Pennsylvania constitution, which Young himself recommended to the settlers. Despite fighting alongside the other colonies in the Revolutionary War, Vermont remained an independent republic from 1777 to 1791.

To grasp how constituent power was tied to settler colonial logics it is necessary to examine the arguments the Vermont settlers made in favor of sovereign statehood. The best expression of the "Vermont doctrine"— the idea that the people have a natural right to constitute a new government independent of preexisting forms of legitimate authority—resides in the Vermont Constitution of 1777.[12] As previously mentioned, settlers modeled the Vermont Constitution on the Pennsylvania Constitution, both of which reflected the basic democratic structure of many state constitutions that were passed after the Declaration of Independence. One of the most innovative features of these state constitutions involved sovereignty clauses asserting that the people were the original source of political authority. The Declaration of Independence notwithstanding, the archetype of this radical assertion of popular sovereignty was the Virginia Bill of Rights, which posited, "That all power is vested in, and consequently derived from, the people; that magistrates are their trustees and servants, and at all times amenable to them."[13] In this formula, the delegated power of elected officials was subordinate to the constituent power of the people. Because the people constituted the government, they represented a higher authority than the state itself. This basic idea of popular sovereignty also surfaced in Article V of the Vermont Constitution: "That all power being originally inherent in, and consequently, derived from, the people."[14]

In upholding the sovereignty of the people as the supreme source of political authority, the Vermont Constitution provided three avenues for the expression of constituent power.[15] First, it granted settlers an explicit right to resist unjust government, affirming the "indubitable, unalienable and indefeasible right to reform, alter, or abolish government in such manner as shall be by that community judged most conducive to the public weal."[16] To justify the ongoing colonial rebellion, the "alter and abolish" clause affirmed the right of the people to resist civil government and eliminate existing forms of unjust authority. To specify the conditions under which this right could be justified, the Constitution clarified, whenever "the great ends of government [i.e., security and protection of community] are not obtained."[17] Second, the Vermont Constitution allowed for the expression of constituent sovereignty through the right to constitutional revision. Specifically, it granted a council of censors the authority to call for a constitutional convention for the purpose of "amending any article of this constitution which may be defective."[18] These two expressions of constituent power undoubtedly derived from the "alter and abolish" clause of the Declaration of Independence.

While these first two are common expressions of constituent sovereignty, the third avenue is peculiar to conceptions of constituent power in settler constitutionalism. Article XVII of the Vermont Constitution proclaimed "That all people have a natural and inherent right to emigrate from one State to another, that will receive them, or to form a new State in vacant countries, or in such countries as they can purchase whenever they think that thereby they can promote their own happiness."[19] Few commentators have appreciated the significance of the emigration clause for American political thought. To some extent, this neglect is understandable. The emigration clause was excised from the Constitution in 1786, and even in its short nine-year lifespan the Vermont Supreme Court did not decide on a single case concerning the provision.[20] Regardless, I want to suggest that the sovereignty clause and the emigration clause worked together to retroactively authorize the origins of the settler state. The emigration clause operates less as the assertion of a present political right than as a fictive device for imagining the legitimate foundations of settler democracy constituted through the constituent power of the people. Put differently, the emigration clause provides an ideological justification of the origins of a democratic state founded on settler colonization.[21] In the emigration clause, settler claims to democratic self-government cohere around representations of vacant land. If the people of New York played any significant role in settling the New Hampshire Grants, then the sovereign claims of settlers were void. Representations of vacant land helped settlers assert that the origins of civil government in Vermont were due to the efforts of settlers themselves.

Emigration and colonization thus operate as forms of constituent power by which settlers constitute democratic community. In explicating the logic of constituent power, the radical democratic theorist Antonio Negri asserts that modern political orders are marked by a revolution-constitution dialectic in which the constituent power of the people upends the constituted order only to be recaptured again in settled constitutional forms. If constituent power expresses the revolutionary potential of the people to both destroy and create political order, it is in inherently at odds with the constituted power of constitutional government. While constituent power opens a revolutionary process by which the people break the ties that bind citizen and government, the exercise of constituted power by the state short-circuits the revolutionary movement and reestablishes political and social order. These effects of constituted power, however, are never without remainder. The revolutionary force of constituent power does not completely dissipate when political order is re-created but rather retreats underground only to reemerge in a new revolutionary situation.[22]

With the emigration clause, a similar dynamic occurs in what I call the *colonization-constitution dialectic*. In settler constitutionalism, colonization represents an alternative constitutional mechanism—distinct from the right of revolution and constituent assemblies—that allows the people to exercise constituent power, to untie the bonds of government and erect new institutions. The emigration clause upholds the right of settlers to "form a new State in vacant countries . . . whenever they think that thereby they can improve their happiness." A few important features of the clause stand out here. The first is the negative right of settlers to extricate from an existing state by migrating to vacant land. When delegated powers no longer secure the happiness of its citizens, those same citizens obtain an inherent sovereign right to remove from the mother country and reconstitute a self-governing community in a new political space. This negative right also involves the disavowal of indigenous sovereignties by representing the new territories to which settlers emigrate as vacant and empty. In its positive aspect, settlers have the right to constitute a new political order that better ensures public happiness. In the colonization-constitution dialectic, the further emigration of settlers threatens to upend the constituted order of settler colonial empire insofar as settlers assert separation as a necessary correlate of settler sovereignty. Rather than a revolutionary right of resistance against unjust government, constituent power in settler constitutionalism entails the natural right of settlers to colonize a new country.

The claim that Vermont settlers made on sovereign statehood against both New York and the British Empire derived from a theory of colonization that affirmed the right of settlers to plant their sovereign claims to self-government in what they deemed to be unpeopled land. Like the Declaration of Independence and the Constitution of Pennsylvania, the preamble to the Vermont Constitution announced independence within the terms of the right to revolution. Because the Crown had withdrawn protection of the colonists and waged "a cruel and most unjust war against them," settlers claimed that "all allegiance and fealty to the said King and his successors, are dissolved and at an end, and all power and authority derived from him, ceased in the colonies." Yet where the Vermont Constitution was wholly original and differed from the Declaration was in the way it cast constituent power in broader terms than just the right to revolution. In asserting their independence, the Vermont settlers had to abolish the authority of the British Empire and the state of New York. In doing so, the preamble provided a lengthy explanation of how the colonial governors of New York used fraud and deceit to make "an unjust claim to those lands, which greatly retards emigration into, and the settlement of, this State."[23] Read alongside the emigration clause, the preamble suggested that the prevention of further settlement represented a violation of natural rights grave enough to warrant independence.

Constituent power is the sheerest expression of the basic maxim that the consent of the governed is the only foundation of legitimate government. With the right to revolution, citizens withdraw their consent through resistance to civil government. In settler constitutionalism, conversely, norms of democratic consent operate through the right of emigration and the potential of settlers to colonize new land. The settler colonial logic of the emigration clause and its attendant notions of democratic consent can be adequately grasped by briefly examining Lockean notions of consent in social contract theory. In a passage that perfectly characterizes the constituent power of settlers to found a new political order, Locke famously wrote, "political societies all began from a voluntary union, and the mutual agreement of men freely acting in the choice of their governors, and forms of government." In this contractual fiction, "people free and in the state of nature . . . met together incorporated and began a common-wealth."[24] In the contractual scenario that marks the origins of civil government, "express consent"—the explicit acknowledgment of one's obligation to obey government—is enough to make "any man entering into society . . . a perfect member of that society, a subject of that government." The problem arises, for Locke, when considering individuals who have not granted their express consent or subsequent generations who were not part of the original founding compact. What obligates an individual who did not grant their express consent to obey civil government? To solve this problem, Locke introduces the concept of "tacit consent." Despite the lack of overt consent, "every man, that hath any possessions, or enjoyment, of any part of the dominions of any government, doth thereby give his tacit consent, and is as far forth obliged to obedience to the laws of that government, during such enjoyment, as anyone under it."[25]

The political theorist Jimmy Casas Klausen argues that notions of vacant space available for further colonization actualize Locke's theory of consent by ensuring that there is "room enough" for those who wish to revoke their tacit consent to civil government.[26] When Locke suggests that the enjoyment of security in property is enough to solicit one's tacit consent to civil government, he is explicitly talking about possession of land. So long as any individual utilizes the protection of landed property provided by government, they grant their tacit consent to that government. Nevertheless, "whenever the owner, who has given nothing but such a *tacit consent* to the government, will, by donation, sale, or otherwise, quit the said possession, he is at liberty to go and incorporate himself into any other common-wealth; or to agree with others to begin a new one, *in vacuis locis* [in empty space], in any part of the world, they can find free and unpossessed."[27] In other words, the theory of tacit consent partially depends upon empty space that provides outlets of colonization for individuals or groups who seek to revoke their obligations to the state. Without the possibility of emigration, the theory of tacit consent unravels. Absent clear opportunities to remove oneself from an already constituted polity, the idea of tacit consent transforms into its opposite—i.e., "tacit coercion." Klausen asserts that the Lockean theory of consent not only "enables and justifies settler-initiated colonialism; it ideologically requires it insofar as natural liberty relies on the availability of open space for full actualization."[28] The exact same assumptions about open space and vacant land animate the emigration clause. Insofar as representations of vacant space necessarily discount the legitimacy of indigenous modes of governance, the notions of consent and constituent power embedded in the emigration clause require colonization and native dispossession.

In key respects, the theory of constituent power embodied in the Vermont Doctrine serves as a microcosm for the constitution of the nation as a whole. The importance of the emigration clause is less in the protection of an actual political right than in the way that it provides for an *ex post facto* justification of a society founded on settler colonization. The importance of colonization and settlement as fictive devices for imagining the origins of settler society is further evident in Thomas Paine's *Common Sense*. In the first section on the "origin and design of government in general," Paine begins by making his famous distinction between civil society and government. In doing so, he invites his readers to "suppose a small number of persons settled in some sequestered part of the earth, unconnected with the rest, they will then represent the first peopling of any country, or of the world."[29] What is important in this initial formulation of "the first peopling of any country" is that human beings are not simply found in a state of nature. They settle it and thus emigrate to it. In addition to upholding the classic assumption of American space disconnected from the European international system, Paine's origin story relies on the assumption that English settlers were America's first native inhabitants.

As this initial settlement develops further, Paine speculates that natural sociability would bring individuals to form a society defined by informal bonds of family, religion, and commerce. Paine writes, "Thus necessity, like a gravitating power, would soon form our newly arrived emigrants into society, the reciprocal blessings of which would supersede, and render the obligations of law and government unnecessary while they remained perfectly just to each other." In these early stages, necessity and mutual dependence provided the glue holding society together, which made law and government unnecessary. Over time, as life became more comfortable, these bonds loosened and vice arose, creating the need for "some form of government to supply the defect of moral virtue." As "the colony increases" and the bonds of natural sociability in civil society slacken, government became necessary to provide freedom and security for individuals. Because civil society is prior and thus superior to government (Paine would say the constituting power of government), the consent of settler-civil-society is necessary for the legitimacy of government.[30]

Unlike Rousseau or Locke, who imagine the origins of government in terms of a hypothetical state of nature and/or an anthropological stage of human development, Paine used colonization as the conceptual linchpin to theorize the origins of government founded in the consent of the people. In Paine's theory of democratic consent, settlers are not born in a state of nature. They migrate to it. In order to sustain the temporal separation between state and civil society, Paine must imagine settlers traveling to a vacant space unburdened by preexisting modes of governance. Conceiving of the state of nature in terms of an anthropological stage of development would not allow for a strict separation of civil society and government because it could not place the emergence of civil society prior to the emergence of government without the speculative stance of philosophical anthropology (thus offending common sense). It is crucial here to remember that in Lockean theories of consent there is no separation of state and civil society. For Locke, society and civil government were interchangeable terms. A member of civil society was de facto a member of civil government.

The problem with philosophical-anthropological understandings of the state of nature, for Paine, is that they cannot explain the absolute origin of civil society in common-sense terms. This failure to do so conflates the origins of society and government. Conceiving of the state of nature in terms of concrete practices of colonization provided Paine with a narrative device by which to place the emergence of society before the emergence of government. In this regard, Paine's liberal notion of limited government derived from a founding act of constituent sovereignty emerged from within the settler colonial spatial imagination.

Constituent Power on the Frontier

The trope of the state of nature grounded conceptions of good government in the settler imagination. Settlers claimed that their rights inhered not simply in their person but also in their own sense of community and for that reason were not contingent upon the territorial jurisdiction of states. Instead, they held that they had exchanged obedience for protection and that when civil and political rights were no longer secure, they were "thrown into . . . a state of nature" and had the right to dissolve the bonds linking state and citizens.[31] Yet in many instances, the appeal to the constituent power of the people did not result in the revolution-constitution dialectic where the people abolished existing tyrannical governments and created new republican states. Rather, settlers exercised their constituent power by removing from the jurisdiction of existing states and constructing their own jurisdictional entities based on settler sovereignty. Within the terms of settler constitutionalism, the history of western settlement after the American Revolution followed a "pattern of self-constituting local jurisdictions contesting the established claims of seaboard centers of power."[32]

The concept of constituent power in settler constitutionalism, however, posed significant problems to the American settler colonial empire in the revolutionary period. It is important to remember that settlers saw their sovereignty as partially autonomous from the authority of metropolitan institutions, which raised the threat of separation and imperial disintegration. Relying on the basic principles of settler constitutionalism, settler communities along the Trans-Appalachian frontier such as Wautauga Association, the Cumberland Compact, and the State of Franklin asserted their natural right to found separate democratic communities independent of preexisting states and the federal government. Overall, what made the tradition of settler constitutionalism unique was not the actual constitutional forms they constructed. For the most part, these projects of constitutional state-building mirrored the precedents they had before them. What was original about settler constitutionalism was the way it used colonization as a means of ensuring democratic consent and actualizing constituent power in the founding of a new constitutional order. In delineating the constitutional development of these settler polities, Frederick Jackson Turner famously proclaimed, "It is the fact of unoccupied territory in America that sets the evolution of American and European institutions in contrast. . . . There was in the Old World no virgin soil on which political gardeners might experiment with new varieties."[33] By migrating to an uncultivated state of nature, these "political gardeners" adapted old institutions to new contexts to cope with the exigencies of the colonial frontier.

The problem of settler sovereignty for American expansion in the early republic arose from the efforts of settlers to constitute new states on the eastern edge of the Appalachian Mountains, most notably in what is present-day Tennessee. On the southwestern frontier, this process of settler constitutionalism and the impulse for separation and independence began with the Watauga Association of 1772. In his famous history of western settlement, *The Winning of the West* (1889), Theodore Roosevelt held that the Watauga settlers provided the prototype of democratic expansion insofar as they "outlined in advance the nation's work."[34] As the last chapter illustrated, the Royal Proclamation of 1763 sought to restrict the expansion of settlers into territory west of the Appalachians. Yet despite its best intent, the proclamation line failed to curb frontier violence between settlers and natives. In hopes of placating settler desires for land, British officials negotiated the Treaty of Fort Stanwix with the Iroquois Confederacy in 1768, which in turn extended the proclamation line further west. Both the Shawnee and Cherokee nations, however, made contested claims on the territory ceded by the Iroquois Confederacy.[35]

Nevertheless, by 1769 settlers from Virginia, Pennsylvania, and North Carolina created the first permanent colony in the territory along the banks of the Watauga River. At first, the Watauga colony was thought to be an extension of Virginia, but by 1771 land surveyors found that the colony was within the territorial limits of land granted by North Carolina's colonial charter. Feeling that they were in a state of legal limbo, settlers constituted a new government and struck a treaty with the Cherokee Nation that granted an even larger tract of land than the Fort Stanwix treaty. As the colony attracted more settlers, the need for a civil authority to settle land disputes and punish criminals became imperative.[36] By 1772, two leaders of the colony—John Sevier and James Robertson—seized the settlers' "characteristic capacity for combination" and composed the Articles of the Watauga Association. Roosevelt wrote of the articles, "It is this fact of the early independence and self-government of the settlers along the head-waters of the Tennessee that gives to their history its peculiar importance. They were the first men of American birth to establish a free and independent community on the continent."[37] Insofar as they established "a purely democratic government with representative institutions, in which . . . the will of the majority was supreme," the Watauga Commonwealth represented the first self-constituted community in North America beyond the initial English colonies.[38]

Beyond establishing a colonial covenant regulating communal life on the frontier, the Watauga Compact asserted the primacy of settler sovereignty in providing a course of Indian policy that would protect settler landholdings. In a 1776 petition to North Carolina, the Watauga settlers defended their land claims on the basis of the fact that they held "their lands by their improvements as first settlers" and "held a Treaty with the Cherokee Indians, in order to purchase the lands of the Western Frontiers."[39] What is most significant in these claims is less the quasi-Lockean assertion of property rights through appeals to agricultural improvement than how the identity of "first settlers" constitutes the legitimate basis of democratic sovereignty. Historian Jean O'Brien explains that practices of "firsting" and "lasting" in historical discourse allowed settlers to construct a sense of belonging to the land by presenting themselves as the first inhabitants and indigenous inhabitants as the last remnants of a dying race.[40] Settlers represented the colonial state as the "first" genuine civilization with its own authentic history and culture. Narrating the colonial origins of the settler state constituted the centerpiece of Wataugan claims to settler sovereignty. The petition asserted, "We have shown you the causes of our first settling and the disappointments we have met with, the reason of our lease and of our purchase, the manner in which we purchased and how we hold of the Indians in fee simple; the causes of our forming a committee, and the legality of its election."[41] In an attempt to justify their sovereign claims to territory against metropolitan authorities, settlers constructed narratives about the causes of settlement as an important part of stories of settler peoplehood. Origin stories about settler communities thus became a crucial way of asserting settler sovereignty.

The further significance of the Watauga Compact is in the precedent it established for the development of settler constitutionalism in the revolutionary era. In 1779, many of the Watauga settlers, again led by Sevier and Robertson, broke off and migrated further west along the Cumberland River and eventually settled around what is now Nashville. Soon after, settlers convened to ratify articles of agreement for the purpose of constituting a new government that would guarantee basic rights of self-government and individual liberty.[42] The outcome of these efforts was the Cumberland Compact, which established "ARTICLES OF AGREEMENT . . . entered into by settlers on the Cumberland River, 1st May, 1780."[43] The radically democratic Cumberland Compact provided universal suffrage for all men over the age of twenty and instituted frequent elections in order to keep delegated powers accountable to the people. In a distinctive twist on modern social security policies, the Compact also stipulated that "when any person shall remove to this country with intent to become an inhabitant, and depart this life . . . before he shall have performed the requisites necessary to obtain lands," his children "shall be entitled . . . to such quantity of land as such person would have been entitled." In other words, the very fact of their parents' migration, and not the value of the improvements they made, entitled settler children to land.[44]

What is more significant about the Cumberland Compact than the specific form of constitutional government it created, however, is how it integrated a theory of colonization into constitutional theory as a means of authorizing the precarious and violent foundations of settler democracy. Like the Vermont Constitution, the Cumberland Compact cast consent and colonization as intricately connected. The compact proclaims:

> That as this settlement is in its infancy, unknown to government, and not included within any county within North Carolina, the State to which it belongs, to derive the advantages of those wholesome and salutary laws for the protection and benefit of its citizens, we find ourselves constrained from necessity to adopt this temporary method of restraining the licentious, and supplying, by unanimous consent, the blessings flowing from just and equitable government.[45]

In Lockean fashion, the original social contract establishing civil government requires the unanimous consent of colonists. Although Locke claims that "the act of the majority passes for the act of the whole" in an already constituted civil government, the legitimacy of the original constituting act depends on unanimous consent. For any man who wishes to withdraw his consent from the founding act of government, Locke advises, "let him plant in some inland, vacant places of America."[46] As with the Vermont Constitution, the Lockean theory of consent at work in the Cumberland Compact treats vacant land as an outlet for further colonization for those who wished to cast themselves outside the initial founding compact. The theory of unanimous consent thus entails the natural right of settlers to colonize vacant land.

The claims of Roosevelt and others notwithstanding, there is very little to suggest that either the Watauga or Cumberland settlers understood their founding social contracts as creating separate and independent governments. Aside from Vermont, the first truly independent republic that existed autonomously from the Confederation government was the State of Franklin, a union of settler republics along the Tennessee frontier. In response to the mounting difficulties that North Carolina faced in securing property claims against indigenous polities on the Tennessee frontier, settlers declared themselves an independent state in 1784. The first article of the Declaration of Independence of the State of Franklin proclaimed, "That the Constitution of North Carolina declares that it shall be justifiable to erect new States westward whenever the consent of the Legislature shall countenance it; and this consent is implied, we believe, in the cession act."[47] Settler sovereignty does not simply involve the unanimous consent of colonists in the founding of settler contracts; it also involves the consent of the mother country—the nest from which settlers emigrate who continue to claim territorial sovereignty over newly settled land. Following the lead of the Virginians, who ceded territory granted in their colonial charter to Congress in 1781, North Carolinians finally made a similar cession in 1784, only to soon revoke it a few months later. Franklinites argued that the cession act necessarily implied the consent of the North Carolina legislature. Because North Carolina was unable to provide law and common government on the frontier, settlers argued that their necessary efforts in self-constituting a democratic polity justified separation and independence.

Another key argument made in favor of independence was that the Constitution of North Carolina recognized the right of settlers to emigrate from existing states to constitute a new polity in the western territories. A petition imploring recognition of Franklin's independence argued that the consent of North Carolina was implicit not just in the 1784 cession acts but also in "a clause in your wise and mild Constitution, setting forth that there might be a state, or states, erected in the West whenever your Legislature should give consent for same."[48] The clause the petition referred to was taken directly from Section XXV of the Declaration of Rights of the Constitution of North Carolina (1776), which stated, "That it shall not be construed so as to prevent the establishment of one or more governments westward of this State, by consent of the Legislature."[49] Although not embracing the strong language of the Vermont emigration clause, the North Carolina emigration clause did not impede the creation of new states in western land grants. Like the case of Vermont, the emigration clause embraced the assumption that North Carolina ceded "certain vacant territory to Congress," which in turn justified independence.[50] Here again, the theory of consent animating Franklinite claims to independence embraced settler colonial logics of indigenous disavowal. Despite the continued wars and treaties necessary for settlers to secure their claims over expropriated land, the refusal to acknowledge native sovereignty underlined colonial theories of democratic consent. Representations of vacant land in settler constitutionalism thus represented an aspiration that grounded claims to democratic legitimacy rather than a political reality.

On the basis of these arguments, Article V of the Declaration of Independence of the State of Franklin announced, "We unanimously agree that our lives, liberty and property can be more secure and our happiness much better propagated by our separation; and consequently that it is our duty and inalienable right to form ourselves into a new independent State."[51] The drive for independence exemplified the ambiguous position of settler sovereignty in larger visions of colonial empire. In a sense, the tradition of frontier constitutionalism represents a continuation rather than a break with the earlier revolutionary tradition. Like revolutionary settlers such as Bland and Jefferson, the settlers of the Appalachian frontier also saw their sovereignty in terms of inherent rights that traveled with them to new colonies. In asserting "the political rights of settlers in vacant regions," the Franklin Constitution applied the principle of settler separation derived from the Declaration of Independence to their own situation.[52] Rather than separation from an empire organized around the subjection of colonial entities, the Franklin Constitution enshrined the right of settlers to separate from existing states. Settler claims to sovereignty, then, exist uneasily in imperial political thought. Because settler sovereignty entails an inherent right to democratic self-rule independent of imperial authority, it always runs the risk of fomenting imperial disintegration.

During the constitutional and revolutionary periods, the rise of new settler collectives on the frontier threatened to undermine the federal state's imperial sovereignty. Squatters clamoring for land had their own ideas about rights and liberties that involved the unbridled right to expansion. Reflecting common notions of *terra nullius*, which disavowed indigenous dominion and sovereignty over western territory, one squatter spokesman confidently proclaimed, "all mankind . . . have an undoubted right to pass into every vacant country, and there to form their constitution" independent of Congressional authority.[53] As late as the Whiskey Rebellion in 1791, radical democrats along the frontier continued to assert that the right of "colonizing this distant and dangerous desert" was a "natural right" inseparable from the cause they had fought for in the Revolution.[54] It is not far from there to argue that a violation of this right constitutes a just reason for insurrection, posing the acute problem of settler revolt and the threat of the separation and independence of settler collectives. Moreover, the right to remove oneself from one's country of birth and settle new communities in western territories was a central element of democratic republicanism. At least three state constitutions—Pennsylvania, Vermont, and North Carolina—upheld the natural inherent right of settlers to emigrate and establish new communities in vacant countries.

To obviate the threat of separation entailed by settler sovereignty, the Northwest Ordinance engendered a vision of settler colonial empire that cast the constituent power of settlers to create new democratic polities on expropriated land as the engine of territorial expansion. The Northwest Ordinance integrated conceptions of constituent power in settler constitutionalism into its framework in Article V by allowing for the self-replication of democratic polities across the Trans-Appalachian West. What characterized settler colonialism was how the constituent power of settlers to establish law and sovereignty became the organizing feature of colonial expansion. Article V of the ordinance captured this feature of settler colonialism in giving the settlers of the Northwest Territory the "liberty to form a permanent constitution and State government; provided the constitution and government so to be formed, shall be republican."[55] By granting settlers themselves the sovereign right "to form a permanent constitution," Article V ensured that new states were granted through the constituent power of settlers. Yet in limiting the specific form of constitutional government to republican forms, the ordinance also circumscribed settler state building. By mandating that new settler communities be organized as republican states, the ordinance codified a direct relationship between colonization and self-government in the law.

The ordinance, however, did not allow settler communities to remain separate and independent. Rather, it provided for the incorporation of settler colonies into a larger territorial empire on terms of consent and equality with other states. The explicit purpose of the ordinance was "extending the fundamental principles of civil and religious liberty, which form the basis whereon these republics, their laws, and constitutions are erected; to fix and establish those principles as the basis of all laws, constitutions, and governments, which forever hereafter shall be formed in the said territory."[56] By unilaterally imposing the civil and religious liberty on the organization of settler colonies, the ordinance preempted the threat of separation and independence. It thus wrote the civil and political rights of settler communities into the law by allowing for the transfer of the metropolitan status of colonists from the eastern seaboard to the western frontier. In doing so, it enabled settlers who emigrated to retain their civic standing in the nation.[57]

The Northwest Ordinance thus provided a framework for the expansion of the federal-imperial state by encouraging settlers to move west and establish new political communities in an ordered and regulated fashion. One of the effects of the Northwest Ordinance was to defuse settler demands for independence by granting settlers rights and liberties equal with eastern states. The cunning of constitutional reason resides in the process by which constituent power "is absorbed, appropriated by the constitution, transformed into an element of the constitutional machine."[58] In this process, constituent power becomes a formal feature of government that upholds the legitimacy of the state rather than solely as a founding power that remains superior to delegated powers. The colonization-constitution dialectic comes full circle. Article V of the Northwest Ordinance integrates the capacity of settlers to constitute new political orders into the colonial-constitutional machinery. In the same manner that the constitution absorbs constituent power and transforms it into the legitimate basis of constitutional order, the Northwest Ordinance incorporates colonization qua constituent power as the engine of imperial expansion. Just as the Constitution was a means of containing democratic excess in the state legislatures, Article V contained the democratic excess of settler sovereignty on the frontier. Through the principle of federative replication, the Northwest Ordinance offered a new world conception of empire driven by the constituent power of settlers to found self-constituted governments.

The Empire of Liberty

If there is a single document that outlines the ideological architecture of US settler colonialism, it is the Northwest Ordinance as much as the Constitution itself.[59] The Northwest Ordinance was one of the few laws of the Confederation government retained by the 1787 settlement, and it established the institutional logic by which the Constitution itself became a powerful instrument of empire in the modern world. One of the most pervasive assumptions uniting the participants in the Constitutional Convention was that the expansionist framework laid out by the land ordinances would be retained in the new government.[60] Indeed, the language of empire permeated the constitutional debates of the 1780s. In his journals of the federal convention, James Madison approvingly recorded the common sentiment that the men present had convened for the purposes of "laying the foundation for a great empire."[61] Publius similarly opened the first of the *Federalist Papers* by observing that the new union concerned the "fate of an empire in many respects the most interesting in the world." According to Publius, there were three ways of constituting an imperial republic: chance, conquest, and consent and reason.[62] Publius insisted that the ability of Americans to found a state based on rational consent depended on the providential bounty of empty and open land: "Providence has in a particular manner blessed [independent America] with a variety of soils and productions and watered it with innumerable streams for the delight and accommodation of its inhabitants."[63]

Perhaps the most forceful vision of this new world conception of empire to emerge during the revolutionary period was Thomas Jefferson's notion of an "empire of liberty." Less than three years before the Constitutional Convention of 1787, Madison expressed to Jefferson his belief that the health and stability of the new republic depended upon the "free expansion of our people" and "the settlement of the Western country."[64] Yet the powerful and revolutionary realities of constituent power on the frontier perpetually plagued Madison's vision of imperial expansion. In ongoing debates over US claims to the Mississippi River Valley, Madison expressed profound anxiety about the prospects of settler expansion. "Will the settlements which are beginning to take place on the branches of the Mississippi," he wrote, "be so many distinct societies, or only an *expansion* of the same society?" Madison feared that settlers expanding westward would morph into a "hostile or a foreign people" rather than remain "bone of our bones and flesh of our flesh."[65] Implicit in this fear was the tacit recognition that colonization potentially engendered a form of constituent power. The power settlers claimed to create self-governing political bodies could be turned against the mother country—the states of the eastern seaboard from which settlers left. In order to contain the constituent power of settlers, Madison sought a framework of regulated expansion that enshrined the democratic and republican aspirations of settler colonists.[66]

It is in this context that Jefferson famously expressed his notion of an empire of liberty. Jefferson wrote to Madison, "We should have such an empire for liberty as . . . never surveyed since the creation; and I am persuaded no constitution was ever before so well calculated as ours for extensive empire and self-government."[67] Jefferson never expanded on what he meant when he suggested that the constitution was uniquely calibrated to democratic expansion, but at least one potential meaning resides in the principle of federative replication exemplified in his authorship of the land ordinances of the 1780s. While the first dimension of federative replication—the principle of imperial equality—was outlined at length in the last chapter, it is worth reiterating its basic features in Jefferson's thinking. In Jefferson's imperial vision, democracy expanded through the decentralized power of settler sovereignty free from the dictates of an absolutist state. This notion of empire rhetorically established distance between his brand of democratic expansionism driven by the power of the people and Hamilton's federalist imperialism in which expansion was directed by a centralized state rather than by the force of the people. Further posing an antagonism between US colonial expansion and the despotic empires of Europe, the phrase also carried connotations of liberating the western territories from the yoke of Spanish, British, and French rule. Reflecting the imperial ideology embedded in the Northwest Ordinance, the democratic element of the empire of liberty arose from the fact that westward expansion would result in the democratic equality of new states instead of their subjection to a colonial administration or centralized government.[68]

A common point against Jefferson's Louisiana Purchase hinged on the fear that the alienation involved in the imposition of great distances between west and east will result in settlers forming political identifications with other imperial states or forming independent republics, jeopardizing the place of American power in the international order.[69] In a defense of the Louisiana Purchase in his second inaugural address, Jefferson asked, "Who can limit the extent to which the federative principle may operate effectively? The larger our association the less will it be shaken by local passions; and in any view is it not better that the opposite bank of the Mississippi should be settled by our own brethren and children than by strangers of another family?"[70] Directly responding to Madison's anxieties about the separation of settler polities, Jefferson asserted that the model of settler colonial expansion provided by the Northwest Ordinance allowed for the replication of the same society across the frontier rather than the creation of newly independent and potentially hostile states. By privileging the equality of new states over relations of colonial dependency, the principle of federative replication ensured that colonial expansion would proceed through the reproduction of settler polities rather than the separation of colonial offspring from the mother country.

If the first dimension of federative replication captures the underlying organizational principle of settler colonial empire, the second dimension—the coloniality of constituent power—expresses the principle of its movement. In Jefferson's vision of democratic empire, expansion proceeded through the democratic force of popular sovereignty rather than the power of a consolidated state. For Jefferson, popular sovereignty and imperial sovereignty were closely aligned, with the *demos* rather than the state acting as the primary agent of expansion. Rather than the centralized power of the national state, he saw settlers as the vanguard of American expansion. In a letter envisioning the prospective course of settler expansion across the continent, Jefferson invited a "philosophic observer to commence a journey from the savages of the Rocky Mountains" toward the eastern tidewaters. In this journey, the philosopher would observe the earliest stage of civilization, composed of savage Indians living in a lawless state of nature. Next, he would find Indians on the "frontiers in the pastoral state, raising domestic animals to supply the defects of hunting." Then he would witness "our own semi-barbarous citizens, the pioneers of the advance of civilization," pushing progress westward from the most developed state of "our seaport towns." Jefferson's account of historical development transformed the stadial view of history marked by the cyclical rise and decline of empires into a linear model of progress. For Jefferson, the course of settler expansion mapped onto the "progress of society from its rudest state to that it has now attained." As the primary agents of expansion, the settlers that blazed the path of civilization wielded imperial sovereignty.[71]

In order to transform the founding capacities of settlers into a colonial force, Jefferson's Land Ordinance of 1785 (which provided the basis of the Northwest Ordinance) instituted a survey system that split western land into square-mile plots. To recruit commercially minded settlers with the ability to improve western territories and found new townships, Congress auctioned off land to the highest bidder. But beyond simply commodifying the land to facilitate commercial expansion, the 1785 ordinance "created a checkerboard whose square mile parcels were assembled as building blocks for townships," which laid the basis for localized settler sovereignty.[72] If Jefferson's republican citizen required landed independence to cultivate democratic habits, the land would need to be transformed into a geometric grid capable of ensuring private possession. Jefferson's grid not only morphed land into a commodity, it provided the geometric coordinates within which democratic sovereignty could be located both at the individual and collective level. Jefferson wedded the principle of constituent power to the constitutional machinery of settler colonial expansion through the grid system. But for Jefferson's grid to root democratic sovereignty in the land, it must first erase customary relationships to land claimed by the pre-democratic, indigenous past, relationships that Jefferson envisioned as archaic, anti-modern, and thus feudal in nature.

In this regard, Jefferson's grid "constituted an erasure, a cartographic overcoding of indigenous spatial practices" that replaced indigenous relationships to the land with settler proprietary arrangements based on the commodification of the landscape.[73] In reaction to this erasure of indigenous relations with the land, Native American political theorists asserted alternative understandings of the land in opposition to the logic of native elimination. In the lead-up to the Creek War (1813), the Shawnee leader Tecumseh sought to unite the Creek and Shawnee nations to resist assimilation and settler encroachment. Tecumseh drew inspiration from the teachings of his half-brother, Tenskwatawa, who called for the revitalization of traditional Indian cultures in opposition to the spread of Anglo civilization. As a longtime opponent of treaties with the federal government, which sought to transfer indigenous occupation of land to settlers, Tecumseh resisted the efforts of previous indigenous leaders who preached assimilation and accommodation. He took accommodationist chiefs to task for selling land to the federal government without the consent of the people. In opposition to the tribal elite, he resisted the very idea that land could be legitimately sold or purchased as a sign of inequality and corruption, calling on "all the Redmen to unite in claiming a common and equal right in the land." In opposition to the commodification of land that enabled settler sovereignty, Tecumseh mocked the very notion of selling land as an abdication of native sovereignty and tribal identity: "Sell a country! Why not sell the air, and the great earth, as well as the sea?"[74] For Tecumseh, customary land tenure was integral to the cultural and political autonomy of indigenous peoples. In challenging the free trade in Indian land and resources, Tecumseh significantly presaged decolonizing critiques of free trade in the twentieth century.[75]

In a similar manner, the Sauk Chief Black Hawk also refused settler sovereignty by critiquing the transformation of land into property and the defilement of his ancestral homelands. In articulating an alternative cultural mapping of western land, Black Hawk provided a counter-narrative of settler colonialism that both challenged the commodification of land and exposed the treaty system as a fiction of consent. Regarding the former, he proclaimed, "My reason teaches me that land cannot be sold. The Great Spirit gave it to his children to live upon. . . . Nothing can be sold, but such things as can be carried away."[76] To the extent that land embodied historical connections of people to past ancestors, the sale of land would bring the decimation of the Sauk people. "Rather than a grid of exploitable pieces of property, Black Hawk saw the landscape as embodied national history."[77] Black Hawk also revealed how democratic principles of consent undergirded the treaty system and in turn acted as an ideological force of compulsion masking the colonial violence of the treaty relation. In showing how the treaty system was designed to push native peoples off of their land, Black Hawk asserted that "myself and band had no agency in selling our country."[78] As Mark Rifkin has put it, "Representing land as purchasable seeks to make native landholding compatible with U.S. legal geography by dislodging it from its cultural context."[79] In challenging the principles of consent in the treaty system and the commodification of land, Black Hawk created counter-geographies of land that redefined it in terms of the social relations and cultural stories imbued with customary and ancestral meaning.

Considering the role of the land ordinances in sustaining the exercise of constituent power on the frontier prompts a dramatic reconsideration of the radical aspects of Jeffersonian democracy. It is no secret that Jefferson was obsessed with the coming of a new, modern political order, and that his penchant for radicalism and revolution stemmed from his disdain of aristocratic society. In his well-known argument that no generation has the right to bind future generations to their laws and constitution, Jefferson famously declared, "The dead have no rights. They are nothing and nothing cannot own something."[80] Jefferson's assertion here, read contrapuntally, applies to white aristocrats and their social systems of privilege as well as to the native civilizations of what he saw as the ancient American past.[81] For Jefferson, Indians who sought to retain their customary modes of politics clung to the dead weight of tradition. Native polities constituted vanishing civilizations, and so their customs and traditions inherited through time ran counter to the historical progression of American democracy. The resurgence of ancient tradition meant the return of ancestral privilege that Jefferson deemed antithetical to democratic equality. Maintaining a free and equal settler state thus entailed the assimilation-extermination of Indian nations seeking the regeneration of their customary political forms. Jefferson directed his democratic assault on the past not only at the last remnants of aristocratic conservatism in America but also at the enduring efforts of native peoples to retain their inherited cultures, what the Iroquois people (Haudenosaunee) call *Gaiwiio*, or "the Old Way."[82]

The logic of Jefferson's approach to native erasure is also evident in his inaugural addresses, often taken jointly as a classical statement of democratic-republican principles. In his first inaugural address, Jefferson expounded a classic vision of American empire: "A rising nation, spread over a wide and fruitful land, traversing all the seas with the rich productions of their industry . . . advancing rapidly to destinies beyond the reach of the mortal eye." Reflecting a progressive understanding of history, Jefferson viewed the United States as the forefront of the democratic movement, and a central feature of this movement was the eradication of religious intolerance. By his second inaugural address Jefferson turned the principle of religious tolerance into a justification of native expropriation. While many native peoples were rightly convinced of the superiority of white civilization and willingly assimilated into white-settler culture, there still existed the "action and counteraction of good sense and of bigotry" among some "anti-philosophers who find an interest in keeping things in their present state." Embracing an irrational and "sanctimonious reverence for the customs of their ancestors," indigenous leaders such as Tecumseh and Black Hawk, who preached the preservation of native traditions, impeded the expropriation of native land by infecting the population with an anti-philosophical penchant for ancient customs.[83] By equating native polities and traditions with pre-Enlightenment values, Jefferson imputed European feudality onto native societies and in the process cast the erasure of native political forms as a precondition for the emergence of modern democracy.

To the extent that it represents natives as either absent or in the process of becoming absent, Jefferson's narrative of democratic expansion reinforces logics of native elimination. For Jefferson, colonial expansion made America democratic. In justifying settler colonization, he engaged in the historical practices of "firsting and lasting" in which settlers constructed their modernity through what they perceived as fading native societies. In such narratives, "Indians reside in an ahistorical temporality in which they can only be victims of change, not active subjects in the making of change."[84] By disavowing the agency of indigenous peoples in the creation of the modern world, Jefferson constructed a new world vision of democracy out of the narrative termination of native histories. Jefferson's account of settler expansion was predicated not only on a process of spatial colonization that normatively condoned the spread of democratic cultural forms and republican civilization across the frontier. It also implied temporal colonization that, through the acculturation of native peoples into the democratic order, produced the "termination of their history."[85] It is only by erasing the historical presence of native polities that America comes to appear as a novel democratic experiment. Just as American settler democracy represented a break from the European feudal order, it also entailed the eclipse of indigenous orders still marking the North American landscape.

Yet despite Jefferson's disavowal of the indigenous past, he at the same time used indigenous histories to ground the authority of the American democratic founding. In *Notes on the State of Virginia* (1785), Jefferson famously likened the "eloquence in council" of indigenous orators such as Chief Logan to Roman and Athenian republicans like Cicero and Demosthenes. In counteracting the European image of native peoples as degenerate and "wanting genius," Jefferson reconstructed an honorable indigenous past to refashion the republican foundations of the new nation.[86] In contrast to this image of savage nobility, Jefferson asserted that the differences between Africans and white settlers were "fixed in nature" and that any attempt to assimilate blacks into white settler society was not only doomed to fail but would likely proliferate white prejudice and racial violence.[87] Because he believed racial equality to be impossible, Jefferson argued instead for the colonization of freed Africans outside the territorial borders of the United States. Unlike blacks, Jefferson allowed for the possibility that indigenous peoples might assimilate into white society. Thus, while natives and white settlers occupied different stages along the same developmental trajectory, blacks and white settlers occupied entirely different historical and cultural trajectories.[88] By identifying a distinctively native American past and allowing for the assimilation of indigenous peoples into white settler society, Jefferson naturalized American democratic identity as a product of the land even as he allowed for the erasure of indigenous peoples from that landscape.

Conclusion

Rather than antithetical dynamics, the basic categories of American democratic thought (i.e., popular consent, constituent sovereignty) emerged through a mutually constitutive relationship with ideologies of settler colonialism. In modern democratic thought, James Tully argues that the "norm of democratization" has served to "legitimate the coercive imposition" of Western forms of politics, economy, and society on the non-West. This "imperial right" manifests itself in different ways in free trade imperialism and neocolonialism, which subject colonized societies to economic dominance rather than formal or informal political control. In the context of settler societies such as Canada, Australia, and America, imperial right is vitally linked to democratic authority. With these forms of "replication imperialism," the norms and institutions of modern democracy were built upon the eradication of indigenous political forms and the systematic appropriation of native land.[89] Following Tully, this chapter has examined how the concept of constituent power in modern democratic thought became a colonial practice. Far from a neutral category of political experience, constituent power was an essential component of settler ideology in American democratic thought.

More broadly, this and the previous chapters have outlined how the two dimensions of the principle of federative replication served as the organizational form and principle of action for American settler colonialism. Attending to the settler colonial dimensions of American federalism also amends contemporary accounts of the relationship between empire and federalism. Tully has usefully drawn a distinction between two forms of federalism in the modern world that stand in contrasting relation to empire. On the one hand, Tully recovers a tradition of treaty federalism grounded in principles of mutual recognition, consent, and cultural continuity. Stemming from early modern treaties between settler communities and indigenous nations, this model productively accommodates cultural diversity in pluralistic societies by preserving the sovereignty of each pole yet encouraging intercultural dialogue.[90]

On the other hand, cosmopolitan federalism, derived from Kantian liberalism, seeks global federation as a means of ensuring universal and perpetual peace. As Tully rightly argues, however, this form of federalism contains a homogenizing impulse that assimilates non-European into European cultural frameworks. In Kant's model, federative cooperation depends upon shared frameworks of republican government. To the extent that non-Western societies fall outside of this, Western powers are justified in coercively imposing republican government.[91] The framework of settler colonial federalism examined here captures an alternative tradition of federalist thinking. Distinct from Kant's cosmopolitan federalism, federative replication seeks not the cultural assimilation of indigenous societies to integrate them into an egalitarian federative framework, but rather the elimination of indigenous sovereignties as a means of integrating principles of popular and imperial sovereignty.

PART TWO

Settler Colonialism and Democratic Culture

3 Colonial Dispossession and the Settler Social State

> "In the United States, it is not only legislation that is democratic; nature itself works for the people. . . . Everything about the Americans is extraordinary, their social state as well as their laws; but what is more extraordinary still is the soil that supports them."
>
> —Tocqueville, Democracy in America (1835)

From Alexis de Tocqueville to Louis Hartz to Seymour Martin Lipset, the absence of feudalism has served as an enduring theme in explaining the presence of the liberal democratic tradition in the United States.[1] More than simply a constitutional form of government, modern American democracy, for these commentators, is best captured as a social condition defined by the collapse of feudal hierarchies that characterized European society. Through the colonization of the Americas, the feudal order marked by rigid hierarchies of social rank and inherited status gave way to a social order grounded in radical principles of social equality. As the crumbling ruins of feudal society were swept away by the winds of the democratic revolution, principles of popular sovereignty stood in for aristocratic systems of rule. European settlers in North America created a new egalitarian social order on a territorial ground marked by the absence of feudalism. Yet what is unspoken in these accounts, though tacitly thematized, is that the democratic social state rests upon settler colonization. Such narratives implicitly define American democracy in terms of a double absence—the absence of feudalism and the absence of indigenous sovereignties.[2] Obscured in this interpretive interplay of presence and absence, however, resides the central disavowal of indigenous peoples and colonial conquest as having any significance for democratic thought and practice. In this regard, the historical trope of the absence of feudalism ideologically masks the foundation of American democracy in settler conquest.

This and the subsequent two chapters fundamentally recast Tocqueville's notion of the democratic social state as a settler-colonial social formation, what I call "the settler social state." Aziz Rana has recently argued that populist and republican principles in American constitutional thought issued in the legal exclusion of indigenous peoples from the principles of liberty and equality embedded in the constituted order. Yet Rana's account of how settler ideologies "fused ethnic nationalism . . . and republicanism to combine freedom as self-rule with a commitment to territorial empire" resides solely at the level of constitutional development.[3] If "the imperial settler state" points to the formal constitutional norms and structures that, in Rana's words, "politically necessitated" settler expansion and external domination of colonized subjects, "the settler social state" captures how the physical and conceptual erasure of native sovereignties provided the social and cultural foundations of settler democracy.[4] Democratic principles of popular sovereignty and social equality emerge not just through the constitutional form of democracy, but also through the deeper foundations of the political culture and social condition of American settler society. A key aspect of the democratic social condition, for Tocqueville, was the unique configuration of law, geography, and territoriality that enabled the emergence of democratic norms and values. Yet when Tocqueville mapped the geography of the democratic landscape, he evacuated North American land of its indigenous presence. Although he recognized that settler colonization was central to the American democratic experience, his representations of North American land obscure the constitutive role of settler conquest and colonial dispossession in the creation of the democratic social state.

Greater focus on the place of settler colonialism and questions of land and indigeneity in liberal democracy lends new insights into the role of race and racial hierarchies in Tocqueville's thought. Although discussions of his relationship to racial and imperial ideologies in the nineteenth century abound, existing accounts have neglected the role of settler colonial ideology in Tocqueville's thought, and by consequence American democratic thought, by focusing exclusively on racial representations of the colonized other at the expense of spatial representations of land. Practices of race-making and space-making align in Tocqueville's text in a way that cannot be captured through exclusive attention to ascriptive hierarchies,[5] categories of identity/difference,[6] or racial representations and civilizational categories.[7]

The relationship between democracy and colonial dispossession cannot be understood solely through categories of identity and difference because they neglect how race, identity, and difference are all constructed through settler geographies that produce indigenous absence. At stake in settler colonial ideology is not simply racial assumptions about the inferiority of indigenous bodies, but, more saliently, the spatial absence of indigenous peoples in geographic mappings of land.

The first section of this chapter focuses on the first chapter of Democracy on "the external configuration of North America" in order to illuminate how Tocqueville's understanding of democratic sovereignty rests upon a conception of territoriality defined by the absence of indigenous sovereignty. By understanding territory merely as a container for popular sovereignty, Tocqueville naturalizes the foundational role of settler conquest in the emergence of American democracy. The second section examines how the democratic social state was constituted through settler conquest, giving particular attention to how processes of settler colonization established the social and cultural foundations of American democracy. The third section recasts the chapter on "the three races in America" by distinguishing between slavery and settler colonialism, and the distinct racial logics they produce. Looking at his extended correspondence with the German-American philosopher Francis Lieber, the last section turns to Tocqueville's comparative analysis of American and French settler colonialism to foreground the centrality of his disavowal of indigenous conquest in the American case.

The External Configuration of Democracy

Although analyses of Tocqueville's treatment of indigenous peoples in the tenth chapter (Volume I, Part 2) of Democracy abound, very little attention has been paid to the first chapter of the book on the "external configuration of North America." In beginning his account with a geographic portrait of the land, Tocqueville follows the conventions of travel writing as well as the Montesquieuean tradition of delineating the natural conditions of politics. In both analytic modes, land, territory, and geography mark the outer perimeter of political form and thus provide a container for politics. Natural conditions such as climate and geography establish the setting in which mores, values, and customs arise. Because he sees politics and democracy more significantly in terms of its social and cultural rather than strictly constitutional foundations, Tocqueville gives priority to the spatial determinants of democratic character. Yet much more than merely a neutral description of North American land, he relies on settler geographies that disavow the native presence in North America and in turn constitute the very conditions under which popular sovereignty take root.

As if to reenact the discovery of "the new world," Tocqueville begins by surveying the "general features" of the North American landscape, casting his gaze over "a simple and majestic arrangement" of "two vast regions" divided "in an almost equal manner." Littered amongst the "extreme variety of tableaux," Tocqueville observes tangled rivers and streams, mountains that attest to "the revolutions of the earth," immense forests sprung from a "primitive ocean," arid and sterile terrain, and the "traces of an unknown people."[8] Cataloging the continent's prior inhabitants along with the natural features of the region, he reads these ancient traces as one among many features of the continental topography. Shrouded in darkness, the continent projects an air of mystery making it impenetrable to science, history, and modern rationality. Surveying the territory east of the Mississippi River, Tocqueville asks why a "great river of woods" gave way to a "boundless prairie," wondering whether nature refused the "seeding of trees" or if the forests had "instead been destroyed by the hand of man." Despite his surprising speculation about human intervention in the natural environment, he notes that the present state of the land was an "immense wilderness" occupied by a "few small tribes" who "wandered under the shade of the forest or in the pastures of the prairie."[9]

In other parts, Tocqueville further speculates about the role of human intervention in shaping the natural landscape. Hearing of the pyramidal mounds of the Mississippi Valley at sites like the ancient city of Cahokia, he reflects that at one point America may have been occupied by large, flourishing civilizations. At the center of these monuments lie "strange instruments, arms, utensils of all kinds . . . recalling usages unknown to current races." The passage of time, however, has separated the present ancestors from memory and knowledge of these "ancient republics," who were "more civilized" and "more advanced" than the "primitive" inhabitants currently occupying "these same regions." Unable "to give any information about the history of that unknown people," one can only conclude that indigenous societies in America represent declining and vanishing civilizations. Tocqueville writes, "A strange thing! There are peoples who have so completely disappeared from the earth that the very memory of their name has been effaced; their languages are lost, their glory vanished like a sound without an echo."[10]

Without history and continued traditions rooted in the soil, and without a civil society attached to a solid place and location, Tocqueville cannot conceive of any legitimate land claim that natives might have over North American territory. He writes, "The Indians occupied [the wilderness], but they did not possess it."[11] The impermanency of civilization and the absence of settled customs prevented natives from attaining any sense of political peoplehood and thus loosened any claim to land or territory that they might make. "Providence," Tocqueville writes, "placing them in the midst of the wealth of the New World, seemed to have given them only a short lease on it; they were, in a way, only in the meantime [sic]."[12] This suggestion that Indians possessed North American land "only in the meantime" institutes a temporal rupture between an autochthonous old world and the democratic new world. In consigning native peoples to a premodern space and time—America's own feudal past—Tocqueville enacts a vision of manifest destiny by treating the land as always-already belonging to European settlers.

What matters here is not simply that Tocqueville's representation of North American land is wrong or misleading, but rather that it produces, through a process of interpretive colonization, that which it seeks to represent. The absence of indigenous peoples and the logics of native elimination in *Democracy* operate not as a neutral description of land and territory but as a "performative representation" that enacts the erasure of indigenous sovereignties, cultures, and histories as a precondition for the establishment of democratic sovereignty.[13] As Henri Lefebvre has argued, "Representations of space . . . have a substantial role and specific influence in the production of space."[14] Insofar as they produce salient social meaning for settlers, representations of native land as empty engender social effects that are politically significant far beyond their factual correspondence to reality. In engendering native dispossession, such representational practices enable settlers to naturalize their land claims and cultivate a spatial sense of belonging to the land through the disavowal of native histories and cultures.

Tocqueville's representation of North American land as the "external configuration" of democracy thus produces a set of representational effects that both eliminate native sovereignties and naturalize the foundational violence of settler colonialism. Territoriality is important to notions of democracy and popular sovereignty not simply because it marks the outer perimeter of the body politic, as Tocqueville suggests. As settler colonialism's "irreducible element," land is more than a container for sovereignty.[15] Conceptualizations and geographic mappings of land constitute liberal democratic sovereignty as such, laying the very foundations upon which democracy arises, rests, and comes into being. Presenting territoriality as a container depoliticizes the construction of democratic identity by separating form from content—if an egalitarian and antiaristocratic identity is the content of democratic peoplehood, then territory is merely its container or form. In representing territory in this way, Tocqueville places issues of land appropriation outside of democratic development and treats colonial dispossession as irrelevant to the constitution of democratic society. As a result, he naturalizes the possession and ownership of North American land by European settlers.

Tocqueville's attempt to root democratic society in the geographic conditions of North America thus conceals the contingent origins of modern democracy in settler conquest. In Tocqueville's account, democratic sovereignty appears as a by-product of nature rather than as a hierarchical process of colonial expansion. By naturalizing democracy as inherent in the landscape, he makes the relationship between land and democracy appear as prepolitical and thus outside the bounds of political contestation. Space does not emerge organically over time but is a social and political process in its own right. Rather than a natural category, space and spatial representations of land are elements of broader configurations of power and ideology. To represent land and territory as the "external configuration" or as a mere container for democracy is to turn attention away from the practices of colonization and land appropriation that figure into the production of liberal democratic sovereignty as such. If Tocqueville's settler geography naturalizes indigenous absence, a critical cartography of settler democracy would seek to unmap settler space by uncovering the ideologies and practices of conquest and colonization that have constituted the basis of democratic sovereignty.[16] As a work of political theory, Democracy is thoroughly cartographic. Tocqueville's primary aim was to guide his readers through the "confusing terrain of American political life."[17] To map the political landscape, however, is not merely to describe the preexisting natural and social order. It is to constitute democratic order as such through representational practices of space making. Understood in this way, the gaps and disavowals in Tocqueville's settler geography regarding indigenous peoples are not simply misrepresentations. They centrally figure into the construction of democratic sovereignty.

The utility of the critical cartography of settler democracy comes into focus by illustrating how Tocqueville erases the productive effects of conquest. One gets an immediate sense of the forms of conquest and elimination that have been effaced in *Democracy* by considering his travel essay, "Two Weeks in the Wilderness," written about his trip to the furthest reaches of the American frontier. In this essay, Tocqueville paints a portrait of the pioneer whose habits and pride have allowed him to brave "exile, solitude, and the countless disasters of the primitive life." The pioneer is an "unknown man," a representative of a race to which the "future of the New World belongs." This "nation of conquerors" bears the savagery of the wilderness for the sake of bringing democratic culture to the "furthest limits of European civilization." If the American pioneers were to make a home of the harsh "wilderness and empty space untouched by clearing" they must give the wilderness content not only by settling communities full of democratic cultural practices but by also clearing the land of its savagery so as to make it inhabitable.[18] Tocqueville describes this process of settlement thusly: "an ancient people, the original and rightful masters of the American continent melting away daily like snow in the sunshine and disappearing before our eyes from the face of the earth. In the same areas another race rises in their stead at an even greater pace."[19] Despite his claim that natives are "the original and rightful masters" of the land, his imagery of indigenous absence in *Democracy* reinforces the notion that North American land providentially belongs to white settlers.

When Tocqueville describes the indigenous condition and the North American political landscape in *Democracy*, the realities of conquest and dispossession are barely visible in his settler geography.[20] In his account of "the principle causes tending to maintain a democratic republic in the United States," he affords special importance to the geographic conditions that define the democratic social state. In doing so, he draws a crucial comparison between the Spanish colonization of South America and the English colonization of North America. In the former, Spanish conquistadors found concentrated civilizations that, despite being "less enlightened," had "already appropriated the soil by cultivating it." Thus, to "found their new states, they had to destroy or enslave many populations." If colonial violence played a central role in the founding of South American colonies, the social state of North American settlers allowed them to pursue a course of expansion that was without conquest. Composed of "wandering tribes," North America was, "properly speaking, an empty continent, a wilderness land that awaited inhabitants."[21] With minimal effort and violence, by merely nudging indigenous peoples off the map, Anglo-settlers could take swift control of the continent.

Tocqueville's assertion that the absence of indigenous peoples in North America enabled a unique mode of settlement also extended to his treatment of the colonization of Texas. He closed Volume I of *Democracy* with a discussion of American expansion across the western frontier and into the Pacific. While the United States already occupied a vast degree of territory, he noted that however "extensive these limits are, one would be wrong to believe that the Anglo-American race will always be contained within them." Pekka Hämäläinen has provocatively shown how one of the most significant problems facing the colony was the persistent threat of Comanche raids. Beyond the theft of human beings and cattle, the Comanche empire exacted tribute from Texas, which further posed considerable financial burdens on the already poor Mexican province. Continued raids left Mexico both militarily and financially weak throughout the 1820s and 1830s. As a result, the United States' ability to gain control of the Southwest was aided by the destabilization provided by the Comanche empire.[22] Yet despite the powerful presence of the Comanche empire, which destabilized Spanish rule in the Southwest and enabled Anglo-settlers to gain a foothold in Texas, Tocqueville claims, "Beyond the frontiers of the Union toward Mexico extend vast provinces that still lack inhabitants. The men of the United States . . . will appropriate the soil, they will establish a society on it, and when the legitimate proprietor finally presents himself, he will find the desert fertilized and foreigners sitting tranquilly on his inheritance."[23] What is important in this portrait is that settlers are appropriating land from Mexico, and not from indigenous communities already inhabiting that territory. For Tocqueville, Anglo settlers in Texas acquired territory not through dispossession but by cultivating empty land and planting their culture and society in the soil.

Tocqueville further develops this characterization of American settler expansion through a contrast with the Russian empire of Tsar Nicholas I. While both empires were "advancing toward the same goal," they had different principles of expansion. If American expansion represented the triumph over "wilderness and barbarism," Russian expansion opposed the advance of "civilization." Tocqueville further writes, if "the conquests of the American are made with the plowshare of the laborer, those of the Russian [are made] with the sword of the soldier. To attain his goal, the first relies on personal interest and allows the force and the reason of individuals to act, without directing them. The second in a way that concentrates all the power of society in one man. The one has freedom for his principal means of action; the other servitude."[24] He thus portrayed US expansion as a process executed through the enterprise of independent farmers operating under a form of enlightened self-interest, which then coalesced into a broader social force. For Tocqueville, American expansion gathered its force from the initiative of individuals acting freely in civil society.

By casting "the people" as the driving force of expansion rather than military conquest and the directing power of the imperial state, Tocqueville constructs an image of a democratic empire driven by the modern movement of the *demos* and their universal demand for equality. Furthermore, as we see in the contrast of American with Spanish and Russian expansion, the foundations of democratic society rest on a spatial imaginary defined by indigenous absence and thus by the absence of conquest. For Tocqueville, the "level of an egalitarian civilization has been laid upon" a landscape emptied of indigenous others. Rather than a social order composed of competing and separate estates, the American social state "consists everywhere of the same elements."[25] Lacking concentrated populations that would need to be eliminated for settlers to expand, Tocqueville concludes that the spirit of conquest is alien to the liberal ethos cultivated in the democratic social state.[26]

Settling Democracy

The work of erasing the continent's native inhabitants in the first chapter of *Democracy* both narratively precedes and conceptually underpins Tocqueville's attempt to explain the "point of departure" for American democracy in the unique mode of colonization by which the New England colonies were settled and founded. If there was any single factor that contributed to the development of democracy in North America, it was the original process of colonization that established the equality of conditions and the basis of popular sovereignty. Tocqueville explained that the "social state of the Americans is eminently democratic" and that it acquired this unique character from "the birth of the colonies."[27] Although he speaks the familiar language of "colonies," few commentators have appreciated how this process of settler colonization represents a distinct mode of colonial expansion that departs from the traditional model of European imperialism and exploitation colonialism. If exploitation colonialism justifies the continued exploitation of native labor and the rule of colonial administration, the strategies of exclusion in settler colonialism are oriented toward rationalizing indigenous dispossession and land appropriation.[28] To obscure the coloniality of settler societies, settler imaginaries require the foundational disavowal of indigeneity and colonial dispossession.

The true origins of the democratic revolution in America, for Tocqueville, are not in the Declaration of Independence or the American Constitution but in the settlement of the original American colonies. Tocqueville went so far as to say that there is not a single event, opinion, custom, or law in America that this "point of departure" does not explain. Two key features of the American point of departure combined to lay the foundation for a form of government founded on "the principle of the sovereignty of the people."[29] First, the principle of popular sovereignty arose from what Tocqueville called "the spirit of liberty" marked by the civic and participatory freedom of township governance as well as the individual and liberal freedom of commerce. All the English colonies, "from their beginning, seemed destined to offer the development of freedom, not the aristocratic freedom of their mother country, but the bourgeois and democratic freedom of which the history of the world had still not offered a complete model."[30] Through this process of settlement, the New England colonial governments embraced a new form of liberal democratic freedom combining respect for individual liberty with the exercise of popular power. "Affairs that touch the interest of all," Tocqueville proclaimed, "are treated in the public square and within the general assembly of citizens, as in Athens."[31] Second, the principle of the sovereignty of the people also found unique expression in "the spirit of religion." "Puritanism," Tocqueville writes, "was not only a religious doctrine; it also blended at several points with the most absolute democratic and republican theories." To establish a "civil body politic," the Puritans drew on congregational principles as a model of colonial self-rule premised on voluntary consent.[32]

In explaining how "the spirit of liberty" and "the spirit of religion" arose in new world conditions, Tocqueville turns to the colonial settlements of New England. What made English colonial society unique stemmed from the system of colonial organization by which settlements were founded. While imperial authorities elsewhere in Europe subjected American colonies to rules legislated in the metropolis, the English system of colonization gave "emigrants the right to form themselves into a political society under the patronage of the mother country, and to govern themselves in everything that was not contrary to its laws." The authority it granted settlers to organize and constitute themselves as a self-governing society comprised the characteristic feature of the English colonial system. "The new settlers did not derive their incorporation from the seat of empire, although they did not deny its supremacy; they constituted a society of their own accord."[33] As a form of constituent power involving the constitution of a new social order, settler sovereignty is also a form of foundational violence that enacts the eradication of prior identities to make way for the new democratic order.

Combined with this model of colonization that rejected the imposition of dependency status on the colonies, the transfer of metropolitan customs and culture to new territory also helped produce the democratic social state. But what is significant in this process is less what settlers brought with them than what they didn't. Although the North American colonies contained "the seed of a complete democracy," it was less the positive qualities of settler political culture than the qualities settlers lacked that shaped the democratic features of colonial society. In departing from the mother country, settlers lacked notions of natural superiority and attachment to aristocratic hierarchies. Instead, they privileged social equality over feudal arrangements and institutionalized this ideal through the abolition of primogeniture and entail. Although "great lords" did come to America and sought to establish "a hierarchy of ranks," the difficulties of colonization thwarted these efforts. Because land had to be cleared before it could be cultivated, feudal lords did not see adequate returns on investment due to the labor-intensive process of agriculture. It was only the "constant and interested efforts of the property owner" applied to small tracts of land that could lead to the adequate cultivation of the land. For this reason, Tocqueville asserts, "American soil absolutely repelled territorial aristocracy."[34]

Despite his sympathetic lament over the Trail of Tears, the disavowal of indigenous sovereignty grounds Tocqueville's account of the foundation of democratic society. Drawing on the doctrine of discovery, he notes that European settlers generally thought that "the lands of the New World belonged to the European nation that had first discovered them."[35] He thus affirms that the sovereign who sent fleets and armies to discover and conquer new land had the sole right to establish dominion and sovereignty over that land. While the discovery doctrine was more concerned with justifying territorial sovereignty in relation to competing European powers, it combined with the doctrine of terra nullius to rationalize the expropriation of indigenous land. The doctrine of terra nullius (land belonging to no one) held that new world territories were empty and uncultivated wilderness without property or government. Because native societies lacked political institutions analogous to modern European sovereignty, states justified their sovereign claims to territory considered *terra nullius* without native consent. Settlers planted themselves in lands designated *terra nullius*, replacing states of nature with civil societies through the creation of new governing institutions that excluded natives.[36] Absent legitimate forms of social organization, Tocqueville reflects that North America at the time of colonization was the "still-empty cradle of a great nation." On top of this land, "civilized men were to try to build a society on new foundations."[37]

The importance of geography in explaining the character and stability of American democracy is so pronounced that Tocqueville considered a liberal-democratic republic to be the "natural state of the Americans." He writes, "In the United States, it is not only legislation that is democratic; nature itself works for the people." Due to the material abundance of land, the perceived absence of native inhabitants, and the virtual lack of immediate territorial threats, the "boundless continent" of North America allowed Americans to "remain free and equal."[38] Political liberty and social equality acquired their material basis in the geographic conditions of democratic society, granting a degree of stability to democratic institutions that prevented them from degenerating into anarchy.

For Tocqueville, social equality enabled by widespread property ownership ensured political stability and public order in democratic societies. Like Aristotle, Tocqueville divided society into three classes: the rich, poor, and the middle class. In an ideal social state, both the poor and rich should be few and impotent while the middle classes who stand between these two extremes should "possess sufficient property to desire the maintenance of order." To ensure such a state of affairs and prevent political instability, Tocqueville stipulated that measures must be taken to ensure that the people acquire a "share of property" that enables the spirit of liberty to take root.[39] Organized in such a way, the democratic social state guarantees a "political form that equally favors the development and prosperity of all the classes of which society is composed."[40] Although reforms in property law helped in this regard, Tocqueville also understood that granting the poor a stake in society required the settlement of western lands.

In American settler thought, the trope of the frontier symbolizes not just the expectation of social mobility and economic advancement but also the promise of free and equal self-rule. Settler expansion maintains a bourgeois class order that places sovereignty in civil society rather than in the aristocracy of the rich or the socialism of the poor. Settler colonialism is thus a political-economic system by which modern society spatially displaces its contradictions to an alternative geographic space to prevent the dissolution of social order. It enacts the "sublimation of politics" by projecting class conflict and broader social conflicts to an elsewhere through the colonization of indigenous land.[41] The centrality of colonization to American democratic thought is not simply in the satisfaction of the economic interests and proprietary aspirations of settlers. It is that liberal-democratic values—"the spirit of liberty" and "the spirit of religion"—that stabilize bourgeois society are cultivated in part through dispossession and settler colonization, which enable an egalitarian social state. In this way, settler colonialism constitutes "empire as a way of life," a durable and institutionalized collection of cultural values and norms that define the democratic social condition.[42] If the values of liberty, social equality, and popular sovereignty at the heart of democratic citizenship were attained through settler expansion, then democracy's material reality resides in a settler-colonial social formation.

Race, Space, and Indigeneity

Examining *Democracy in America* through the lens of settler colonialism sheds new light on the last chapter of Volume 1 on the "three races in America." In this chapter, Tocqueville posits a crucial distinction between logics of racial slavery that rely upon anthropological representations of the racial other that cast black capabilities as inferior and logics of settler colonialism that rely on spatial representations of empty land. The racial logics of settler colonialism rest less upon anthropological constructions of native capacities than they do on the presumed absence of indigenous political forms. In this regard, race operates not just through racial representations of indigenous bodies but more precisely through representational practices of space making that in turn reproduce settler colonial hierarchies. Too often scholars collapse Tocqueville's treatment of racial slavery and native dispossession into the homogenous and undifferentiated category of "racial exclusion" or "ascriptive hierarchy" without attending to the distinct racial logics embedded in these different forms of domination and dispossession.[43]

Although both highlight the way American settlers have constructed what scholars have variously called a "white republic,"[44] "herrenvolk democracy,"[45] or "racial polity,"[46] chattel slavery and indigenous dispossession represent distinct structures of colonial domination that rely on different practices and ideologies of racialization. The distinction between the racial logics of chattel slavery and settler colonialism is immediately evident in the problem Tocqueville laid out in the very beginning of the chapter on the three races. There Tocqueville notes that there are three "naturally distinct and . . . inimical races" in North America. He writes, "Fortune has gathered them on the same soil, but it has mixed them without being able to intermingle them, and each pursues its destiny separately."[47] The puzzle that Tocqueville grapples with is why each race has been destined to pursue its own path separately, and specifically, why natives and blacks (whether freed or enslaved) face different prospects in America. Tocqueville does emphasize continuities across the experiences of the two oppressed races. Both, for instance, have experienced dispossession and alienation from their ancestral homelands. The Negro has "lost even the memory of his country" and has no home to speak of other than his master's hearth. European settlers also dispersed indigenous families and appropriated their land, and in doing so broke the bonds of memory and custom connecting them to the past. Both suffer from tyranny and oppression, but "the effects are different."[48]

Tocqueville is worth quoting at length on these different effects faced by natives and freed and enslaved blacks:

> The Negro makes a thousand useless efforts to introduce himself into a society that repels him; he bows to the tastes of his oppressors, adopts their opinions, and in imitating them aspires to intermingle with them. . . . The Indian, on the contrary, has an imagination filled up with the pretended nobility of his origin. He lives and dies in the midst of these dreams of his pride. Far from wanting to bend his mores to ours, he attaches himself to barbarism as a distinctive sign of his race, and he repels civilization perhaps less in hatred of it than in fear of resembling the Europeans. . . . The Indian could up to a certain point succeed at it, but he disdains the attempt.[49]

Underneath these somewhat opposed situations lies a puzzle: Why can natives succeed at integrating themselves into white society while blacks cannot? Freed and enslaved blacks sought integration into white society, but the intensity of white racial prejudice dashed any hope of equality. Because white views of Indians were often rooted in spatial assumptions about natives as a vanishing race rather than anthropological assumptions about the inferiority of native bodies, white settlers were, in many cases, willing to accept natives into white society through assimilation and acculturation.[50]

Natives could thus succeed at assimilating into white society, but according to Tocqueville they recoiled at the thought of such an idea.

Tocqueville's observation here points to the difference, as regimes of dispossession and domination, between slavery and settler colonialism. Whites, he suggested, would accept Indians into their culture because they want their land, not their labor. The obstacles to black inclusion, even in the North, where Tocqueville notes that white prejudice toward blacks is in fact stronger than in the South, are rooted in the legacy of southern slavery. To continually justify the exploitation of black labor, slaveholders treated their slaves as separate from the dominant racial group and constructed ideological justifications that relied on the inferiority of African bodies (yet that made them particularly suited for physical labor). Ultimately, Tocqueville suggests, even freed slaves internalized this inferiority complex, which both prevents freedmen from asserting their rights and further fans the flames of white prejudice. Even in Northern states that abolished slavery and lacked formal legal barriers separating the races, the "trace of slavery" lives on in the souls of freedmen and the prejudice of whites, preventing full assimilation into white society. Tocqueville asserts that even in the absence of formal slavery, "The remembrance of slavery dishonors the race, and race perpetuates the remembrance of slavery."[51] Slavery, Tocqueville profoundly grasps, lives on in culture and customs in the same instance as it is abolished in law.

If slavery and its racial logics are rooted in an economic system aimed at the exploitation of labor, settler colonialism revolves around the logic of native elimination and land expropriation. As Patrick Wolfe has argued, "Whatever settlers may say . . . the primary motive for elimination is not race (or religion, ethnicity, grade of civilization, etc.), but access to territory."[52] Tocqueville's text clearly reflects the assimilative logic of settler colonialism. He famously reflects the enduring nineteenth-century trope of the vanishing Indian when he writes, "I believe that the Indian race of North America is condemned to perish, and I cannot prevent myself from thinking that on the day that the Europeans will have settled on the coast of the Pacific Ocean, it will have ceased to exist." Despite this grim prognostication, Tocqueville offers "two options for salvation: war or civilization; in other words, they had to destroy the Europeans or become their equals."[53] Although he sees civilization as a path to equality (evidenced in examples like the Cherokee people), he fails to grasp the settler colonial logics embedded in the very pursuit of equality. Insofar as it implies equality on terms established by the settler social state, civilization and assimilation entail the loss of native sovereignty. In a perverse sort of logic, the salvation of natives by means of civilization becomes their elimination. Ultimately, settler colonial dispossession—whether through means of removal or assimilation—focuses on the expropriation of indigenous land rather than the exploitation of native labor. "The Americans of this part of the Union," Tocqueville claims, "look jealously on the lands that the natives possess; they feel that the latter have still not completely abandoned the traditions of the savage life, and before civilization has attached them solidly to the soil, they want to reduce them to despair and force them to go away."[54]

Of course, none of this is to say that anthropological representations of native capacities for settled agriculture are irrelevant to Tocqueville's account of colonial dispossession. Rather, it is that anthropological representations of the indigenous other operate in relation to spatial representations of North American land as empty. Indian culture, for Tocqueville, was entirely incompatible with republican self-government. Drawing on common prejudices during the Jacksonian era concerning Indian forms of cultural life, Tocqueville argued that the "great fault" of Jesuit and Puritan missionaries "was not to understand that to succeed in civilizing a people, one must before everything else get them to settle, and one can only do that by cultivating the soil; it was therefore a question first of turning the Indians into farmers." Absent sedentary forms of agriculture that provided the foundation for township self-government, Indians were unable to incorporate into the democratic movement sweeping across North American.[55] Based on the incompatibility of native and settler cultural forms, Tocqueville saw the process of American expansion in explicitly colonial terms, as the replacement of native sovereignty with settler sovereignty *qua* democratic sovereignty. Describing his travels through the American frontier, he wrote, "everywhere the savage's hut had given way to the civilized man's house; the woods had fallen, the empty spaces were coming to life."[56] Distinct from his representations of North American land in *Democracy*, Tocqueville conceded that the emptiness of territory is less a natural fact than a condition produced through the process of settlement.

In any case, natives (and the vanishing civilizations they represented) symbolically condensed those elements of European political order that Tocqueville deemed absent from the American landscape—i.e., class conflict and feudal aristocracy. Regarding the former, in "Two Weeks in the Wilderness," Tocqueville recounted scenes from his first sight of American Indians, whom he saw congregating at an Indian agency in Buffalo to receive payments for lands ceded to the government. Tocqueville expressed severe disappointment at the sight. Having read Chateaubriand's *Natchez* series and James Fenimore Cooper's *Leatherstocking* tales, he expected to see the magnanimous nations of romantic lore and "those proud virtues fostered by the spirit of freedom." Instead, he saw a devastated people with only the shambles of what was once a thriving civilization. Tocqueville was especially troubled by the fact that the people he witnessed collecting the money were part of "the final remnants of that renowned confederation of Iroquois . . . one of the most famous tribes of the old American world." Describing the despair and indigence of the Iroquois people, he remarked, "Their facial features heralded that profound degradation which the lengthy abuse of the blessings of civilization alone can produce. One might have described these men as belonging to the lowest rabble of our great European cities. And yet they were still savages."[57] As if to recognize the irony in the policy of assimilation pursued by Jefferson, Knox, and others, Tocqueville conceded that policies of payment and purchase encouraged rather than impeded native elimination.

Yet what is more important for present purposes is the direct comparison Tocqueville draws between the Iroquois and the European rabble. In *Democracy*, Tocqueville draws a similar equivalence between Indians and the impoverished masses when he stated that democracy in France has "been abandoned to its savage instincts."[58] By symbolically likening the degradation of native peoples with the impoverishment of the European masses, he projects class conflict away from North America and imputes it onto European political space. In this way, the coming absence of indigenous peoples helps ensure the absence of European-style class conflict and ideological struggle in America. The appropriation of indigenous land lays the material foundation for a bourgeois class order premised on the destruction of feudal hierarchies and the elimination of class struggle. Under conditions of social equality, which emerged from the removal and conquest of native peoples, Americans found themselves in a social and political order that was without entrenched class divisions.

On the other hand, Tocqueville also equates vanishing indigenous orders with the eclipse of European feudalism in the Americas. In this way, the notion of American democracy as defined by the absence of European-style feudal hierarchies itself reproduces the same logics of native elimination Tocqueville lamented. In a crucial passage in the chapter on the three races, he evocatively likens American Indians and the French aristocracy, suggesting that both are in the process of being decimated by the providential torrent of democratic equality and thus share the same fate of being uprooted from their native soils. "The Indian, in the depth of his misery in his woods, therefore nourishes the same ideas, the same opinions as the noble of the Middle Ages in his fortified castle. . . . What a singular thing! It is in the forests of the New World, and not among the Europeans who people its shores, that the old prejudices of Europe are still found today."[59] In likening two separate classes of people desperately clinging to archaic notions of honor and glory despite the dominant egalitarian tendencies, Tocqueville reinforces the production of indigenous absence in the text.

Read in light of Tocqueville's point about the absence of feudalism as a defining feature of the democratic social state, the equivalence he draws between the feudal order and indigenous orders is especially revealing. For Jefferson as for Tocqueville, landed expansion sustains the democratic experiment by guarding against the resurgence of aristocratic hierarchies and feudal land title. The novelty of modern democracy necessarily entails the deracination of the old order. Yet in both thinkers the absent-feudalism trope displaces the centrality of colonial dispossession to the emergence of modern American democracy. Just as America provides a solution to the European social question, Europe symbolically condenses a set of constitutive absences that have been displaced from North American space. As registered in the Tocquevillean imagination, Anglo-American democracy projects indigeneity away from the Western Hemisphere and onto Europe in the form of ancient feudal hierarchies. Tocqueville's constative statement that America lacks a feudal past (i.e., the absent), which in turn defines that which is vitally present (i.e., democracy), obscures the production of native absence upon which the democratic social state rests. The inevitable force that leads democracy to triumph over feudalism is the same colonial force that embraces the elimination of native peoples.

America and Algeria

American practices and ideologies of settler colonialism come into more direct focus by emphasizing the transnational circulation of colonizing practices in the nineteenth-century imperial order. In addition to writings on American democracy, Tocqueville was also a prolific writer on the French conquest and colonization of Algeria in the 1830s and 1840s. Serving as an official in the Chamber of Deputies, Tocqueville was also an expert on the "Algeria question" and issued several reports on the matter.[60] In accounting for the peculiar blend of democratic and imperial principles in Tocqueville's thought, Jennifer Pitts points to his anxiety about the dangers of democratization in France, which contributed to his support for French expansion in Algeria despite his obvious awareness of the violence that colonial policy required. In substituting national glory for France's lost aristocratic virtue, which was softened by the ascendance of bourgeois social values, colonial expansion reinvigorated French liberal democracy, thereby stabilizing liberty in the metropole.[61] Tocqueville's concern for the stabilization of liberty in France can be understood in settler colonial terms. Just as colonization helped stabilize and constitute the democratic social state in America, the colonization of Algeria would reconfigure French democracy. Put differently, Tocqueville promoted the colonization of Algeria because he thought it would resolve the contradictions of French social order generated by democratization and the transformation of the aristocratic social order.

Throughout his writings on French colonialism and the Algeria question, Tocqueville turned to the American precedent of settler colonization.[62] In an extended correspondence with the German-American philosopher Francis Lieber—one of his primary interviewees and philosophical influences in his research for *Democracy in America*—Tocqueville pondered the possibility of importing the American model of colonization into French Algeria.[63] His primary question was how to people North Africa with French Europeans. "The most important issue today is colonization. How to attract and, above all, to retain a great number of European farmers in Algeria? We already have 100,000 Christians in Africa without counting the army, but almost all of them are settled in towns which become great and beautiful cities, while the country side remains depopulated. It is impossible to deal with the colonization of Africa without thinking of the great examples given by the United States on this issue."[64] The problem of colonization involved replacing existing North African Arabs with French settlers. To deal with this issue, Tocqueville asked Lieber if any books concerning the theory and practice of colonialism had been published in the United States.

Instead of providing a list of reports and studies, Lieber honored the request by supplying his own comparative analysis of US and French colonial expansion. To Tocqueville's dismay, Lieber asserted that the "cases of America and Algeria are essentially different" based on what he saw as three fundamental divergences in "the elements which constitute and characterize our process of peopling."[65] The first set of divergences between the American and Algerian cases of colonization concern the different political cultures of France and the United States. Lieber wrote to Tocqueville, "There is in the Anglican race an instinctive impulse of establishing governments with the principle of vitality and self-action within, not depending upon a *vis matrix* [a womb] from without—there is a *nisus* [an impulse] . . . of so forming polities in this race, that people no more speak about it than about the fact that the settlers eat, sleep, and walk."[66] Lieber's cryptic prose indicated that the impulse of English colonization stemmed not from an outside force but from political values that are internal to the democratic organization of Anglo-Americans. The "principle of self-action" that resides within the hearts of Americans referred not only to a political culture that encourages settlers to colonize distant lands but also to the peculiar founding capacity of Anglo-Saxons to create new governments. He thus advised that while the "Teutonic race have a readiness of emigration . . . the French have not."[67]

Lieber's reflections here derived from his own philosophical work on the idea of civil liberty, which he thought was peculiarly suited for expansion and colonization. Lieber understood civil liberty as synonymous with what he called "Anglican liberty," which was bound to cultural hierarchies that carved out a central role for Anglo-Americans to bring civilization, liberty, and progress to the world. Lieber wrote, "We belong to the Anglican race, which carries Anglican principles and liberty over the globe, because wherever it moves, liberal institutions and . . . *the principle of an expansive life*, accompany it." It is the obvious task of Anglo-Americans to "rear and spread civil liberty over vast regions in every part of the earth, on continent and isle."[68] If Gallican (i.e., French) liberty was marked by "imperial absolutism" and the predominance of centralized state power, Anglican liberty combined colonial expansion with the preservation of individual freedom. Lieber saw in US settler expansion a "great process of expansion of liberty," and he celebrated the spread of "the most fruitful principles of Anglican self-government in the widening colonies, north and south of the equator."[69] American liberty, in this regard, had an expansionist tendency deeply woven into its cultural fabric.

A second divergence between American and Algerian colonization concerns the distinct configuration of law and territoriality in North America. Lieber wrote, "Although the land belongs to the U.S., the pre-emption law makes it for all purposes of first settling as though it absolutely belonged to no one. You settle down and clear land where you list."[70] In the 1830s, partially due to the efforts of labor radicals, the US government shifted its western land policy away from an approach focused on the sale of land by auction aimed at increasing government revenue to a policy of granting virtually free land grants to settlers who expended the labor of agricultural improvement. One of the first key precedents to the Homestead Act of 1862 was the policy of preemption. Passed by Congress in 1838, the Preemption Act granted squatters the right to purchase at a minimum price land that they settled before the government could survey it. While Tocqueville focused on the abolition of primogeniture and entail in North America as a defining feature of the "equality of conditions"—which prevented the consolidation of centralized land holdings and the emergence of a feudal aristocracy—he neglected laws concerning the distribution of western land. For Lieber, it was not simply inheritance laws regulating the transmission of landed property but also colonization laws granting cheap land to settlers that made the democratic social state uniquely attuned to settler expansion.

A related aspect of American colonization concerns the fertile and undisputed territory of North America. Lieber counseled Tocqueville that Americans "have to do with no enemies except Indians, who recede with the buffalo. Besides what are they, compared to your Arabs?"[71] For Tocqueville as for Lieber, American Indians were a vanishing race that receded with the surge of settlers westward. Distinct from the condition of indigenous absence in America, the Arab presence in Algeria posed a powerful obstacle preventing French settlement. In his 1841 "Essay on Algeria," Tocqueville posited that the "right of war authorizes us to ravage the country . . . either by destroying harvests during the harvest season, or year-round by making those rapid incursions called razzias, whose purpose is to seize men or herds." Such were the "unfortunate necessities" that "any people that wants to wage war on the Arabs is obliged to submit."[72] As Margaret Kohn has argued, Tocqueville viewed the rule of law not as a universal right but as a "technique of government" that was applicable only to communities that had cultural forms supportive of liberal and consensual social relations. The "laws of war," conversely, were a political technology that applied to those collectivities that lacked the social relations and cultural practices characteristic of liberal democracy. The blind devotion of Arabs to Islam and nomadic liberty led them to resistance and to respect only power and force, thus making the use of conquest as a tool of colonial governance justifiable and inevitable.[73]

The third and most important difference between American and French Algerian patterns of colonization concerns the unique modes of colonial organization at work in each. While he did not call it out by name, Lieber described to Tocqueville the colonial protocol of the Northwest Ordinance in which "the regular government, i.e. Congress establishes a 'Territory;' the self-constituted government [i.e., the colonial government] passes over into or furnishes the rudiments of a legalized one." Especially important to Lieber was that colonial legislatures in new territories were self-constituted, which ensured that the localized sovereignty of settlers would remain somewhat autonomous in relation to the federal government. By showing no favoritism to old states, the "wisdom of Congress" was in providing for a regularized process of settlement that placed citizens of new territories in a condition of imperial equality. Moreover, by privileging settler-popular sovereignty over imperial sovereignty in the constitution of new settlements, Congress created a process of colonization by which settlers retained their standing in the civic community when they emigrated. Lieber wrote, "Every American who emigrates knows he does not sink into a colonist; he is and remains full citizen, which aids much in inducing people to emigrate."[74]

Despite his belief that the French could learn important lessons from the Anglo-Americans in the art of colonization, Tocqueville begrudgingly agreed with Lieber that the different social conditions of French Algeria and North America prevented the wholesale adoption of American colonizing practices. Nevertheless, although the first two differences were too great to overcome, he hoped that France could facilitate the conquest of Algeria by adopting Anglo-American models of colonial organization. One of Tocqueville's primary arguments in the "Essay on Algeria" was that conquest (the displacement of natives) and colonization (the settlement of colonists) must proceed together. If the objective of Algerian colonization was to create a new society on top of conquered territory, it was impractical to think that colonization could occur without war and domination. To establish French sovereignty in Algeria required transplanting the French population to the shores of Africa. Tocqueville noted, "until we have a European population in Algeria, we shall never establish ourselves there but shall remain camped on the African coast."[75] The objective in colonizing Algeria was to transport the European population from one place to another. Rather than separate processes, the settlement of Algeria by French colonists and the conquest of Arabs by the French military must be simultaneous.

But the simultaneity of conquest and colonization posed difficulties to the task of encouraging settlers to migrate to the colonies. As long as France was at war with Algerian Arabs, and as long as the French military remained a powerful presence in North Africa, settlers risked the loss of rights and liberties when they settled in a conquered territory. The problem is evident in considering what settlers lose in leaving France (i.e., civil and political rights). Tocqueville wrote, "The tribune, liberty of the press, the jury, electoral right, do not exist in Africa." Conversely, "In his own country, the Frenchman takes part in the government of affairs either directly through elections or indirectly through freedom of the press. The laws are made by powers that he either elected or oversees." Without the "guarantees of security and liberty," settlers lacked incentive to emigrate.[76] It was thus necessary that settlers who arrived in Africa "feel exiled as little as possible, and that they encounter, if possible, a perfect image of their homeland."[77] While American settler expansion proceeded without conquest through the disavowal of indigenous sovereignty, the centrality of conquest to the settlement of French Algeria posed formidable problems that discouraged further colonization. Nevertheless, despite Lieber's analysis, Tocqueville maintained that colonization and conquest could occur in tandem if French imperialists adapted the American model of colonial organization to the Algerian context in an effort to protect the rights and sovereignty of settlers.

Conclusion

Driven by modern ideals of equality and self-rule, Tocqueville believed that the colonization and conquest of North America was part of the same providential movement that drove the spread of democratic equality in the modern world: "One must therefore not believe that it is possible to stop the surge of the English race in the New World. . . . No power on earth can close off . . . this fertile wilderness, which is open on every side to industry and offers a refuge in all miseries." The "march of equality" in this passage, as Francis Fukuyama puts it, operates in both a metaphorical and a literal sense: as the steady progression of democratic equality, signaling the rise of modernity; and as the steady march of settlers across the western landscape, which offered citizens the promise of social mobility and economic independence through the appropriation of native land.[78] Tocqueville saw the emergence of popular sovereignty and social equality largely in terms of a theory of political development that cast democracy as a socio-cultural rather than as a constitutional form. In this socio-cultural concept of democracy, settler expansion guarded against the resurgence of feudal land title in the new world by ensuring the primacy of civic equality in the context of an expanding political economy. Regimes of settler colonialism and indigenous dispossession constituted the very foundation of American democracy by shaping the values, habits, and customs that defined the boundaries of popular sovereignty. Although Tocqueville recognized that settler colonization was central to the American democratic experience, his representations of North American land obscured the constitutive role of conquest and colonial violence in the creation of the democratic social state.

While the previous two chapters focused on constitutional arguments aimed at integrating settler sovereignty and the democratic self-rule of colonies into imperial frameworks, this and the following two chapters focus on democracy as cultural form and social state. The argument in this chapter thus moves beyond existing accounts of the vexed relationship between democracy and dispossession that focus on constitutional dynamics. Insofar as it maps the democratic landscape through settler geographies, *Democracy* reveals the entwined legacies of democracy and dispossession. Tocqueville's unique perspective on political development emphasizes the social and cultural foundations of constitutional democracy rather than simply its constitutional foundations. As such, the entwinement of democracy and colonial expansion resides at a deeper level than the constitutionality of settler empire and legally codified forms of exclusion. Not only does American democratic society and culture rest upon settler colonization, the boundaries of democratic peoplehood and the intelligibility of the people as a subject of rule in American political discourse emerge through indigenous disavowal. Sheldon Wolin has written, "One of the great mythemes of *Democracy* is the appearance of the people as full-fledged political actors continuously involved in the exercise of power."[79] Settler colonialism both established the boundaries of popular sovereignty and drives the process by which "we the people" became an acting and active agent of popular self-rule. By locating the analysis at the socio-cultural level of democracy—in what I have called "the settler social state"—rather than solely at the constitutional level, the centrality of settler colonization to establishing the foundations of modern democratic sovereignty comes into more critical focus.

4 Manifest Destiny and the Safety Valve of Colonization

"The warlike proceedings of the Americans in Mexico were purely exceptional, having been carried on principally by volunteers, under the influence of the migratory propensity which prompts individual Americans to possess themselves of unoccupied land."
—John Stuart Mill, Considerations on Representative Government (1861)

The idea of manifest destiny is one of the most enduring legacies of American colonial thought. Although its complex and contested legacy cannot be attributed to one single source, the basic idea of manifest destiny is that the United States had the right and duty, as a matter of divine providence, to expand over the whole of the North American continent, spreading democracy and freedom as settlers marched to the Pacific. By expanding westward and conquering foreign populations in the way, American settlers were carrying out the will of God. The millennial destiny of the American people was to enter a new historical age that transcended past historical epochs. Situated in space rather than time, the new millennium of American democracy derived its novelty from the boundlessness of land and territory. The dominance of American power in North America foretold not only the ascendance of a new international power, but also the emergence of a new democratic age. As a divine agent in the historical redemption of humanity, American power was an exception to the rule of classical empires that expanded through conquest and violence. Because it followed a different path of historical development, American empire possessed an alternative collective destiny that was superior to the international role of other European empires.

By casting the right to expand as a world-historical mission to free enslaved populations from the chains of dogma and superstition, the divinely ordained destiny of American settlers was to be a "redeemer na-tion."[1] A central motif of manifest destiny was the notion of Americans as a "chosen people" who possessed a divine calling to bring about a state of global democratic redemption. Walt Whitman epitomized this idea when he envisioned a hierarchical image of world order in which American moral leadership stemmed from its status as "the first nation on the earth." Imag-ining US colonial expansion as a democratic process by which free settlers planted democratic institutions in a barren and under-cultivated landscape, Whitman proclaimed, "We claim those lands, thus, by a law superior to parchments and dry diplomatic rules."[2] Presaging the ideology of American exceptionalism that sustained US imperialism throughout the twentieth century, Whitman held that the projection of American power was exempt from the traditional moral constraints of international law. The mission to spread liberty and democracy over the continent represented a higher claim to "imperial right" than traditional justifications in international law such as discovery and conquest.[3]

Despite the prevalence of studies of manifest destiny, none have analyzed it as a distinct theory of settler colonization.[4] While several commentators probe the political theology of manifest destiny and its attendant notions of Americans as a "chosen people," there has been little work situating the discourse in the larger context of settler colonial ideology in the Anglo-American world.[5] The idea of manifest destiny was closely connected to what is called the "safety-valve theory of colonization." More than a sym-bol in antebellum culture of the promise of uncultivated "virgin land," the safety-valve theory of colonization was a central aspect of emergent forms of democratic theory that saw the absence of feudalism and legalized social hierarchies as the hallmark of an egalitarian society. In the safety-valve theory, outlets of open land in the West available for colonization provided relief from the pressures of urbanization and industrialization in the East. Closely connected to the Jeffersonian dream of an independent, agrarian citizenry, the safety-valve theory instituted a temporal rupture in which the democratic time of the new world transcended the social ills of the old. In this way, historical consciousness in the antebellum democratic imagina-tion emerged from within a settler colonial ideology in which the presence of unsettled land in the Americas drove the historical transition from an aristocratic to democratic stage of political development.

The metaphor of the safety valve served as the conceptual linchpin for antebellum conceptions of democracy. Extending Tocqueville's argument about the settler social state, the safety-valve theory forcefully illustrates how modern democracy acquired its unstable foundation through the expropriation of indigenous land. This chapter explores the central place of the safety-valve theory of colonization in shaping the emergence of antebellum democratic thought and culture, focusing particularly on the contexts of the annexation of Texas (1845) and the Mexican-American War (1846–1848). Notions of manifest destiny and the safety valve of colonization have received little attention from historians of political thought because it is believed that they express no more than symbolic manifestations of the American "legitimizing myth of empire," more a "rhetorical flourish" than a "sincere expression of principles."[6]

Against these interpretations, I treat manifest destiny and the safety-valve theory as enduring features of modern democratic thought.[7] One of the hallmarks of nineteenth-century American thought was the idea that modern democracy resided more firmly in the social and cultural conditions of the democratic polity than in its constitutional form (Chapter 3). This chapter extends this analysis by exploring how the safety-valve theory of colonization represented more than a simple argument for the total conquest and colonization of North America. It was a theory about the social and cultural foundations of modern democratic politics. Focusing less on manifest destiny as a political theology of divine mission, I explore the idea of the safety valve as a democratic theory of settler colonization. In the safety-valve theory, democracy represented a distinctive social and cultural formation that acquired its character from the plentitude of land readily available for settlement. As a social form, modern democracy stood in opposition to archaic social forms represented by both indigenous peoples and European feudal structures. The safety-valve theory of colonization thus provided a powerful argument for the expropriation of indigenous land as a means of insulating the democratic political economy from the social problems of rampant poverty and class conflict plaguing European society.

By placing the political thought of John O'Sullivan and Ralph Waldo Emerson in the context of settler colonialism, this chapter outlines the safety-valve theory of colonization through three key phases. The first phase reads O'Sullivan's journalistic writings in *United States Magazine and Democratic Review* as important instantiations of democratic theories of settler colonization. In O'Sullivan's concept of manifest destiny, the temporal and messianic destiny of the United States derives from the distinct configuration of North American land as empty and boundless. Closely connected to this was the notion of western land as the "safety valve" of democracy, which drove the progressive transition from the aristocratic to democratic stage of history. The second section reads O'Sullivan's writings on the conquest of Mexico against the Treaty of Guadalupe Hidalgo (1848), which concluded the Mexican-American War and provided for the consensual inclusion of conquered Mexicans into the American imperial order, and the Treaty of Dancing Rabbit Creek (1830), which facilitated the dispossession of the Choctaw people under the Indian Removal Act (1830). I find in these political practices a logic of "consensual colonization" in which settlers elicit the consent of the colonized in their attempts to eliminate the political presence of Mexican and indigenous peoples. The third section examines Emerson's writings and lectures on colonization, which romanticize the safety-valve theory of colonization by envisioning the cultivation of nature as a source of democratic ethos. The values of democratic citizenship that stabilized the American polity were cultivated through processes of settlement, colonization, and indigenous disavowal.

John O'Sullivan and the Safety Valve of Colonization

Even though John O'Sullivan coined one of the most important (and most amorphous) concepts in American political thought, there is little extant scholarship that seriously examines his political thinking. After the United States annexed Texas in 1845, O'Sullivan first introduced the language of manifest destiny in the *United States Magazine and Democratic Review* as a means of asserting American territorial claims in North America against the British Empire. In reaction to both Whigs and British diplomats who sought to check American expansion, O'Sullivan railed against those who remained intent on "limiting our greatness and checking the fulfillment of our manifest destiny to overspread the continent allotted by Providence for the free development of our multiplying millions."[8] In an editorial for the *New York Morning News*, O'Sullivan similarly asserted that America's "true title" to Oregon stemmed from the superiority of its democratic way of life. The claim to Oregon, O'Sullivan pronounced, "is by the right of our manifest destiny to overspread and to possess the whole of the continent which Providence has given for the development of the great experiment of liberty and federative self-government entrusted to us."[9] O'Sullivan was unaware that his term would coalesce into a powerful political discourse, but it became a potent expression of America's "providentially or historically sanctioned right to continental expansion."[10]

Although little appreciated as a political thinker, O'Sullivan distilled many aspects of the ideology of democratic empire throughout the late 1830s and 1840s in a series of editorials for the *United States Magazine and Democratic Review*. After some help from Andrew Jackson and Martin Van Buren in recovering a family fortune, O'Sullivan started the *Democratic Review* in 1837 to give the Democratic Party a cultural base in mass society. In an attempt to politically recover from crippling economic depression, President Van Buren sought a broad base of popular support, which the journal aimed to provide. Despite the persistent illusion of formal independence from the Democratic Party, Van Buren helped O'Sullivan's vision of a democratic journal of thought and culture come to fruition and ensured its continued success by promoting it among the party ranks. Having shared O'Sullivan's vision for a literary and political journal of democratic ideas, Jackson himself was among the first subscribers. Through his position in networks of political and cultural elites in New York and Washington, O'Sullivan published leading political and literary voices of the antebellum period such as Walt Whitman, Orestes Brownson, George Bancroft, and Ralph Waldo Emerson.[11]

In his introductory editorial for the inaugural issue of the *Democratic Review*, O'Sullivan established democracy as the central theme of American national identity by showing the importance of the "democratic principle" to "our political system and literature." The emergence of democracy in America, according to O'Sullivan, required the wholesale reevaluation of Western political theory: "All history has to be re-written; political science and the whole scope of moral truth have to be considered and illustrated in the light of the democratic principle."[12] As a momentous event that fundamentally altered the course of world history, the rise of democracy rendered the previous categories of political thought insufficient to grasp the theoretical novelty, operation, and significance of modern democratic politics. To reorient political theory in a democratic direction, O'Sullivan outlined the primary features of "that high and holy DEMOCRATIC PRINCIPLE which was designed to be the fundamental element of the new social and political system created by the American experiment."[13] Without fully grasping this principle and embedding it in its national literature, the American polity would be unable to achieve its unique democratic destiny.

O'Sullivan identified three key features of the democratic principle. First, "the principle of democratic republicanism" entailed "an abiding confidence in the virtue, intelligence, and full capacity for self-government of the great mass of our people." By investing power in the sovereign people and "the supremacy of the will of majority," the public good would be more vigorously pursued than by a self-interested minority.[14] The second aspect involved "the VOLUNTARY PRINCIPLE," which furnished a "system of administration of justice" and then left "all the business and interests of society to themselves, to free competition and association." Repeating a phrase that was emblazoned on the masthead of every issue of the *Democratic Review*, O'Sullivan maintained, "The best government is that which governs least."[15] Third, he asserted that "the pervading spirit of democratic equality . . . constitutes our point of departure." He saw democratic equality not just in terms of "the natural equality of the rights of the human race" but more importantly as the abolition of "artificial social distinctions."[16]

All in all, O'Sullivan's sketch of the democratic principle was not particularly innovative. What make his reflections worthy of theoretical consideration was how he envisioned democratic time and space as both progressive and expansive in its scope and duration. During the constitutional period, political thinkers saw democracy as an archaic and unstable form of self-rule confined to small-scale politics. James Madison, for instance, understood democracy as an ancient political form relegated to small political units such as colonies, townships, and city-states. Temporally, Madison asserted that democracies were "spectacles of turbulence and contention," inherently prone to the rise-and-fall cycles of history. Because it was subject to continual decomposition and decay, democracy was the political form of the past, unable to drive America into the future.[17] O'Sullivan, in contrast, wrote that "the democratic principle . . . is borne onward by an unseen hand of Providence, to lead our race toward the high destinies of [the] human soul."[18] Democracy, in O'Sullivan's eyes, was no longer an archaic institutional form relegated to the confined space of the Athenian polis or New England township, but was a social form that directed its gaze toward the future and moved beyond its spatial limits.

In O'Sullivan's hands, manifest destiny was more than a clever ideological ploy to extinguish the territorial claims of Britain and Mexico; it represented a whole new way of interpreting the time and space of democracy.[19] In an 1839 editorial from the *Democratic Review*, O'Sullivan presaged the language of manifest destiny in proclaiming that "our country is destined to be the great nation of futurity" because "the principle upon which a nation is organized fixes its destiny."[20] The democratic principle posed a radical rupture in history in which America departed from the historical laws that governed European development. In entering a new stage of history, American democracy drew no inspiration from European political traditions: "We have no interest in the scenes of antiquity, only as lessons of avoidance of nearly all their examples."[21] Separated from the influence of European politics, America represented an exemplary model of democratic government. The annals of American history "describe no scenes of horrid carnage, where men were led on by hundreds of thousands to slay one another, dupes and victims to emperors, kings, nobles, demons in the human form called heroes."[22] Lacking a history of conquest, America transcended the violence of past European empires, propelling the nation into a future of universal peace.

In charting a unique collective destiny for the fledgling democratic nation, O'Sullivan seamlessly conflates spatial and temporal metaphors. "The expansive future is our arena," O'Sullivan writes, "and for our history. . . . The far-reaching, the boundless future will be the era of American greatness. In its magnificent domain of space and time, the nation of many nations is destined to manifest to mankind the excellence of divine principles." He goes on to assert that the modern principles of "individual equality and political liberty" were produced through the "onward march of the multitude . . . through the present and the future."[23] What is significant in these formulations is the peculiar conjunction of space and time. For O'Sullivan, the future is "expansive" and "boundless," just as history is an "arena." The democratic multitudes march not just through space but also through time, or more precisely, they march through time by marching through space. O'Sullivan conceptualizes colonial expansion as historical destiny by tying the projection of power in space to the future development of the democratic principle. Manifest destiny thus enacts the "spatialization of time": time is subordinated to space, or rather derived from space such that historical progress rests on settler colonial expansion.[24]

The "spatialization of time" also surfaces in the implicit notion of *translatio imperii* inflecting O'Sullivan's argument for manifest destiny. The concept of *translatio imperii* embodied the idea "that civilization was always carried forward by a single dominant power or people and that historical succession was a matter of westward movement."[25] The historical development of civilization has a spatial direction: human progress moves westward. As such, the seat of civilization was continually moving west, from the Orient to Greece and Rome to Britain and now, at the height of the modern world, to the Americas. North America was, in other words, the frontier of the world-historical process. This process would find its consummation in a new order of the ages when the civilizing process had traversed the entire globe, bringing the entire planet into the domain of its rule. The expansion of the United States to the Pacific would result in the "end of history" because North America was considered the space of the final phase of history before modernity engulfed the globe. As US expansion stretched to the Pacific, the seat of empire approached the ancient origins of civilization.

Hegel, in his *Philosophy of History*, systematized this understanding of world history when he wrote, "America is therefore the land of the future, where, in the ages that lie before us, the burden of the World's History shall reveal itself. . . . It is a land of desire for all those who are weary of the historical lumber-room of old Europe." While Europe was crashing under the duress of its own contradictions, largely generated by economic and political modernization, America became the vanguard of Western civilization. Having escaped the social revolution and class conflict plaguing European states, America was what Hegel called "the land of the future." In Hegel's formulation, America was a space that existed beyond the laws of history, foretelling the future possibilities and promises of a new universal form of humanity.[26] The concept of *translatio imperii* partakes in an exceptionalist discourse that "placed the new nation outside of time, and so exempted the United States from the cycle of rise and decline, or foundation and decay." Combined with the "providential bounty" of western land that made boundless expansion possible, colonization "provided a spatial solution to the problem of republican temporality" by suspending time and forestalling the threat of imperial decline.[27] Colonial expansion promised institutional stability and temporal duration by suspending the process of historical development through a democratically organized mode of expansion. It was the movement of American democracy through space that compelled its progression from one stage of civilization to another.[28]

One sees this idea clearly expressed in O'Sullivan's stadial theory of political development elaborated in a little-discussed article first published in the *Democratic Review* titled "The Course of Civilization" (1839). The stadial theory of history is most closely associated with the republican temporality of the Scottish Enlightenment. Adam Ferguson famously developed a theory of historical development by which civil society passed through several stages of growth: in the earliest stages of civilizational growth, primitive societies were based on hunting and gathering economies; in the middle stages, societies were agricultural and pastoral; and in the later stages societies became commercial, luxurious, and corrupt, and eventually led to social decay. The idea of *translatio imperii* joined stadial history to modernist conceptions of linear time as means of breaking the political cycles of rise and decline. Through imperial expansion and the expropriation of North America's abundant land, the United States could forestall the inevitable decline into corruption and class conflict.[29]

O'Sullivan drew on Ferguson's stadial theory of history and adapted it as a theory of political development rather than civil society. He began in grandiose terms by asserting that North America "was destined to become the birth-place of a new society, constructed in a new spirit and on a new plan, attaining the highest reach of civilization, and ordained to work a thorough change in the structure of European government."[30] In outlining this process, he traced the ascendance of democracy through five stages of political development. Political man first begins his historical journey in a "state of savage individualism" unrestrained by any notions of higher law or morality. The second order of political civilization was the theocratic state of ancient India and Persia, in which people were governed by the "mastery of impulse" rather than reason. In the theocratic stage, humanity had barely departed from the savage state. Nevertheless, the theocratic stage represented a modest degree of improvement over the savage state through the development of art and religion.[31]

The third phase was the state-centric stage of ancient Rome and Greece. Art, science, literature, and religion were all deeply interwoven with and subordinated to matters of the state, which embodied the public good. The hold of the state over the mind of the individual was so great that it extinguished the very thought of resistance. Ancient writers, for all their education and philosophical excellence, "uttered no word of individual freedom." Although this stage saw advancement in science and art, it remained a state of despotism. State supremacy infiltrated the informal customs and laws of society.[32] The fourth phase was the aristocratic state of feudalism, which exhibited "the spirit of exclusive rank and class" that prevailed in Western Europe. Distinct from the condition of democratic equality prevalent in North America, the feudal stage of history was marked by inherited hierarchies. It was with this last stage that democracy had to contend most vigorously. In North America, the cultivation of "the free spirit of the new-born democracy" required separation "from the influences of ancient arrangement."[33]

In this stadial view of history, the fifth and final stage came with the triumph of the democratic principle. "The last order of civilization," O'Sullivan proclaimed, "received its first permanent existence in this country."[34]

O'Sullivan defined democracy in a rather simplistic sense as "the supremacy of the people, restrained by a just regard to individual rights."[35] Yet what is again significant here is less his simplistic idea of democracy than the way he registered a profound shift in the spatio-temporal coordinates of the democratic imagination. Cast in the guise of O'Sullivan's pen, democracy represented the highest stage of civilization, a durable mode of rule capable of projection in time and expansion in space. Such changes in dominant conceptions of time as a progressive process of universal history served radical purposes by challenging the authority of feudal order. Through expansion in space, democracy arose as a new stage of civilization by uprooting the feudal system. Democracy became modern through settler expansion.

It is out of this stadial theory of history that O'Sullivan more fully developed his notion of the safety valve of colonization, which helped push the transition from the feudal to the democratic stage of political history. While the surge toward the Mexican-American War was clearly geared toward the expropriation of Mexican land, it also had a significant antiaristocratic element directed against the recolonization of North America by Britain. As early as 1844, President James K. Polk had declared that Britain was a foreign power that was violating the Monroe Doctrine by attempting to establish colonial settlement in Texas.[36] Without having fully established claims to Texas and the Oregon territory, democratic expansionists feared that British presence in the regions would provide a foothold for the return of feudalism in America. British principles of aristocratic rule served as a constitutive though negative reference point for democratic imperial ideology. If the British Empire expanded to establish inequality and servitude, democratic empire embraced a civic dimension in expanding to establish the political and economic independence of citizens.

O'Sullivan fully developed these themes in an editorial on what he called one of the great "problems of the age"—i.e., property. In contrasting the American empire of liberty to the British Empire, O'Sullivan mocked the "civilized nation" who "cannot afford bread and meat to the men who produce these." Although Britain possessed a vast extent of "colonies and dependencies," British officials restricted the popular masses to the home territory for the sake of providing a steady stream of industrial labor.[37] In contrast, "The general policy of the democracy is to favor the settlement of land, spread the bounds of the future empire, and to favor . . . the welfare of the settlers."[38] While the United States acquired territories to promote social equality through widespread property ownership, Britain restricted potential settlers from colonizing land and acquiring property in the colonies.

The consequence was that British society was collapsing under the weight its own industrial contradictions, in which the suppression of industrial wages fanned the flames of festering class conflict. In contrast, American political development was spared such a fate. O'Sullivan attributed American fate to the "safety-valve of the public lands." In America, when "workpeople feel the iron hand of competition pressing too harshly upon them, they shall . . . be allowed to escape to the free woods and rich lands of the Far West."[39] First expressed by Edward Evert, who characterized the frontier of the 1830s as a "safety valve to the great social steam engine," the safety-valve theory of colonization held that republican stability depended upon a relative degree of social equality enabled by widespread property ownership.[40] The safety-valve theory was based on the simple principle of classical political economy that vast population growth in urban centers tended to outpace economic growth and production, leading to a surplus reserve army of laborers. Surplus labor in industrial society, in turn, drove down the value of wage labor because of the ready availability of cheap workers. With the declining value of real wages, social discontent further provoked class conflict, pitting the working classes against wealthy elites. By providing the laboring classes with a way out of urban poverty, granting settlers free or cheap land relieved social conflicts generated by industrialization and suppressed wages in the East, further stabilizing democratic institutions by ensuring widespread social equality.

Consistent with this idea, O'Sullivan championed a series of policies of preemption passed through Congress, which granted settlers the right to occupy land that had not been settled and then purchase that land at a low price when it went on the market. For O'Sullivan, this response to industrialization in the East kept the nation from descending into chaos and anarchy.[41] The Pre-Emption Act of 1838, for instance, granted property rights to settlers who illegally settled land prior to the passage of the act. Two features of the act stand out for present purposes. First, it put limits on the size of landholdings, thereby ensuring the equality of conditions and preventing the consolidation of landed property. Second, it enacted a process of native elimination by making preemption rights hinge on "the extinguishment of the Indian title to the land on which such settlement or improvement was made."[42] Quite different from Tocqueville, O'Sullivan attributed the creation of the settler social state not to inheritance laws that regulated practices of entail and primogeniture but to colonization laws that provided for the egalitarian distribution of western lands. The distinct social condition of North America produced through colonization allowed Americans to pursue a democratic path of development that transcended the inequalities and class conflict of European societies rooted in feudal social structures.

O'Sullivan's idea that regimes of colonization propelled America into a new stage of democratic history found a similar yet more systematic expression in Hegel's Philosophy of History.[43] For Hegel, the characteristic feature of modernity was the rise of the bureaucratic state, which emerged to mediate social conflicts between different classes that arise in civil society. The market economy (i.e., civil society as a functionally differentiated sphere of social life from the state) necessarily produced contradictions through the private pursuit of self-interest and the simultaneous accumulation of wealth and poverty. In addressing these social problems, the development of the modern state gave civil society an ethical form through the actualization of universal freedom and the pursuit of the public good that allows individuals to locate their particular interests in the general interest of the community. The market economy that resulted from the formal differentiation of politics and civil society is a fragmenting force, which produced social divisions impeding political unification that only a centralized state can ensure. The development of the modern state, therefore, arose in response to the social conflicts and contradictions generated in modern civil society and the market economy.

While O'Sullivan carved out a positive role for the democratic state in promoting settler colonization, Hegel saw the absence of a modern state bureaucracy as the product of the colonizing process. For Hegel, North America enjoyed a unique condition of democratic equality, which impeded the formation of the bureaucratic state: "A real State . . . [will] arise only after a distinction of classes has arisen when wealth and poverty become extreme." While this condition accurately characterized European state development, North America was "hitherto exempt from this pressure, for it has the outlet of colonization constantly and widely open, and multitudes are continually streaming into the plains of the Mississippi." He went on to say, "Had the woods of Germany been in existence, the French Revolution would not have occurred."[44] Presaging Frederick Jackson Turner's lament over the "closing of the frontier," Hegel speculated that American and European development will converge only after the outlet of colonization vanishes and social classes are forced back upon each other.[45] If vast social and economic inequality in civil society spurred the emergence of class conflict in Europe, the guarantee of social equality through the colonization of western land ensured the virtual absence of social classes in North America and thus the absence of a centralized state.

In focusing on the centrality of colonial settlement to the democratic condition of equality, Hegel engages in the ideological disavowal of colonial dispossession. Comparing North and South American modes of colonization, he claimed that what distinguishes the political development of the two is the fact that "South America was conquered, but North America was colonized."[46] If conquest entails the coercive displacement and subjugation of native peoples, colonization proceeds through the cultivation of unoccupied land. By differentiating conquest from colonization, Hegel reinforced exceptionalist notions of manifest destiny that portrayed American settler expansion as a democratic process. While natives in South America endured great suffering and toil at the hands of Spanish conquistadors, natives in North America "gradually vanished at the breath of European activity." In such a condition, Europe sent its "surplus population" to North America in order exploit the advantages of its "still virgin soil."[47] Hegel casts colonization not as the conquest and displacement of indigenous populations, but as the settlement of empty space.

Consensual Colonization

While O'Sullivan similarly hoped that colonization could proceed without conquest, he had to more realistically contend with the coercive realities of settler expansion. Plagued by a profound degree of ambivalence about the ability of colonial conquest to provide a stable foundation for democracy in the new territories of the American West, he doubted whether Mexico could be incorporated into the union in a manner consistent with "national honor." One immediate option would be to incorporate Mexican states into the union on equal terms according to the principle of federative replication, which granted equality to the constituent units of empire. Yet such a position required that Mexicans already exhibit the requisite capacities for free and equal government. Presaging Social Darwinist arguments about the fitness of racialized subjects for democratic self-rule, O'Sullivan held that Mexicans were unaccustomed to the habits of democracy. Yet conquest and outright legal exclusion (e.g., in the form of colonial dependencies) was equally ill advised because it would contradict American national character:

"Democracies must make their conquests by moral agencies. If these are not sufficient, the conquest is robbery."[48] In his support of the annexation of Texas, O'Sullivan found himself caught between the Scylla of avowing colonial expansion as an important feature of democratic self-rule and the Charybdis of granting citizenship to what he considered an inferior race incapable of self-government.

In navigating this predicament, O'Sullivan drew on a set of practices and principles that I call "consensual colonization," which were first developed in the treaty system used to facilitate the removal of Choctaw and Cherokee peoples under the Indian Removal Act (1830). In brief, consensual colonization sought not the coercive annexation and conquest of territory, but the enlistment of the consensual agreement to the subjection of the colonized to the colonizer. Put differently, consensual colonization is, in Sunil Agnani's words, a form of "soft colonization, in which the interests of the settler and native are unified and the dominance of the settler is established with the voluntary consent of the colonized."[49] Pursued in this manner, the American method of democratic expansion could be rendered consistent with the moral principles that defined the essence of American democracy.

One sees the logic of consensual colonization forcefully at work in the Indian Removal Act of 1830, which authorized the president to "provide for an exchange of lands with the Indians residing in any of the states or territories, and for their removal west of the river Mississippi" to land administered by the federal government as Indian territory.[50] As a means of reconciling conflicts between Indian tribes and southern states who claimed sovereignty over the same territory, the act sought to eliminate indigenous territorial claims. Although it granted the president authority to carry out removal, the actual implementation of the policy required additional negotiation with affected nations. Diplomatic negotiations such as those of the Treaty of Dancing Rabbit Creek gave the Choctaw an ultimatum: either Indians could take up individual ownership over separate parcels of land, at which point each person was free to sell their plot and remove westward, or remain on the land as a tribe subject to state laws. Article XIV of the treaty stated, "Each Choctaw head of a family being desirous to remain and become a citizen of the States, shall be permitted to do so . . . and he or she shall thereupon be entitled to a reservation of one section of six hundred and forty acres of land, to be bounded by sectional lines of survey." By adopting liberal practices of private property and commercial agriculture through the settlement of individual plots, Indians could remain east of the river.[51] One also sees here how practices of land surveying initiated by Jefferson erase customary relationships to the land through the imposition of private property on indigenous peoples. Although Article IV did provide modest protection of tribal sovereignty against state and territorial laws in the West, the treaty nevertheless severed the connection of the Choctaw people to their ancestral homelands through principles of voluntary consent.

In an attempt to mask the coercion and violence of colonial dispossession, O'Sullivan drew on a similar set of practices of consensual colonization. He explicitly racialized conquered Mexicans as indigenous when he applied the logic of Indian removal to the expropriation of indigenous and Mexican land in the Southwest. "The Mexican race now see," O'Sullivan pronounced, "in the fate of the aborigines of the north, their own inevitable destiny. They must amalgamate and be lost in the superior vigor of the Anglo-Saxon race, or they must inevitably perish."[52] As a necessary correlate of America's democratic destiny, O'Sullivan envisioned the temporal and spatial vanishing of both Mexicans and Indians. He claimed that Anglo settlers in Texas have retained their right not only to expropriate unsettled land but to construct a new democratic order in the wilderness: "To say that the settlement of a fertile and unappropriated soil . . . is the aggression of a government is absurd. Equally ridiculous is it to suppose that when a band of hardy settlers have reclaimed the wilderness, multiplied in numbers, built up a community and organized a government, that they have not the right to claim the confederation of that society of States from the bosom of which they emanated."[53] By racializing Mexicans as indigenous, O'Sullivan represented colonization not as a process of colonial dispossession but as the creation of egalitarian social conditions on top of vacant land.

For O'Sullivan, the consensual colonization of indigenized Mexicans required the voluntary assimilation into the American political order. In allowing the "missionaries of our political science" to spread to "every quarter of the globe," O'Sullivan asserted that Mexicans would be led into the domain of American civilization.[54] He treated the assimilation of Mexicans into American citizenship as the moral elevation of conquered subjects. Since Mexicans lacked the individualist capacities for free trade and democratic government, "the great problem" following the war was to "inoculate Mexico with the commercial spirit." This method of inoculation involved the unrestrained spread of American settlers westward: "A strong infusion of the American race would impart energy and industry gradually to the indolent Mexicans."[55] The racial dimensions of settler ideology thus led to the assimilation of Mexicans into the norms of democratic citizenship.

The assimilative logic of consensual colonization is clearly evident in the Treaty of Guadalupe Hidalgo, which ended the Mexican-American War in 1848. Article V of the treaty began by fixing the boundary between the Mexican and American Republics at the Gulf of Mexico, which extended to the mouth of the Rio Grande River. But more than this, the treaty governed the process by which Mexicans were incorporated into American citizenship. Much like the Treaty of Dancing Rabbit Creek, Article VIII granted conquered subjects an ultimatum: either they could retain their property and "continue where they now reside," or they could relinquish their land claims and "retain the title and rights of Mexican citizens." In other words, Mexicans could choose either American or Mexican citizenship. Article IX of the treaty reinforced this provision: "The Mexicans who, in the territories aforesaid, shall not preserve the character of citizens of the Mexican Republic ... shall be incorporated into the Union of the United States and be admitted ... to the enjoyment of all the rights of citizens of the United States."[56] As David Kazanjian has aptly put it, "In promising to recognize Mexicans annexed by the United States as fellow citizens equal on the national stage, [Article IX] offers them a formal and abstract equality whose universality is conditioned upon assimilation to white nationality."[57] Although it concluded a long process of military conquest, the treaty reinforced consensual narratives of democratic empire by granting Mexicans equal citizenship, initiating the cultural conquest and assimilation of Mexicans into the norms of democratic citizenship.

Despite the presumption of formal equality at work in the treaty, incorporated Mexicans were met with rampant discrimination and land appropriation in their new position as US citizens. As Kazanjian has deftly shown, the legacy of discrimination following the treaty did not represent a "broken promise" but rather the fulfillment of its assimilative objectives. If Article IX promised Mexicans formal equality, this grant of citizenship also implied the negation of the "character of citizens of the Mexican Republic" and full assimilation into the norms of American democracy. Moreover, in imposing a division between Mexican and American nationalities, the treaty cast the relationship between the two in hierarchical terms. As a result, it instituted a hierarchical regime of international order that to this day underwrites the neocolonial order of the Western hemisphere. Much more than a border war, the Mexican War thus entailed the hemispheric transformation of the transnational American order.[58]

The erasure of Mexican norms of property and citizenship is further evident in the US Senate's extrication of Article X from the final version of the treaty. Article X held that "All grants of land made by the Mexican government or by the competent authorities, in territories previously appertaining to Mexico, and remaining of the future within the limits of the United States, shall be respected as valid, to the same extent that the same grants would be valid, if said territories had remained within the limits of Mexico."[59] Together with Articles VIII and IX, the deletion of Article X enabled the imposition of imperial citizenship on Mexicans by preventing previous practices of land tenure (which often involved communal land holdings) from having any authority in the newly annexed territories, giving individualized settler land claims legal priority over communal Mexican claims. By granting Mexicans an ostensible choice to adopt American citizenship, the fiction of consent at work in the treaty engendered logics of native elimination by augmenting the assimilative power of American society.

Emerson and the "Sanative Influences" of the Land

The historian Albert Katz Weinberg has provocatively characterized O'Sullivan as "the philosopher of the pioneer movement."[60] O'Sullivan distilled the basic features of manifest destiny into a full-fledged democratic theory of settler colonization. Rather than incidental elements in a romantic expression of nationalist rhetoric, O'Sullivan saw democratic principles and settler colonialism as conceptually, culturally, and materially necessary for each other. Although O'Sullivan is often interpreted as an aggressive expansionist who is largely anomalous to broader currents of antebellum democratic thought, his political thought exhibits profound parallels with that of Ralph Waldo Emerson. Perhaps more than O'Sullivan himself, Emerson illustrates the close connection between democracy and settler expansion. Indeed, a review of Emerson's essays in the *Democratic Review* pronounced, "No man is better adapted than Emerson to comprehend the spirit of the age and to interpret its mission." Thus, not only were there parallels between O'Sullivan and Emerson, O'Sullivan's own journal cast Emerson as the paragon of democratic expansionism.[61] To explore these parallels, this section examines Emerson's writings on empire and colonization in the 1840s. My central claim is that Emerson blends the safety-valve theory of colonization with transcendentalist philosophy to envision the settlement of land as necessary for the creation of the democratic ethos.

To understand how Emerson's conception of democratic equality both reflected and reinforced the burgeoning discourse of manifest destiny, it is necessary to first understand the broader political and cultural context of the 1840s United States. Although the Jacksonian period saw a flurry of mass movements such as workingmen's parties, the period is perhaps best defined by the political and cultural movement called "Young America." As a broad current of political and cultural discourse, Young America represented a democratic awakening in the American political imagination to the possibilities of popular self-rule. To actualize democratic ideals, Young America advocated for free trade, expanded political participation, universal suffrage, limited government, economic development, land reform, national improvements, and territorial expansion. What uniquely characterized Young America, however, was its fusion of politics and culture in service of national development.

On the literary side of Young America, radical ideals of popular self-rule and the formation of a national literature represented two sides of democratic nationalism. First coined by author and frequent contributor to the *Democratic Review* Cornelius Mathews, "Young America" symbolized the ideal of popular democracy along with a conception of national literature in which "the people" were at once subject, author, and audience.[62] For Mathews, the formation of democratic literature not only signified national glory but also provided vital support for popular rule by instilling democratic values and habits in the citizenry. In a similar way, the literary editor of the *Democratic Review*, Evert Duyckinck, held that national literature would both reflect and inform the political institutions of the nation. Paraphrasing the French theorist Germaine De Stael, he wrote that "the form of government, the laws, the private manners and pursuits, and the religion of a people, are reflected by . . . their literature; and . . . these circumstances, in their turn, re-act upon the form of the government."[63]

Beyond its literary dimensions, Young America also had a political component in a group of Democrats who promoted radical land reform as an essential feature of democratic self-rule.[64] George Henry Evans, a radical reformer and leader of the workingmen's movements that took root in New York and Philadelphia during the 1830s, created a journal of radical workerism that also went by the name "Young America." As the founder of the National Reform Association (NRA), a civic organization that actively lobbied Congress for land reform, Evans published a tract, "Vote Yourself a Farm," which was originally distributed as a handbill for the NRA. Its central idea was that social equality and economic independence required the availability of public land in order to ensure the economic independence necessary for popular self-rule and the cultivation of civic virtue. More than a means of eliminating economic inequality, Evans believed that land reform would restructure society through the diffusion of wealth and the democratization of power. Key to such a program was the acquisition and reservation of western land for settlement by independent farmers.[65]

While the idea of Young America represented a distinct current of thought and culture, it was also part and parcel of the broader trans-Atlantic movement of democratic nationalism. In Europe, self-consciously national movements first emerged in the form of "youth movements" that were modeled on Giuseppe Mazzini's cry for Italian unification under the banner of "Young Italy." Mazzini hoped that the cultivation of national consciousness and national literature would free Italy from foreign control and instill national unity. In response, similarly inspired movements took the form of Young Germany, Young France, and Young Ireland.[66] Whereas these European movements were revolutionary in their commitment to the overthrow of monarchical rule, the American counterpart was more moderate in its defense of democratic principles in opposition to aristocratic currents in American politics and imperial geopolitics. In both cases, the trope of youthfulness captured an optimistic faith in new beginnings generated by political and economic modernization, which promised to break the bonds of ancient fetters and replace them with democratic institutions.

Settler expansion stood at the center of Young America and was a key component of its optimistic faith in modern democracy. The progressive ethos of Young America embraced an imperial ideology that promoted the colonial expansion set in place by the market revolution. For the Young Americans, "the essence—and the destiny—of the nation is expansion. And an expanding nation implies the triumph of the democratic principles."[67] Empire and democracy were firmly linked in the discourse of Young America. One editor of the *Democratic Review* wrote that the term "Young America" was a symbol of "sympathy for the liberals of Europe, the expansion of the American Republic southward and westward, and the grasping of the magnificent purse of the commerce of the Pacific."[68]

In his democratic thought, Emerson not only reflected the logic of the Treaty of Guadalupe Hidalgo, he also calcified the ideological structure of democratic empire. What is at stake here is not Emerson's own political position on the Mexican-American War.[69] Rather, two other central claims are in play. First, in elaborating his notions of individualism and democratic equality, Emerson drew on the public hermeneutic of manifest destiny that reflected and reinforced American settler thought. Second, an engagement with his political writings reveals how the values of moral and democratic equality acquired their meaning in relation to settler colonialism.[70]

These dynamics are best illustrated in Emerson's 1844 speech, "The Young American." Delivered before a Boston audience, Emerson articulated the foundational values of the political movement that bore the namesake of his speech. Separated by a generation from the founders of the American republic, Emerson sought to instill in the American public a commitment to the renewal and regeneration of democratic principles. As a means of continuing and strengthening the spirit of 1776, Emerson preached not only independence from the political institutions of Europe but also a cultural declaration of independence from European traditions. In pursuit of both collective and individual autonomy from feudal authority, he emphasized the vast economic development of the North American continent, which provided the foundation for both political self-rule and the intellectual autonomy of the American mind.

In affirming the political and cultural significance of North American colonization, Emerson attached particular importance to the economic transformations associated with the expansion of market society. Based on the supposition of the natural equality of men in morality and intellect, Emerson proposed that "every American should be educated with a view to the values of land."[71] In one regard, Emerson clearly meant the economic value of the land in its provision of individual wealth and national prosperity. But the "values of land" operated in both a moral-cultural and political sense as well. Politically, open land and boundless opportunity ensured social equality among citizens and freedom from feudal authority. Based on republican ideals of landed independence, the settlement and economic development of the land ensured that democratic institutions would prevail over feudal land title. Culturally, land instilled in citizens a respect for individual property and notions of moral restraint that curtail the destructive and appropriative impulses of atomistic individualism. The public morality necessary for civic life grew from the experience of cultivating the land.

The cultivation of the land itself shaped American national character, granting citizens the habits and manners that sustain democratic community. Despite his skepticism of base materialism, Emerson saw capitalist exchange as central to the regenerative potential of American democracy. Clearly reflecting the discourse of manifest destiny and processes of commercial expansion, Emerson wrote, "The American people are fast opening their own destiny. The material basis is of such extent that no folly of man can quite subvert it. Add, that this energetic race derives an unprecedented material power from the new arts, from . . . the railroad, steamship, steam-ferry, steam-mill." Settler expansion provided more than material benefits; it laid the "material basis" for a higher moral purpose. Emerson pronounced, "We are persuaded that moral and material values are always commensurate. Every material organization exists to a moral end, which makes the reasons of its existence."[72] The higher *telos* of settler expansion was not simply economic development, but the moral development of the American citizenry. In Emerson's mind, commercial expansion made man's moral improvement possible. Far from antithetical principles, commercial wealth and public morality were not only compatible but were mutually necessary.

Commercial expansion directly led to the democratization of power and destruction of feudal land title. While the economic organization of land in Europe adhered to an "aristocratic structure," American land was organized on democratic terms. Despite the role of slavery and conquest in American political development, Emerson maintained that the historian of the future "will see that trade was the principle of Liberty; that trade planted America and destroyed Feudalism . . . and it will abolish slavery."[73] Commercial expansion and the settlement of American land provided a bulwark against the resurgence of feudal institutions, leading Emerson to embrace the "anti-feudal power of Commerce." Rather than the land of aristocrats and monarchs, America is the "land of the laborer, of the democrat."[74]

In Emerson's thought, the boundlessness of the modern mind was importantly connected to and drew its energy from the boundlessness of the land. If feudal society was characterized by the confinement of individuals to inherited social rank, which at the same time suppressed the powers of individual imagination, the material boundlessness of North American land led to the democratization of both intellectual creativity and political power. Perhaps more than any other factor, it was the appropriation and colonization of land that encouraged the cultural and moral autonomy of democratic individuals, which in turn prevented the resurgence of old-world political traditions from taking root in America. Emerson wrote, "The land is the appointed remedy for whatever is false and fantastic in our culture. The land, with its tranquilizing, sanative influences, is to . . . bring us into just relations with men and things." Insofar as the colonization of the land instills a new "habit of living" in citizens, it also morally purifies them to make them suitable for community life, reinforcing the solidification of the democratic culture taking root in the American soil.[75]

Emerson's individualism did not simply entail the atomization of citizens and their separation from civic life. Rather, it was fundamentally predicated on a form of moral equality that, much like the safety-valve theory of democratic expansion, rests on settler colonization. The doctrine of democratic individuality, Emerson wrote in his journal, affirms that "there is imparted to every man the Divine light of reason, sufficient not only to plant corn and grind wheat, but also to illuminate all his life, his social, political, religious actions. . . . Democracy, Freedom, has its root in the sacred truth that every man hath in him the divine Reason. . . . That is the equality and the only equality of all men."[76] What is striking in this passage is how the absent ground of the American soil lays the basis not only for democratic practices but also for moral equality. Reason grants men the economic independence to "plant corn and grind wheat" as well as political and moral autonomy from the will of others. Through the cultivation of the land, individuals become free and equal citizens.

Virtue and colonialism, in this regard, maintain each other. The individual becomes a virtuous citizen by engaging in the process of colonization. By grounding material and spiritual independence in the value of individual labor, the cultivation of the soul is one and the same process as the cultivation of the land. More precisely, individuals develop a sense of morality and community through the colonization of the land. Emerson writes, "Any relation to the land, the habit of tilling it, or mining it . . . generates a feeling of patriotism."[77] The moral and cultural bonds that tie together self-reliant individuals thus conceptually and psychologically emerge in relation to regimes of land appropriation. In the context of an expanding political economy, social equality and individual autonomy rely upon territorial expansion to provide the material basis for democratic self-rule. But colonial expansion did more than simply satisfy the proprietary aspirations of individual settlers. It allowed settlers to cultivate the democratic ethos. Emerson thus gave the safety-valve theory of colonization a romantic twist by casting the cultivation of nature as a source of democratic virtue. Just as O'Sullivan's theory of the safety valve embraced the role of colonization in sustaining the democratic condition of social equality, Emerson's romanticization of the safety-valve theory cast colonial settlement as the moral foundation of democratic equality.

Morality, for Emerson, fundamentally depends on settler colonization. "To men legislating for the area betwixt the two oceans, betwixt the snows and the tropics, somewhat of the gravity of nature will infuse itself into the code."[78] The natural world becomes infused into the moral "code" that binds self-reliant individuals in a broader community. To grasp this, it is necessary to understand what Emerson means by nature. According to Emerson, there are two conceptions of nature at work in the development of the American landscape: *natura naturans* (nature as active and savage) and *natura naturata* (nature as civilized and tamed). The process of individuation involves the transformation of wild, uncultivated nature (*natura naturans*) into civilized nature (*natura naturata*). The transformation of nature from an active and wild force to a passive and tamed substance constitutes the "guiding identity" of democratic individuals.[79]

The production of moral identity through the cultivation of nature lays the basis for democratic politics. In Emerson's understanding of the state, "Governments have their origin in the moral identity of men."[80] The fusion of the individual with nature through cultivation determines the individual's moral development. The harmony of man with nature, in other words, produces harmony between citizens. Emerson's point about the formative role of land/nature in guiding the American ethos closely mirrors but also extends beyond O'Sullivan's safety-valve theory of colonization. By envisioning land/nature as a source of both unity and democratic morality, Emerson casts colonial settlement as the central dynamic in the cultivation of the democratic ethos that in turn perpetuates the democratic polity into the future. For Emerson, nature is without conflict, marked by wholeness and unity. If democratic society is rooted in nature, it too could transcend social and class conflicts that divide citizens by instilling common morality in the hearts of men.

In articulating the land as the literal and figurative ground of American democracy, Emerson also reinforced the spatio-temporal imaginary of manifest destiny. The predominance of youthful optimism in the ideology of Young America led Emerson to proclaim, "[America] is the country of the Future . . . it is a country of beginnings, of projects, of designs, and expectations."[81] Like the rhetoric of the "great nation of futurity," Emerson's proclamation derived its meaning from a spatio-temporal economy in which the progression of American nationality into the future stems from the expansion of American democracy in space. In Emerson's democratic thought, native elimination cleared the way for the cultivation of the democratic ethos in a land separated from the feudal space of European society. Freed from its ancient confines in England, Emerson wrote that the "imperial Saxon race" will continue to acquire a "hundred Mexicos." Upon witnessing the prodigious expansion of American settlers, Emerson confidently pronounced that the "first and worst races are dead" and the "second and imperfect races are dying out, or remain for the maturing of the higher."[82]

While these assertions appear to be aggressive proclamations not too distant from the more abrasive ideologies of herrenvolk democracy, Emerson pursued native elimination and the cultural conquest of Mexicans not through physical extermination but through assimilation. He praised the ability of expanding commercial networks to tie together "various threads of national descent" in "one web" through an "hourly assimilation."[83] This process of cultural absorption was closely tied to land appropriation. Emerson pronounced, "The Anglo-American is a pushing, versatile, victorious race . . . it has wonderful powers of absorption and appropriating."[84] The connection between assimilation and land appropriation becomes especially pronounced in Emerson's claim that American settlers have "reached into the Indian tribes of North America, and carrie[d] the better politics of Democracy among the red men."[85] Democracy, for Emerson, enacts both the spatial and temporal colonization of native peoples and Mexicans, subsuming their political and cultural identities into the progressive surge of the Anglo-American race across the continent.

Viewed in this context, Emerson's famous letter to President Martin Van Buren criticizing the Indian Removal Act and the dispossession of the Cherokee people gets cast in an entirely different light. Although Emerson's letter is often taken as a robust critique of colonial dispossession, it subtly relies on the logic of consensual colonization. Throughout the 1820s, the Georgian state government sought to extinguish Cherokee land claims and encourage white settlement. Yet throughout the early nineteenth century, Cherokee political development was guided by assimilationist chiefs who encouraged the adoption of Western-style agriculture, Christianity, and democratic institutions. By the 1820s, the Cherokee adopted a written constitution modeled on the US Constitution and published a national newspaper called the Cherokee Phoenix. As part of their claim to civilizational progress, the Cherokee also often pointed to their mimicry of the institution of slavery.[86] Pointing to such evidence for civilized advancement (with the exception of slavery), Emerson argued, "In common with the great body of the American people, we have witnessed with sympathy the painful labors of these red men to redeem their own race from the doom of eternal inferiority, and to borrow and domesticate in the tribe the arts and customs of the Caucasian race."[87] For Emerson, the sanative influences of settling and colonizing the land had extended to the Cherokee people, raising them from an under-civilized, savage state, to a higher state of sedentary agriculture and constitutional government. Indian removal constituted a violation of justice in Emerson's eyes because the Cherokee had already entered the domain of Euro-American civilization. To defend native claims to self-government, Emerson pointed to the ability of the Cherokee people to assimilate into and replicate white settler culture.

Cherokee leaders who preached assimilation and accommodation drew on a similar set of logics in their claims for native rights of self-government. In his 1826 "Address to the Whites," the Cherokee leader Elias Boudinot called upon this legacy of civilizational progress to challenge stereotypical representations of Cherokee Indians as savage and historically backward. "There are, with regard to the Cherokee and other tribes," Boudinot proclaimed, "two alternatives; they must either become civilized and happy, or sharing the fate of many kindred nations, become extinct." Clearly choosing the first option, Boudinot suggested that the "rise of these people in their movement towards civilization" provided a clear right to native land and self-government. Like Emerson, Boudinot saw the mimicry of white settler culture as evidence of native capacities for civilization and modern democracy. Rather than an entirely separate nation, Boudinot imagined the Cherokee people as a "faithful ally of the United States." By providing evidence to other indigenous communities of the benefits of assimilation, the Cherokee people could aid the US settler state in spreading civilization across western lands: "If she completes her civilization—then we may hope that all our nations will—then, indeed, may true patriots be encouraged in their efforts to make this world of the West, one continuous abode of enlightened, free, and happy people. But if the Cherokee Nation fail in her struggle, if she dies away, then all hopes are blasted, and falls the fabric of Indian civilization."[88] Boudinot thus tied indigenous survival to the civilizing and colonizing process.

Conclusion

Although manifest destiny represented a form of democratic nationalism in which the nation would be united around the simultaneous pursuit of democracy and expansion, the denouement of the Mexican War exposed the contradictions of race and class at the center of the ideology of democratic empire. Just as Europe was crashing under the duress of its own class contradictions with the 1848 Revolutions, democratic expansionists in the United States held to the vision of a democratic empire. For Emerson and O'Sullivan, the United States would escape the contradictions plaguing France and other European states through the relief provided by the safety valve of western land. Nevertheless, the dream of a unified vision of democratic expansion would soon be challenged by the slavery question. In his seminal analysis of Herman Melville, Michael Paul Rogin contrasts what he calls "the American 1848," in which the democratic ideal of a national republic was jeopardized by political conflict over the slavery question, and the European 1848, in which the liberal dream of a national state premised on individual liberty and equal rights "foundered on the . . . social question."[89] That is, if class conflict in Europe was the primary expression of the contradictions inherent in modern civil society, in the United States it was imperial and racial conflict generated by the politics of slavery's expansion. America's own version of 1848 represented not so much a sharpening of sectional conflict as it did the division of the ideology of democratic empire into two competing imperial imaginaries: an empire of free soil and free labor and an empire of slavery and domination.

5 Slavery and the Empire of Free Soil

"It is according to the interest of 'the Few' that colonies should be cultivated. This, if it is true, accounts for the attachment to colonies, which most of the countries, that is, of the governments of modern Europe, have displayed."
—James Mill, "Colony," Encyclopedia Britannica (1825)

The close of the Mexican-American War signaled a crucial shift in the ideology of democratic empire and the dynamics of settler colonization in North America. The hallmark of the Jacksonian coalition that dominated antebellum politics was an agreement to keep slavery off the national agenda so as to maintain a cross-class Democratic movement consisting of southern planters, industrial working-men, urban artisans, and independent farmers. This arrangement was given institutional legitimacy in the Missouri Compromise of 1820, which regulated the expansion of slavery in the western territories by establishing the 36th parallel as the dividing line between free and slave territories. By preventing the expansion of slavery in northern territories, the Missouri Compromise struck a delicate balance between proslavery interests and antislavery sentiment. The political stability provided by the compromise, however, faded with the onset of the Mexican-American War as the Democratic coalition splintered around the slavery question. In 1846, US Representative David Wilmot introduced the Wilmot Proviso, which mandated that if the United States invaded Mexico, any newly acquired territories would be free rather than slave states. In opposing the expansion of slavery into new territories, Wilmot's bill drew on the legacy of the Northwest Ordinance for a framework of settler expansion that privileged principles of free soil over the extension of slavery.

Although the Wilmot Proviso lost in the House of Representatives, it reopened national debate about the relationship between slavery and settler expansion by questioning the basis of the Missouri Compromise. Disaffected with the previous partisan arrangements in which Whigs and Democrats refused to address the slavery question, a faction of antislavery Democrats (the Barnburners) from New York joined radical abolitionists and antislavery Whigs to form the Free Soil Party in 1848. The formation of the Free Soil Party fundamentally altered the national political landscape regarding the slavery question. With slavery back on the national agenda, proslavery interests went on the offensive. To protect the South's "peculiar institution," proslavery politicians offered visions of empire that competed with alternative visions of settler expansion premised on the principles of free soil and free labor. In this effort, proslavery theorists envisioned slavery as a global-imperial institution rather than simply a regional or even national institution.[1] In response to the Wilmot Proviso, proslavery politicians in Congress argued for the wholesale repeal of the Missouri Compromise. While they did not achieve this objective until the 1854 Kansas-Nebraska Act, the Compromise of 1850 extended the line to California and further entrenched slavery by enacting more stringent fugitive slave laws.[2]

After the Mexican-American War, the ideology of democratic empire split into two imperial visions: the empire of slavery and the empire of free soil. The Wilmot Proviso thus shifted the primary cleavage of imperial conflict in American imperial ideology from inter-imperial conflict between the United States and Russia, Britain, and Spain to intra-imperial conflict between the North and South. In this reconfigured ideological conflict, the South provided the "negative reference point" against which free-soil democrats redefined American imperial identity.[3] Free-soil expansionists articulated democratic ideals through discourses of settler colonialism that promoted a form of territorial expansion based on the agrarian political economy of free labor over the slave economy of the South.

While it is tempting to think of slavery and settler colonization as perfectly consistent, they existed in profound tension with one another. Tocqueville, for instance, placed southern slaveholders outside the settler social state. In delineating American democracy's "point of departure" in patterns of English colonization, he emphasized how the "spirit of religion" and the "spirit of liberty" emerged out of the structures of early North American settlement.[4] Especially important was the position of labor in North American colonial society. In the English colonies, land was culti-vated solely by the labor of the individual, not by tenants or landlords who kept laborers in bondage. The primacy of individual ownership prevented the concentration of landed wealth in the hands of the feudal nobility. "All the English colonies," Tocqueville wrote, "from their beginning, seemed destined to offer the development of freedom, not the aristocratic freedom of their mother country, but the bourgeois and democratic freedom of which the history of the world had still not offered a complete model." Tocqueville treated southern colonies as anomalous within this broader trend of settler colonial development. As a colony of "gold-seekers," Virginia was settled not by free laborers but by conquerors who brought slavery with them in pursuit of precious metals (which was eventually abandoned in favor of agricultural slavery). While individual labor was a sign of freedom in northern settler colonies, Tocqueville argued that southern slavery devalued labor and introduced idleness into society, engendering an altogether different social state.[5]

In a similar manner, free-soil ideologists saw settler expansion as antithetical to the expansion of slavery. As I will argue at length in this chapter, the emergence of the Free Soil Party (which eventually morphed into the Republican Party) represented a reconfigured form of settler colonial ideology in the antebellum era, which placed ideals of free labor and free soil at the center of democratic expansionism. In *Wages of Whiteness*, David Roediger shows how ideals of free labor formulated in white working-class culture were shaped in relation and in opposition to perceptions of slave labor and blackness. In their opposition to wage labor, white workers in the antebellum period constructed their dream of a small producerist republic premised on free labor against the "nightmare of chattel slavery."[6] Similarly, this chapter explores how settlers envisioned western territory as the domain of freedom through ideologies of native disavowal. In free-soil ideology, representations of land and territory as "free" from the tyrannical hold of the slavocracy importantly mediated conceptions of free labor. To the extent that free labor meant individual independence, laborers could only inhabit a state of freedom on land that was free in a dual sense: free from regimes of coerced labor and freely available to cultivate independent of oligarchic economic interests and native title. In free-soil ideologies of democratic empire, colonial dispossession provided the absent ground of free labor.

This chapter explores these dimensions of free-soil ideology in three phases. First, I distill the basic features of free-soil visions of empire by examining the settler colonial thought of three prominent politicians who connected ideals of settler expansion to free labor: Galusha A. Grow, Abraham Lincoln, and William Henry Seward.[7] In his support of a homestead bill that granted settlers free land, Grow revised the basic features of settler colonial ideology. Specifically, he provided a theoretical attack on the right of discovery by casting it as an undemocratic doctrine that prevented the free settlement of land. In a similar way, Lincoln opposed the doctrine of "squatter sovereignty" by arguing that the expansion of slavery hindered the colonization of land by free settlers. Seward, in turn, connected free-soil ideology to free-trade imperialism, offering an incipient vision of global empire. The second section mines Walt Whitman's poetry and prose for similar visions of free-soil empire. In these writings, Whitman created democratic poetry out of the experiential raw material of the free expansion of laborers westward. Finally, the third section links Whitman's poetry and famous work of democratic theory, Democratic Vistas (1871), to show how his theory of democratic culture rested on what I call *poetic dispossession*, a process by which indigenous languages and cultures are integrated into democratic poetry but are at the same time historically and spatially removed from the moral development of modern democracy.

Free-Soil Visions of Democratic Empire

With the close of the Mexican War in 1848 and the slavery question back on the national agenda, Walt Whitman joined disaffected Democrats, Whigs, and abolitionists in forming the Free Soil Party in Buffalo, New York, nominating Martin Van Buren as their presidential candidate under the slogan of "Free Soil, Free Speech, Free Labor, and Free Men."[8] The ideals of the Free Soil Party revolved around two central principles. First, the primary mode of labor in the western territories was to be independent agriculture rather than slave or wage labor. Second, free labor based on widespread land ownership entailed free soil in both a figurative and literal sense: the freedom of the soil from regimes of slave labor and the free acquisition of land by settlers. The platform of the Free Soil Party proclaimed, "No more slave states and no more slave territory. Let the soil of our extensive domain be kept free for the hardy pioneers of our land and the oppressed and banished of other lands seeking homes of comfort and fields of enterprise in the new world." To promote such a program, the Free Soil Party called for land to be issued by means of a "free grant to actual settlers" for the purpose of "making settlements in the wilderness," which would ensure the "union of the people under the banner of free democracy."[9]

In this democratic vision, settler expansion ensured the equality of citizens and sustained institutions of popular self-rule. The expansion of slavery represented to the Free Soil Party the triumph of feudal society and aristocratic principles over the principle of popular sovereignty. The language of empire directly underpinned free-soil fears of slavery's expansion. In their opposition to the resurgence of feudal society, free-soil democrats juxtaposed an "empire of freedom" to an "empire of despotism and slavery."[10] To free-soil democrats, feudal rule threatened to undermine democratic institutions and turn the nation into an oligarchy ruled by an economic elite. In this way, the ideological conflict between these two conceptions of empire was a battle between the "Democratic principle" and the "aristocratic element of slave labor society."[11] The empire of slavery violated democratic conceptions in which settler expansion should be pursued for the public good rather than the aggrandizement of the economic elite.

Galusha A. Grow and Man's Right to the Soil

Although a somewhat minor figure in antebellum politics, the Pennsylvania politician Galusha A. Grow provided instrumental leadership in shaping western land policy in the 1850s and 1860s. As one of the primary leaders of the land reform movement that moved under the banner of Young America, Grow used his position as Speaker of the House to usher the Homestead Act of 1862 through Congress. Throughout the 1840s and 1850s, land reform legislation initiated a shift in federal land policy from the survey system to a homesteading system. The first step in federal land reform came with the Preemption Act of 1841, which gave squatters the right of purchasing land at a minimum price if they settled the land before the government could survey it. The Homestead Act of 1862 built on this basic logic by granting settlers the right to appropriate up to 160 acres of uncultivated federal land by making economic and agricultural improvements. This signaled an important shift in federal land policy, to be sure, but my concern here is more saliently with the ideology of settler colonialism that underpinned the Homestead Act. In 1852, ten years before the passage of the bill, Grow issued a report to Congress, titled "Man's Right to the Soil," which offered a sustained theoretical vision of free-soil expansion.

At stake in Grow's theory of settler expansion was a question that equally occupied earlier theorists of settler colonialism, specifically, "the proper disposition to be made of public lands." From the Northwest Ordinance of 1787 until the late 1830s, federal land policy revolved around the Public Land Survey System, in which the federal government surveyed and sold land to the highest bidder to increase government revenue. Like Paine before him, Grow called on Congress to abolish the survey system and institute a homesteading system under the authority of Article IV of the Constitution, which granted the "power to dispose of, and make all needful rules and regulation respecting the territory or other property of the United States." Instead of selling land for purposes of increasing government revenue, Congress should grant land to "the actual settler at a price barely sufficient to cover the cost of survey." The problem was that property was becoming concentrated in the hands of speculators, slaveholders, and other economic interests who were able to consolidate landholdings, which inhibited "the actual settlement and cultivation of land" by inflating its actual market value. Drawing on Painite theories holding land to be "the common treasure of the country," Grow asserted that it was Congress's responsibility to prevent land grants that are "unequal and unjust."[12]

To articulate his defense of the homesteading principle, Grow also drew on Jacksonian theories of democracy. The common interest of the nation resided not in increasing government revenues, but rather the real settlement and cultivation of the land. Citing President Jackson's annual message to Congress in 1832, Grow proclaimed, "I cannot be doubted that the speedy settlement of these lands constitutes the true interest of the Republic. The wealth and strength of a country are its population, and the best part of the population are the cultivators of the soil." The survey system promoted faction and corruption by encouraging "partial and interested legislation" regarding public land. To promote the common good of the nation, Jackson and Grow implored Americans to abandon the idea of public land as a source of revenue. Drawing on Jeffersonian theories of republican citizenship, both believed that providing settlers "the opportunity of securing an independent freehold" helped ensure the vitality of democratic institutions and the freedom of citizens from economic elites.[13] By treating land as a source of revenue, congressional policy worsened the centralization of landed capital plaguing the already precarious republic. Selling land for revenue "opens the door for the wildest system of land monopoly."[14] The survey system privileged wealthy elites in the race for land acquisition, further solidifying entrenched political and economic inequalities.

In addition to Jacksonian and republican theories of independent citizenship, the homestead principle was premised on Lockean notions of natural right, which held that the only valid title to property is the expenditure of physical labor to cultivate and improve the land. Based on the Lockean idea that the labor expended cultivating land provided legitimate title to property, settlers claimed property rights to land by virtue of the fact of settlement. Grow systematized this argument in American discourse in a simplistic fashion when he asserted that each settler shall "apply his labor" to "uncultivated land" to appropriate it for his "exclusive use." Improvements made to the land then become the basis of exclusive rights to land. Grow went on, "For the only true foundation of any right to property is man's labor."[15] Although he justified the unlimited acquisition of wealth, it is a mistake to reduce his use of Locke to liberal influences and neglect its republican dimensions. Grow designated the "public domain" as the "patrimony of labor" not simply to justify the individual acquisition of property but to maintain a state of social equality in the enduring "struggle between labor and capital."[16] Again, the individual settlement of land did not simply satisfy proprietary aspirations; it grounded democratic citizenship in the possession of land.

As any reader of Locke will readily note, Grow's defense of man's "natural rights to the soil" was not by any means novel or peculiar to this phase of Anglo-American colonization.[17] As Barbara Arneil has forcefully shown, Locke's theory of labor and property was "written to justify the seventeenth-century dispossession of the aboriginal peoples of their land, through a vigorous defense of England's 'superior' claims to proprietorship."[18] What made Grow's analysis of labor original was the way he separated the theoretical basis of the homestead principle—labor and settlement as the source of land rights—from the fundamental basis of private property in American constitutionalism—i.e., the doctrine of discovery.

Most forcefully expressed in Chief Justice John Marshall's majority opinion in *Johnson & Graham's Lessee v. M'Intosh* (1823), the doctrine of discovery "gave to the nation making the discovery the sole right of acquiring the soil from the natives and establishing settlements upon it." Although Indians have a "right of occupancy," they do not possess clear ownership rights over the land that must be recognized by international law and European sovereignty. As a result, purchasing or directly appropriating land from natives by individual settlers did not establish sufficient right to property. The implication of Marshall's decision was that the federal government was at the root of all land title in the western territories, because the original fee simple owner of western land was the federal government by right of discovery. Embedded in Marshall's argument was a subtle Lockean logic in which "vacant soil" should be "well settled" for the benefit of "the whole nation." In other words, superior modes of agriculture and practices of settlement established a superior right to proprietorship.[19]

While Marshall blended the labor theory of property with the right of discovery to establish the legal basis of private property, Grow divorced the two by casting the doctrine of discovery as antithetical to free-soil doctrines. In the doctrine of discovery, the state's right as the ultimate owner of the land derived from royalist doctrines holding that the king possesses the "sole proprietorship of the soil of his empire." The sovereign who sent the fleets to discover and conquer land, in other words, had the sole right to direct how it was settled. Going through the history of new world colonization from the Spanish to British Empires, Grow refuted the right of discovery. Like the Castilian Crown who claimed dominion to the new world based on Columbus's expedition, Henry VII also claimed title to North America based on John Cabot's explorations. In both cases, empires asserted dominion over the new world as "fruits of these discoveries." For Grow, the right of discovery violated man's right to the soil by giving the state "the sole and exclusive right to any of the bounties provided by nature for the benefit and support of the whole race."[20] In positioning the rights of the sovereign to land over the rights of labor, the right of discovery promoted an undemocratic system of colonization that placed land under the unjust jurisdiction of state power.

By divorcing the Lockean theory of labor from the right of discovery, Grow treated settler colonization in pacific terms as the cultivation of the soil rather than as a process of colonial dispossession. In so doing, he contrasted settlers with the "soldier of the tented field . . . who [goes] forth at the call of their country." While "soldiers of war" receive significant bounties for their efforts, "soldiers of peace" (i.e., settlers) receive neither glory nor reward for their toil and sacrifice in "leading the van of civilization along untrodden paths." In a condition of new and uncultivated land, "the first and most important labor . . . is to subdue the forest, and convert the lair of the wild beast into a home for civilized man." Like Jefferson, Grow championed the efforts of the settlers in driving natives back in retreat from the spread of civilization. As such, settlers should receive, in exchange for settlement, an undisturbed right to free soil. Yet by contrasting the pacific labor of cultivation with military action, Grow saw colonization not as an act of conquest but as "the labor of your pioneer settler."[21] Notions of colonization as cultivation (as opposed to conquest) at the heart of free-soil doctrines mask the necessary extinction of native land title. The freedom of laborers, in turn, grows out of soil that paradoxically becomes free only through the erasure of native sovereignties.

Abraham Lincoln and the Critique of Popular Sovereignty

While the Republican Party emerged in 1854 out of the organizational and political failures of the Free Soil Party, it largely continued the legacy of free-soil and free-labor principles by redirecting them toward the abolition of slavery. Formed directly after the passage of the Kansas-Nebraska Act of 1854, the Republican Party arose not in opposition to the sectional existence of slavery in the South, but in reaction to the expansion of slavery into "free territories." Ushered through Congress by the Democratic Senator Stephen A. Douglas, the Kansas-Nebraska Act repealed the Missouri Compromise by determining whether slavery would be allowed in new territories through the principle of popular sovereignty. The question of whether Kansas and Nebraska would be free or slave territories hinged on the popular will of white settlers. Also called "squatter sovereignty," the doctrine of popular sovereignty held that settlers were distinct and quasi-autonomous political communities who should be left "to form and regulate their domestic institutions in their own way," free from congressional discretion.[22] At stake in the question of squatter sovereignty was whether the free expansion of settlers could coexist with the expansion of plantation society.

In his 1854 speech on the Kansas-Nebraska Act, Abraham Lincoln sought to answer precisely this question. In arguing for the restoration of the Missouri Compromise, he declared his opposition to the expansion of slavery into free territories. Yet in making this argument, Lincoln held that his opposition to slavery distinguished "between the EXISTING institution, and the EXTENSION of it."[23] In unambiguous language, Lincoln clarified that he opposed slavery only in new territories and not in southern states where it already existed. The thrust of his criticism of the expansion of slavery resided in his belief that "it deprives our republican example of its just influence in the world." In exceptionalist language reminiscent of John Winthrop's notion of "the city on a hill," Lincoln saw America as a model republic, a forceful example of free institutions to the world. The further expansion of slavery eroded the United States' moral reputation among "the liberal party throughout the world," which was becoming increasingly apprehensive about the exemplarity of the American system.[24]

This element of Lincoln's opposition to the Kansas-Nebraska Act should not be ignored, as it comprises a consistent thread that runs through his political thinking. Yet there is a subtle but, for present purposes, more salient basis of his opposition to plantation expansionism that cuts to his vision of free-soil empire. At stake for Lincoln in the principle of popular sovereignty was the way in which it undermined settler colonization based on free-labor and free-soil principles. Squatter sovereignty could not dictate the legality of slavery in the territories because the issue was not the exclusive concern of settlers who currently resided there. "Slave states," Lincoln proclaimed, "are places for poor white people to remove FROM; not remove to. New free states are the places for poor people to go to and better their condition." The nation needed western territories for the "future use" of settlers seeking economic opportunity and social mobility.[25] But by reserving the decision to allow slavery in the territories to current settlers alone and enabling the few to dictate laws to the many, the doctrine of squatter sovereignty eroded the democratic principle and the egalitarian social state. Lincoln thus based his opposition to the expansion of slavery on a conception of settlement as prolepsis rather than present reality. Potential settlers had proleptic claims to territory that exceeded the present and past assignment of land rights. By extension, the projection of colonization into the future displaces and erases the customary land rights of native peoples rooted in ancestral authority.

It is in this context of the expansion of slavery and the Kansas-Nebraska Act that one should understand Lincoln's free-labor ideology. In his 1859 "Address to the Wisconsin State Agricultural Society," Lincoln outlined two competing theories of the relationship between labor and capital in a democratic society. The first—the "mud-sill theory"—posited that capital existed temporally and thus morally prior to labor. That is, individuals only become laborers "in connection with capital," when somebody who owns capital compels another to labor for him. In this theory, whether they are "hired laborers" or "slaves," workers are driven to labor either by necessity or with whip and chain, in either case, "without their consent." In both cases of hired or slave labor, the laborer is considered by capital to be "fatally fixed in that condition for life."[26] Without the opportunity for formal advancement and social mobility, wage labor mimicked slave labor in its basic structure.

James Hammond, a US senator from South Carolina, best expressed the mud-sill theory of labor in exactly these terms in his 1858 speech declaring "Cotton Is King." There Hammond articulated a classical Greek conception of democracy in which freedom for the white community depended on the enslavement of inferior races. "In all social systems," Hammond asserted, "there must be a class to do the menial duties, to perform the drudgery of life." The enslavement of one class by another was necessary for the progress of civilization. To condemn all citizens to the "drudgery of life" would be to subject the intellect of the white race to the dictates of biological necessity, preventing them from guiding the progressive development of society. Because human freedom depended on enslavement, slavery constituted the "very mud-sill of society and of political government."[27] Like Lincoln, Hammond equated slave labor with wage labor by suggesting that although Northern society does not have formal slaves, they too have their separate class of hirelings who endure physical toil to produce wealth and value.

The second—the free-labor theory—conversely posited that "labor is prior to, and independent of capital; that, in fact, capital is the fruit of labor, and could never have existed if labor had not first existed—that labor can exist without capital, but that capital could never have existed without labor." Because it is temporally prior to and creates capital, labor has a moral claim to greater power. This is not to suggest that labor and capital should have no relation, but only that capital should never have superior power over labor. What this meant for Lincoln was that wage labor should be a temporary condition on the path to free and independent labor. As a provisional stage in the life-cycle of labor, wage labor provided workers with opportunities to acquire the means of becoming self-subsistent and free from the necessity of subjection to capital: "The prudent, penniless beginner in the world, labors for wages awhile, saves a surplus with which to buy tools or land, for himself; then labors on his own account another while, and at length hires another new beginner to help him."[28] After demarcating the distinction between the two theories of labor, Lincoln expressed his unequivocal support for the free-labor theory. It is the potential for the ownership and cultivation of land that allows wage laborers to break out of their condition of servitude and get ahead in what Lincoln famously called "the race of life."[29] In addition to providing for equal opportunity and social mobility, the free-labor theory also resulted in the moral elevation of individuals by encouraging "the thorough cultivation upon the farmer's own mind."[30]

What is important here is the way that Lincoln's theory of free labor depends upon a tacit conceptualization of land as potentially available for future appropriation by free settlers. As with his opposition to squatter sovereignty, Lincoln treated setter claims to land not as a present right but as a future patrimony, not by virtue of current capacities for improvement but due to the future potential for cultivation. In Lincoln's theory, the capacity to produce value through labor does not simply extinguish the present right of indigenous others to the land. Rather, it casts the land as always-already belonging to free laborers by projecting the land rights derived from settlement into the future. The conception of freedom through labor implicit in Lincoln's theory rests on a conception of free soil that erases both the presence of slaves and natives in the territories. If soil remains locked up within the legal structure of plantation society or by ancestral rights of native peoples, it cannot be free. And if soil is unfree, labor remains in chains. Thus, Lincoln's theory of free labor does not simply assume the presence of free soil. Rather, it produces that which it takes as its basic supposition. The theory of free labor constitutes rather than represents free soil by erasing the political and cultural existence of indigenous peoples through the temporal projection of future settlement. The labor of settlers to cultivate the land does not occur on top of free soil. It *frees* the soil from its archaic belongings.

Lincoln's colonial thinking embraced another form of colonization that sought to carve out the free territories of the West for exclusive use of white settlers. Although they differed on the question of squatter sovereignty, Lincoln and Douglas agreed that the primary "beneficiaries of territorial expansion must be free white farmers."[31] Another basis of Lincoln's opposition to plantation expansion was that it further encouraged racial amalgamation among black and white and prevented land from being fully available to white labor. In his "Speech on the Dred Scott Decision," Lincoln pronounced, "I have said that the separation of the races is the only perfect preventive of amalgamation . . . [and] opposition to the spread of slavery—is most favorable to the separation [of the races]." Lincoln feared that allowing slavery in the territories would degrade white labor and impede the emigration of free laborers from both Europe and the eastern republic. Because race branded slave labor, free labor could only remain free through racial separation. Lincoln went on to assert that "separation . . . must be effected by colonization."[32] In order to ensure racial separation, Lincoln proposed the colonization of freed slaves to Central America alongside the colonization of free settlers to the West. If free soil was the exclusive reserve of the white race, settler colonization required a program of racial colonization as a way of ensuring racial separation.[33]

In addition to racializing the idea of free soil as the domain of "poor white people," Lincoln also utilized the program of racial colonization to bolster his vision of a free Union based on "the spirit of compromise." In an address to a committee of free African American leaders, Lincoln reaffirmed his support of colonization as late as 1862: "Nevertheless, I repeat, without the institution of Slavery and the colored race as a basis, the war could not have an existence."[34] Lincoln saw racial colonization as a means of releasing the pressure of racial contradictions produced by the continued existence of southern slavery. By attributing the Civil War to the existence of the "colored race" rather than the inherent contradictions of the American republic, Lincoln posed colonization as a way of ensuring the stability of the Union and its guiding "spirit of compromise" in the face of racial radicalization. In this way, he racialized the safety-valve theory by using colonization as a mechanism of suppressing "the irrepressible conflict." Just as the safety-valve theory displaced class conflict by projecting it onto a geographic else-where, racial colonization restored national unity by transporting the source of racial conflict (i.e., "the colored race") to Central America.[35]

William Seward and the Empire of Free Trade

Although free-soil ideology focused on continental expansion, the imperial framework of free-soil democracy encapsulated a much broader geographic scale. The imperial gaze of the free-soil democrats almost always pierced beyond the continental boundaries of North America, fixating on commercial supremacy in the Pacific. No one so perfectly condensed this dimension of Northern imperial desire and its democratic moorings than William Henry Seward, a vocal opponent of the slaveholding empire who was also one of the early architects of America's free-trade empire. While Seward was a not a particularly original thinker, his writings significantly synthesized existing currents of American thought and culture.[36] Specifi-cally, he combined free-labor and free-soil ideals at the center of continental visions of empire with a global vision of American commercial hegemony.

Although originally an antislavery Whig, Seward had long expressed much more democratic leanings than his more conservative counterparts. Where Whigs typically condemned the Mexican-American War from a conservative standpoint as a war of democratic excess, Seward agreed with radical democrats in viewing it as a stage in the inexorable path of demo-cratic modernity. In 1850, he celebrated the Treaty of Guadalupe Hidalgo for allowing the settlement of the Pacific coast and establishing the germ of global empire that would soon spread over the world:

> If, then, the American people shall remain an undivided nation, the ripening civilization of the West, after a separation growing wider and wider for four thousand years will in its circuit of the world, meet again, and mingle with the declining civilization of the East on our

own free soil, and a new and more perfect civilization will arise to bless the earth, under the sway of our own cherished and beneficent democratic institutions.[37]

Seward drew on the discourses of universal history and *translatio imperii* reminiscent of Hegel, in which civilization relentlessly progresses westward, extending from its ancient origins in Asia to its final resting place in the Americas.[38] In doing so, he imagined the extension of American commerce into the Pacific as the triumph of a universal form of democratic civilization on the world stage. As Seward's celebration intimates, American global empire depended on the durability of the Union. Slavery represented to Seward less a wedge of sectional conflict than the central institution in a competing way of imagining empire and organizing civilization.

The idea of democracy occupied a central place in Seward's imperial imagination. Resonating with the free-soil vision of empire, he proclaimed that the "center of political power must rest . . . in the agricultural interests and the masses, who will occupy the interior of the continent."[39] The democratic masses flooding the West constituted the primary source of imperial power. Yet Seward's promotion of settler expansion across the continent existed alongside commercial expansion into the Pacific. The political economy of settler colonialism in the antebellum period is best viewed as a form of agrarian capitalism. Settlers colonize new land not simply to acquire landed independence and construct new forms of democratic government, but also to enhance their own economic opportunity by producing agricultural commodities to sell on global markets. Seward embraced the expansion of free trade into the Pacific as a central aspect of individual independence and popular self-rule. He advised settlers that their attempts to extend their "power to the Pacific Ocean and grasp the great commerce of the east" were vital to "maintaining the democratic system of government."[40] Although free-soil ideology rejected wage labor as a form of economic dependence, it embraced the opportunity for independent farmers to sell surplus commodities on global markets.

Seward's imperial vision positioned settlers as the driving force of colonial expansion. Settlers expanded the scope and authority of modern democracy by colonizing the West and founding new states: "The native colonist no sooner reaches a new and distant home, whether in a cleft of the Rocky mountains or on the seashore, than he proceeds to found a state, in which his natural and inalienable rights shall be secure."[41] This conception of settler expansion directly drew on the Northwest Ordinance, which offered a new imperial vision that institutionalized the equality of the constituent parts of empire, preventing the formation of colonial dependencies. Consistent with this colonial ideology, Seward saw colonization in terms of the replication of democratic societies in a vacant wilderness. A central feature of settler expansion is the inalienable and natural rights of settlers that allow a form of civic equality between separate communities despite their removal from the original community.

The extension of slavery posed a clear threat to Seward's vision of settler expansion. By consolidating landholdings through the colonization of new territory, the empire of slavery represented the resurgence of feudalism in the new world and thus violated national ideals of social equality. The expansion of slavery, Seward feared, would introduce an "aristocratic element" into government based on two principles: "the privileged own the lands" and the "laborer works on compulsion." These two principles, which together comprised a feudal social state, combined to institute an oligarchic government based on the rule of the few. In contrast, free government depended on a democratic social state marked by free soil and free labor.[42]

Much of Seward's criticism of slavery cohered around a civilizational discourse that divided political space into barbarism and civilization. He insisted that the democratic creed embraced a singular idea: "That civilization is to be maintained and carried on upon this continent by federal states, based upon the principles of free soil, free labor, free speech, equal rights, and universal suffrage."[43] The expansion of slavery meant the decline of democratic society. In making this claim, however, Seward had to explain why slavery became so entrenched in the Americas. If the new world represented the pinnacle of democratic society, then slavery's persistence provided counter-evidence to this thesis. Seward explained slavery's persistence in terms of two competing modes of empire. Slavery and the slave trade were "altogether foreign from the habits of the races which colonized these States, and established civilization here [i.e., North America]." In making this claim, Seward drew on imperial discourses of the "Black Legend," in which British imperial architects, influenced by Bartolomé de las Casas's *Destruction of the West Indies* (1542), depicted Spanish colonialism as excessively cruel and exploitative. While Spanish expansionism was premised on conquest, colonial violence, and the exploitation of indigenous resources, British colonialism was premised on benevolence and the soft power of commerce.[44] So as to deflect responsibility away from Anglo-American processes of colonization, Seward asserted that slavery was "introduced on this continent as an engine of conquest, and for the establishment of monarchical power, by the . . . Spaniards."[45] Similar to Tocqueville and others, Seward used the Spanish Empire as the negative reference point for settler colonization by positing a difference between expansion through liberty and expansion through despotism.

Writing at approximately the same time, the British theorist of colonization, Edward Gibbon Wakefield, proposed a more accurate explanation of the relationship between slavery and settler colonization. Wakefield agreed that slavery was introduced into the Americas by Spain, but rather than reduce this dynamic merely to a different model of colonization, he hypothesized that the reason for slavery in the colonies was the abundance of land alongside the scarcity of labor. Modern slavery, Wakefield explained, originated in the Spanish *encomienda* system. When Spanish conquistadors appealed to the Crown for land grants in the Americas, they also requested dominion over natives to make them laborers.[46] The abundance of land available for agricultural labor necessitated an equally available workforce. Wakefield similarly posited that the "original and permanent cause of slavery in [North] America is superabundance of good land."[47] Likewise, the abundance of land in Australia leads large property owners to desire slaves, which encourages the export of convicts to the region. While the form of coerced labor varied in all three cases (i.e., native, racial, and penal slavery, respectively), the colonization of large tracts of land coincided with the emergence of slave labor.[48] Rather than a real portrait of settler colonial history, Seward's narrative exonerated settler institutions and principles from complicity in the political thickening of southern slavery in North America.

Walt Whitman and the Expansion of Free Labor

Uncovering the settler colonial dimensions of Whitman's poetics and political thought is significantly burdened by his reception and mythic status among Marxist literary critics and Latin American radicals. Despite his clear reliance on imperial categories such as manifest destiny, Whitman appears to these writers as a fierce anti-imperial critic. Georg Lukacs, for instance, included Whitman among the ranks of modernism's great anti-imperial writers: "great literature has a powerful historical function, a pioneering role in the true aspiration of the people, in the establishment of true democracy. From Walt Whitman to Anatole France, from Ibsen to Shaw, from Tolstoy to Borski, the leading writers of freedom-loving peoples have fulfilled their mission in the age of imperialism."[49] In Lukacs's rendering, Whitman was a radical internationalist who sought an egalitarian world order in the midst of thickening empires. Of course, anyone familiar with his earlier journalistic writings for the Brooklyn Daily Eagle will readily contest this image of Whitman as an anti-imperial critic. Even then, other commentators more attuned to the breadth of Whitman's writings construct rigid divisions between his imperialist political writings and his more democratic and egalitarian poetry.[50]

By emphasizing the differences between his earlier political writings and his later poetry and democratic theory, however, these commentators neglect the central place of settler colonialism in Whitman's democratic thought. Rejecting such interpretive currents, I show how Whitman's democratic theory and poetry is not separate from but grows out of his earlier political concerns. Democratic poetics and colonial politics, for Whitman, were closely connected. Consistent with his conviction that a self-consciously democratic culture provides the firmer foundations for American democracy, he gave poetic substance to free-soil visions of democratic empire. In turn, narratives of settler expansion also influenced Whitman's poetry at the level of his belief in the formative influence of language and culture on the development of modern democracy.[51] Rather than antithetical aspects of his political thought, Whitman's poetry and political prose both reflect and reinforce settler colonial ideologies.

Whitman, early on in his journalistic writings, established an incipient conception of settler colonial empire rooted in free-soil ideology. Whitman had long been both an opponent of slavery and a proponent of settler expansion, and he explicitly aligned the two in his writings for the Brooklyn Daily Eagle touting the virtues of the war with Mexico. In fact, Whitman's Eagle was one of the first periodicals to actively support the Wilmot Proviso. According to Whitman, the extension of slavery in the territories violated American founding principles and further stretched the chasm between the ideal and the real in American politics. In an 1846 editorial, Whitman condemned slavery as a "disgrace and blot on the character of our Republic, and on our boasted humanity!"[52] At the same time, however, Whitman trumpeted the conquest of Mexico and further expansion into the West as the triumph of democratic principles.

What made Whitman so central to ideologies of settler colonialism was how he attached radical-democratic principles of popular sovereignty to broader frameworks of settler expansion. In line with the safety-valve theory,

Whitman's notion of democracy upheld a conception of political space in which the underpopulated and "uncultivated acres of land" in the West provided land reserves for the overpopulated spaces of the "crowded East."[53] Similar to the relationship between the democratic social state and settler expansion, Whitman's democracy acquired its energy through the transfer of the settler population to western territory. In providing the material basis for self-rule, Whitman praised "The boundless democratic free West!" The "cheapness of land" in the West erases hierarchy and inequality, producing a social condition that frees citizens from "conventionalism" and "common want." Like Emerson's romantic reconstruction of the safety-valve theory, Whitman held that the experience of settling the West produced creative intelligence and a "Democratic vitality" that made the common man suitable for self-rule.[54] The individual labors of cultivating the land led to an elevation of mind that prepared men for the intellectual rigors of democracy.

Whitman's political tract, "The Eighteenth Presidency!" (1855), also illustrates the role that free-soil ideology played in his cultural conception of democracy. The objective of the tract was to incite the American people into mass electoral action against the proslavery Democratic Party. Yet although Whitman's views were closely aligned with the Republican and Free Soil Parties, "The Eighteenth Presidency!" was more than a piece of campaign literature. In speaking not to sectional interests or partisan factions, but rather to the American people as a whole, Whitman held that the question of slavery versus liberty in the territories was much larger than partisan politics, for it cut to the very heart of American democratic identity.[55] The relationship between democracy and settler expansion provided the animating thread of "The Eighteenth Presidency!" Whitman framed his discussion in terms of the identity of the sovereign, posing the question, "First, Who are the Nation?" Whitman writes, "Before the American era, the programme of the classes of a nation read thus, first the king, second the noblemen and gentry, third the great mass of mechanics, farmers, men following the water, and all laboring persons." The modern American era inaugurated a new "theory of government" that privileged the power of the third class above the first two.[56] Estimating that around six million workingmen made up the nation and only 350,000 slaveholders, Whitman grouped the latter class among "noblemen and gentry." If the slaveholding class comprised the oligarchic element of society, the workers, farmers, and sailors made up the democratic element.

The question of land in the western territories was a question of which class would constitute the primary force of colonization. In grappling with this question, Whitman cheered the "national tendency toward populating the territories full of free work-people," which was the program of colonization most consistent with the promulgations of "the fathers." The project of settling the West with the free population was "vital to the life and thrift of the masses of the citizens." To allow the expansion of slavery would be to put democratic society "violently . . . back under the feet of slavery."[57] With the further consolidation of landholdings in the hands of the slaveholding oligarchy, the democratic masses would be kept from forming state governments based on the freedom and equality of citizens. If slavery was not prohibited from the American territories, "there will steadily wheel into this Union . . . slave state after slave state, the entire surface of the land owned by great proprietors, in plantations of thousands of acres, showing no more sight for free races of farmers and work-people than there is now in any European despotism or aristocracy."[58] As a result, American politics would be characterized by institutionalized hierarchy and the master-slave relationship rather than democratic equality. Throughout his poetry and prose, feudalism served as the constitutive outside against which Whitman defined democracy and American identity. If democracy was the cultural form of the future, feudalism represented a decaying form of civilization.[59] Whitman viewed feudalism not only as a form of politics but also as an economic system in which the mass of laborers was exploited for the benefit of the ruling aristocracy. His opposition to the expansion of slavery, which he thought would subject the mass of free laborers in the West to economic hierarchy, thus fueled his fear of feudalism.

In his opposition to the expansion of slavery, Whitman saw settlers not only as the bearers of democratic expansion but also as soldiers destined to reconquer the East from proslavery forces. Although Whitman subscribed to a Hegelian view of universal history in which civilization moves westward, the expansion of slavery complicated the directionality of settler colonization. In "Facing West from California's Shores," Whitman imagined himself standing on the shores of the Pacific, witnessing the triumph of democratic modernity as civilization completed its global circuit and found its final resting place in California. Yet Whitman experienced the triumph of modernity less as a victory than as a form of loss, for he remains "seeking what is yet unfound."[60] His ambivalence was driven by anxiety about the potential triumph of slavery over democratic empire in the West. In a tribute to the global reach of modernity, Whitman ended not with the spread of democracy into the Pacific, but with a vision of American settlers marching back toward the Atlantic from their settlements in California: "They shall now also march obediently eastward for your sake Libertad."[61] With the onset of the Civil War in 1861, he celebrated the agents of empire returning east to reclaim American power from the slaveholding oligarchy.[62]

Whitman closed "The Eighteenth Presidency!" by drawing on one of the main poetic tropes that would come to shape his poetry throughout his career: the idea of the poet as the representative voice of the nation. In the closing sections of the essay, he cast himself as the representative poet of the masses: "Circulate and reprint this voice of mine for the workingmen's sake." The expansion of the democratic masses portends for Whitman a new order of the ages in which the disintegration of old-world hierarchies culminates in a new vision of humanity. At the center of this was the democratic-settler as representative man: "Never was the representative man more energetic. . . . He urges on the myriads before him, he crowds them aside, his daring step approaches the arctic and Antarctic poles, he colonizes the shores of the Pacific, the Asiatic Indias, the birthplace of languages of and of races, the archipelagoes, Australia."[63] The representative man that Whitman praised as the embodiment of the democratic spirit was also a settler colonial. But perhaps more significant is how Whitman imagined the further colonization of the Pacific as a source of democratic poetry in which the mass of democratic settlers provided the imaginative raw material for a national epic.

Whitman's personification of the settler-citizen as the force of democratic expansion also shaped his poetry. In "Starting from Paumanok," which references the Algonquian name for Long Island (where he was born), Whitman personified the nation's expansionist drive across the continent in his own autobiography. In doing so, he saw himself as a pioneer ushering in the democratic promise of the "New World."[64] Similarly, in his paean to settler expansion, "Pioneers! O Pioneers!," Whitman included himself among the ranks of settlers and free laborers seeking a new world of equality and fraternity in the West: "All the past we leave behind, / We debouch upon a new mightier world, varied world, / Fresh and strong the world we seize, world of labor and the march."[65] Whitman further imagined "successions of men, Americanos," flooding into the western territories. In Whitman's settler imagination, the "vast trackless spaces," as "countless masses debouch upon them," provided the basis for an enlarged notion of individuality that is commensurate with the political life of the community.[66] Through the individual labors involved in the self-constitution of the community, the individual locates himself in the democratic community. Whitman's masses, composed of otherwise disparate individuals, bind themselves together through the experience of conquering new spaces and constructing new democratic forms on top of expropriated land.

Colonial dispossession operates in Whitman's poetry in a distinctively linguistic and poetic sense, not simply as the physical displacement of indigenous peoples. Specifically, his democratic poetry enacts a form of poetic dispossession in which indigenous disavowal enables the emergence of a political language suitable to the expression of the democratic ethos of the nation. By the close of "Starting from Paumanok," Whitman pauses to consider the fate of the "red aborigines" that previously occupied the new world: "Leaving natural breaths, sounds of rain and winds, calls as of birds and animals in the woods, syllabled to us for names, / Okonee, Koosa, Ottawa, Monongahela, Sauk, Natches, Chattahoochee, Kaqueta, Oronoco, Wabash, Miami, Chippewa, Oshkosh, Walla-Walla, / Leaving such to the States they melt, they depart, charging the water and the land with names."[67] A characteristic feature of Whitman's poetry was the use of native names to construct a native American vernacular that was distinct from British English. As Ed Folsom has put it, "It was the heroic and noble side of the natives, their healthy attachment to American landscape, that Whitman believed he could absorb into the American consciousness via native words, stories, sounds."[68] In his essay "The Spanish Element in Our Nationality," Whitman posited that Indian and Spanish names would provide the essential parts of the "composite American identity of the future." While indigenous languages left an imprint on American identity, indigenous communities "must gradually dwindle as time rolls on, and in a few generations more leave only a reminiscence, a blank."[69]

Whitman thus integrated indigenous names into American democratic identity at the level of language, yet he evacuated the American landscape of its indigenous presence. Viewed through the lens of colonial dispossession, Whitman's poetry continues to weave the thread of his earlier journalistic and political writings praising settler expansion. In an 1846 article on "Indian Life and Customs," he more fully developed his theory of democratic language that sustains the cultivation of a unique American identity distinct from European cultural precedents. Responding to the common charge of European critics like Tocqueville and Sir Walter Scott that "we have no fit themes for poetry and imagination here," Whitman drew on indigenous languages and traditions to construct the outlines of democratic poetry. "While Europe may boast of her age of chivalry and of the deeds of her knights and princes . . . her castles and moss covered fortresses—her gothic cathedrals" represent the eclipse of a bygone period.[70] Yet rather than deny that America had an epic past, Whitman encouraged inquiry into indigenous languages and histories as a way of giving substance to democratic identity. Comparing European feudal relics to the American past, he wrote, "We may love the traditions of the hapless Indians—and cherish their names—and bestow those names on rivers, lakes, or States, more enduring than towering monuments of brass." In his attempt to infuse indigenous languages into the landscape, Whitman asserted that "the course of events" will cause "every tangible representative of Indian character [to] have passed from sight." In Whitman's mind, "hardy Westerners" engaged in "the labor of 'extending the area of freedom' into the confines of Indian territory" resulted in the complete displacement of the "weakened, degraded, and effeminate beings who prowl in our frontier towns."[71]

What struck Whitman about the United States was that the nation spoke itself into existence in a singular act of poetic self-creation through the Declaration of Independence. As Whitman wrote in the preface to *Leaves of Grass*, "The Americans of all nations at any time upon the earth have probably the fullest poetical nature. The United States themselves are essentially the greatest poem."[72] Yet what is essential in such acts of poetic self-constitution is that the words of the Declaration and the subsequent formation of democratic poetry were expressed in a democratic and native American vernacular that distinguished American political language from its European counterparts. The language that America used to speak itself into existence was a unique indigenous language that, like the nation itself, was common, democratic, and egalitarian, accessible to all.

In its appropriation of indigenous languages, Whitman's democratic poetry exemplifies the "typical settler narrative." Settler narratives rely on two complementary forces: (1) the "effacement of the indigene" proceeds alongside (2) the "concomitant indigenization of the settler."[73] By integrating indigenous languages into his poetry, Whitman distinguished US democratic culture from the language, culture, and poetics of the European homelands from which settlers emigrated. Without an indigenous element, American poetry would be unable to mark itself off from European poetry, and thus unable to establish itself as democratic.

Democratic poetry, which gave poetic voice to the democratic identity of the new nation, flowered on top of a ground prepared by conquest even as it incorporated indigenous linguistic elements. Indian-ness thus serves the function of what Jodi Byrd calls a form of transit—a discursive circulation of presence, absence, and repetition. Although they provided a symbolic source of democratic culture and identity, Indians figure into Whitman's democratic poetry as "past tense presences." This absent-presence of indigenous peoples provides the ontological ground upon which American democratic empire constituted itself.[74]

Poetic Dispossession in Whitman's Democratic Theory

By the time of Reconstruction, Whitman turned to prose writing and came to synthesize his poetic vision of democratic expansion into a political theory of American democracy. Outlined in his essay "Democratic Vistas" (1871), Whitman's democratic theory flowed out of his poetic reflections on the relationship between democracy and settler expansion. Although colonial and imperial themes are subtler in "Democratic Vistas" than in his earlier poetry, reading his theory of democracy through his earlier poetry and political writings illustrates that settler expansion shaped his moral vision of democratic community. The incorporation of indigenous elements into settler vernaculars grounded Whitman's theory of democratic culture as the foundation of American democracy. Insofar as the assimilation of indigenous elements into settler-democratic languages entailed the disappearance of actual indigenous cultures, Whitman's democratic theory acquired its force and originality through colonial dispossession.

In Whitman's democratic theory, democracy rests less in its constitutional form than in the social relations and cultural bonds that unite citizens. "Democracy was not to be a constitutional device for the better government of given nations, not merely a movement for the material improvement of the poorer classes. It was to be a social and a moral democracy and to involve an actual equality among all men."[75] Like Tocqueville and Emerson, Whitman invests his hope in the social condition of democracy rather than in its political form. For Whitman, "democratic literature" and "democratic sociology" are closely connected, both of which constitute the "chief influence in modern civilization."[76] Literature has an expressly sociological role in shaping the cultural values and moral bonds that tie citizens together in a broader community. Democracy is not simply a set of political institutions that ensure general suffrage. It provides a "literature underlying life . . . handling the elements and forces with competent power, teaching and training men." In conceiving of democracy in this way, Whitman offers a novel form of democratic theory. His answer to the "great question of democracy" is not "the result of studying up in political economy, but of the ordinary sense, observing, wandering among men, these States, these stirring years of war and peace."[77] Whitman's theory of democracy stems from the human experiences of settler expansion that provide the content for his poetic vision of democracy.

Whitman considers democratic literature to be a form of democratic theory because it provides the primary justification for American democracy. He justifies democracy not through a set of abstract principles but through an account of the moral and spiritual benefits that democracy offers. Democratic culture gives a "moral identity" to the political community as defined by its "Constitutions, legislative and judicial ties."[78] After the Civil War, Whitman wrestled with the question of the relation between the one and the many in giving shape to the political community. To this end, he sought to reconcile democratic individuality with "democratic nationality."[79] In offering a solution to this problem, the binding force of democratic culture operates on two levels: it binds individuals to the community by offering a cohesive sense of national identity; and it binds the separate states into a larger federal union, what Whitman called a "compacted imperial ensemble."[80]

On the first level, individuals must experience a sense of moral autonomy but also experience themselves as members of a political community. For Whitman, individualism and political democracy must be made commensurate by developing the political personality of citizens. To discern the shape of this political personality, Whitman called for a "democratic ethnology of the future," the aim of which was to discover a new political species. He argued that "to practically enter into politics is an important part of American personalism," suggesting that political participation is a vital element of the new democratic character.[81] Yet Whitman's ethnology was indistinguishable from democratic literature because its objective was not to discover this new political specimen as an empirical fact, but to create and constitute a new form of democratic subjectivity through poetic regimes of representation.

On the second level, Whitman offered his notion of federalism not as an alternative to empire but rather as an alternative understanding of democratic empire that would transcend "history's hitherto empires or feudalities." The "moral and spiritual idea" at the center of American democracy is vital to "carrying out the republican principle to develop itself in the New World." Like the individual, each state is afforded a relative degree of autonomy from the federal government within its own sphere. Federalism requires that popular sovereignty be institutionalized in both federal and state governments. Whitman considered this to be the "original dual theory and foundation of the United States."[82] Federalism, however, provided more than an institutional theory of government that balanced state and federal authority. It provided a moral vision that united separate communities into a larger imperial union.

Based on this theory of moral democracy, Whitman offered a theory of democratic development that divided American history into three stages. The first involved establishing the "political foundation" of democracy by inscribing the rights and liberties of the "immense masses of people" in the Constitution, Declaration of Independence, and the state governments. This first stage was primarily a form of political development in which electoral institutions of universal suffrage granted the will of the people legislative force. The second stage was a form of economic development that established prosperity and opportunity for the masses through the expansion of commerce. Although Whitman thought both stages were essential, they were insufficient to prompt evolution to the higher stage of moral democracy. Mere political institutions served as an insufficient adhesive for the democratic community. Without a moral identity, the nation would remain a fragile confederation of states and individuals each pursuing their own economic interests. And without a moral and cultural dimension, economic prosperity would degenerate into base materialism. The third stage was thus a form of social and cultural development that would establish a "sublime and serious Religious Democracy."[83]

Like John O'Sullivan's stadial theory of politics, the primary force pushing American democracy from its political to economic to moral stage, in Whitman's theory of democratic development, is settler colonization. As Benjamin Barber puts it, modern democracy was "able to root itself in firm soil only because of the deracination of those who came before."[84] Like Marx, Whitman sees the obliteration of feudal hierarchies that restrict the development of regimes of free labor as necessary to the construction of a new modern order. In the context of American democracy, this fear of feudalism involves restricting the spread of slavery. But underneath the destruction of feudal hierarchies lies the deracination of indigenous sovereignties that previously occupied the new world. Whitman contends that "democracy can never prove itself beyond cavil, until it founds and luxuriantly grows its own forms of art, poems, schools, theology, displacing all that exists, or that has been produced anywhere in the past."[85] American democracy rests upon the displacement of indigeneity not simply for the material benefits of open land but more precisely for the sake of the geographical conditions that provide soil for the moral growth of democracy. Directly rooted in the settler ideals of the free-soil movement, Whitman demanded that a "programme of culture" be formed "with an eye to the practical life, the west, the working-men, the facts of farms and jack-planes and engineers."[86]

Although not predetermined, Whitman's conception of history is teleological. His democratic theory is not a simple justification of the present state of affairs, for without the third stage of moral and cultural development American democracy would remain mired in the second, materialistic stage of development. The cultivation of a democratic literature and a new democratic personality, Whitman affirms, would lead to a "spiritualization" of politics that will "offset . . . our materialistic and vulgar American democracy." The futurity of the democratic personality, however, is contingent upon the continued process of settler expansion. Recapitulating the discourse of manifest destiny, Whitman pronounced that the "Almighty had spread before this nation charts of imperial destinies."[87] Yet the teleology linking settler expansion to the formation of moral democracy is not automatic. Whitman calls upon the democratic masses to march upon the West to make moral democracy a material and spiritual reality.

Although taking root in the new world, Whitman insists that modern democracy remains "unperform'd." Despite largely succumbing to the ideological impulses of manifest destiny, he departs from this broad ideological formation in one key respect: he sees the future as marked by contingency, not locked into a deterministic process guided by Providence. While it might stand to reason that this distances him from the idea of manifest destiny, Whitman remains confined within the ideology of democratic empire. Although he anxiously proclaims, "No one knows what will happen next," he prophetically performs the future of democratic modernity by intoning the "irresistible power" of democracy. In proclaiming that modern democracy remains "unperform'd," Whitman calls on settlers to instantiate a new democratic order. Although the future was yet to be written, he interpolates settler constituencies as democratic constituencies, calling on the settler masses to theatrically perform the future of American democracy.

For Whitman, democratic expansion involved more than a form of political and economic development. It was a form of cultural and moral development by which individuals located themselves in a democratic community, leading to a higher state of individuality and political organization. In becoming a new "empire of empires" that will "dominate the world," American settlers would inaugurate a "new . . . history of democracy" that transcended the violence and conquests of "old-world dynasties."[88] What is essential in this unique and complex theory of democracy is the way in which Whitman's conception of democratic culture emerged out of the linguistic raw material provided by indigenous languages. For Whitman, the use of "indigenous" vernaculars of the common people fundamentally marked democratic poetry. The self-creation of a democratic community depends on the poetic use of native language that departs from European literary forms. To the extent that it stems from his earlier reflections on settler colonization and indigenous languages, Whitman's democratic theory is significantly shaped by the logic of colonial dispossession.

PART THREE
Unsettling Democracy

6 William Apess and the Paradox of Settler Sovereignty

> "What, then, shall we do? Shall we cease crying and say it is all wrong, or shall we bury the hatchet and those unjust laws and Plymouth Rock together and become friends?"
>
> —William Apess, "Eulogy on King Philip" (1836)

Questions of political foundations and what political theorists have called "the paradox of sovereignty" have become of central concern to contemporary democratic theory. In its broad contours, the paradox of sovereignty suggests that any constitutional order rests on forms of exclusion that are beyond the realm of legal legitimacy. Because attempts to draw the boundaries of popular sovereignty can never be done by purely democratic means, law and sovereignty always rest on violence and exclusion. Instead of a disabling problem to overcome, many contemporary democratic theorists see the paradox of sovereignty as an enabling dilemma that generates a productive politics of conflict and contestation.[1] By exposing the contingency of modern rule, the paradox of sovereignty produces sites of contestation that allow political actors to challenge unjust legal exclusions and produce new political possibilities.

Although it has been given much theoretical treatment in recent years, scholars have largely failed to locate "the paradox of sovereignty" in the context of one of the most enduring problems of democratic modernity—the relationship between European settlers and indigenous peoples in settler societies. While the example of native conquest is often taken as an archetypal case of founding violence, which in turn creates paradoxes of legitimacy and sovereignty that stand at the heart of liberal democratic states, few have fully explored these dynamics in much detail. This neglect is likely symptomatic of a broader failure of political theorists to take seriously

Native American political thought, and it is further compounded by the fact that native dispossession represents one of the most forceful examples of founding violence. Yet despite the emergent framework of "comparative political theory," Native American and indigenous thought remain virtually unstudied by academic political theorists.[2]

This chapter seeks to correct these fissures and erasures by examining a specific moment in American history when the paradox of sovereignty was explored and exposed as a problem in both political thought and practice. It examines the thought and politics of the Pequot Indian William Apess, a polemical writer and orator who was involved in a conflict between the Mashpee Indians and the Massachusetts government in 1833. To further the cause of native rights, Apess wrote two political tracts explicitly dealing with questions of sovereignty and political foundings: "Indian Nullification of the Unconstitutional Laws of Massachusetts" (1835) and "Eulogy on King Philip" (1836). Immediately evident from the title of the former work, questions of constitutional authority loomed large in his political thought. But how should we make sense of his activation of constitutional discourse in his defense of native self-determination? Prevailing accounts posit that he articulated a hybridized Indian-American identity to demand inclusion into the US political order. The most vocal proponent of this view, David Carlson, argues that Apess forged a discourse of "Indian liberalism" that revolves around liberal conceptions of the self and contractual freedom in American political discourse. The rhetorical effect of Apess's work was thus to implore white settlers to affirm the rights of indigenous peoples as liberal subjects.[3]

Two problems with this reading arise, however. First, it assumes that liberal legal discourse was adequate to the task of articulating the wrongs imposed upon Indians. Liberal discourse, however, is unable to capture the settler colonial foundations of American democracy because it lacks the concept of "conquest" in its theoretical repertoire. As Michel Foucault notes, the notion of the contract in liberal thought operates to obscure the role of conquest in the formation of modern sovereignty.[4] Absent an idea of "conquest" to express native peoples as conquered nations, liberal discourse casts Indians as paternalistic wards of the state unable to make political claims on their own. The language of liberal democracy is thus unable to express the American founding as an instance of colonial conquest. To navigate this predicament, Apess developed "Indian nullification" as a political-rhetorical form that Jacques Rancière calls *dissensus*, a disruption in the hegemonic ordering of who counts as a legitimate political subject that occurs when colonized subjects speak in a language they are not entitled to use.[5]

Second, as Robert Nichols has forcefully argued, the surest way to provide for the legitimacy of the settler state is to require colonized subjects to contest injustice in terms of a gap between the real and the ideal. In other words, treating indigenous contestation of settler rule as a means of exposing the failure to fulfill in practice what that state professes in principle actually reinforces the universality of settler authority.[6] My contention is that in using the constitutional language of "Indian nullification," Apess sought to displace and dislocate rather than extend the universality of American democratic ideals by exposing the manner in which settler colonialism—the systematic appropriation of native land and elimination of native sovereignty—established the cultural and political foundation of American democracy.

Through his rhetorical deployment of "Indian nullification," Apess confronts what political theorists have identified as the fundamental paradox of law and sovereignty in modern democracies: the fact that any constitutional order rests on forms of exclusion that are beyond the realm of legal legitimacy. Lacking clear guidelines to demarcate "the people" that rule in democracy, delineating the boundaries of popular sovereignty necessarily entails exclusion. Any democratic state requires, in Chantal Mouffe's words, "drawing a frontier between 'us' and 'them,' those who belong to the *demos* and those who are outside it."[7] In the case of settler states, however, the fundamental line demarcating the boundaries of popular sovereignty is the "settler-indigene divide."[8] Frantz Fanon, in *Wretched of the Earth*, argues that settler societies rest on a compartmentalization of social and legal institutions into "settler" and "native." For Fanon, settler colonialism produces a dualism of political space in which settler space is governed by liberal principles and native space is governed through conquest and occupation. Fanon goes on, "For it is the settler who has brought the native into existence and who perpetuates his existence. The settler owes the fact of his very existence . . . to the colonial system." This chapter extrapolates this point to suggest that the political subjectivity of settlers—marked by notions of equality and popular sovereignty—are similarly produced through practices of settler conquest.[9]

Indeed, the transnational circulation of colonial practice and discourse back and forth between the American and French Algerian settler colonial contexts forcefully demonstrates the shared connections between the decolonial politics of Fanon and Apess. Rejecting "the colonial politics of recognition"[10]—which reproduces colonial relations through the state-sanctioned, reciprocal recognition of indigenous tribes and racial-colonial difference—both Fanon and Apess engage in a refusal of rather than simply resistance against settler sovereignty. "Where resistance looks for lacuna and interruptions in the constancy of power, refusal denies its very legitimacy."[11] If resistance seeks gaps of legitimacy in the exercise of colonial power to renegotiate power relations, refusal destabilizes the very ground of sovereign legitimacy claimed by the settler state.[12]

In capturing the fundamental division that anchors American democracy, Apess employs the concept of nullification less as a feature of institutional design than as a refusal of American settler sovereignty, and more precisely as a narrative mode of exposing democracy's constitutive exclusions, the way in which liberty and equality rest upon settler conquest. Indian nullification, consequently, is not a simple demand that the boundaries of liberal citizenship be expanded to include Indians. For Apess, the problem facing the Mashpee and other indigenous peoples in Jacksonian America is not exclusion from the rights of equal citizenship, but rather colonial dispossession and land expropriation. Accordingly, Apess rejects solutions involving the inclusion of native peoples into a preexisting constitutional order in favor of the continued contestation of settler sovereignty. Yet rather than reject democracy entirely as a mode of colonial imposition, Apess employs constitutional discourse to articulate claims for the political autonomy of indigenous communities. In this manner, he resignifies the meaning of nullification in a way that exceeds the initial context to which it was originally intended to correspond. As a result, nullification becomes an indigenous concept that marks the limits of settler authority and asserts the political autonomy of Indian communities.[13]

The Mashpee Revolt of 1833

A Pequot Indian by birth, Apess became a vocal and influential proponent of indigenous rights in New England and national politics through his involvement in a small but significant conflict between the Massachusetts government and a community of Wampanoag Indians in a Cape Cod town called Mashpee. As an itinerant Methodist preacher in the late 1820s, Apess heard of increasingly strained relations between settlers and Indians and went to Cape Cod to offer his services. He went to Mashpee in May 1833 and found a struggling town, one of the sole remaining Wampanoag settlements that had survived after the Puritans went on a wave of extermination during King Philip's War of 1676. The plantation was settled in 1667 on land provided by the Reverend Richard Bourne. In accordance with the Crown charter and Bourne's will, Mashpee was organized as a self-governing community.[14]

Throughout the eighteenth century the Mashpee people continually clashed with New England settlers encroaching on tribal lands. In this context, the Mashpee developed their own institutions of self-government that combined political practices of Wampanoag council democracy and the English plantation system. To assert their customary land rights, the Mashpee instituted a series of meetings that mimicked though did not replicate the New England town meeting. In response, the Massachusetts General Court in 1746 legislated a new system that appointed three white guardians to oversee the affairs of Mashpee and other Indian settlements. Under this law, the guardians had the authority to lease land to white colonists, the revenue of which was put at the sole discretion of the overseers. In defiance of the Crown charter and Bourne's will, the General Court and local settler communities asserted their unilateral rights to appropriate native land. After petitioning the General Court for redress to no avail, the Mashpee Indians took their case directly to the Crown, which led to three years of investigation and the eventual incorporation of Mashpee as a self-governing town in 1763.[15]

In 1788, the Massachusetts government fully rescinded Mashpee rights of self-government and reinstated the guardianship system of 1746. Although the stated reason for the law was that natives were incapable of self-government, the more probable motivation was the state's unwillingness to enforce laws preventing non-Indian trespassers from acquiring Mashpee land. Mashpee was rich with resources, with eight thousand acres of pitch pine and two thousand acres of oak and another two thousand acres of cleared and arable land for agriculture. The official rationale for the guardianship system was premised on the common law principle that orphans and other physical or mental dependents with property claims should have a court-appointed guardian to administer their affairs and prepare for the future. Despite (or perhaps because of) its paternalistic motives, the law authorized the direct expropriation of native land. Operating under the Lockean assumption that surpluses in real estate could justifiably be expropriated under natural law, the General Court authorized guardians to dispose of Indian surpluses in wood and land to white farmers, a practice that continued into the 1830s.[16]

After being adopted by the tribe, Apess assisted the Mashpee people in writing a list of their grievances and presenting them to the Massachusetts governor. The outcome was the "Indian Declaration of Independence," a series of resolutions declaring Mashpee political autonomy and nullifying the laws establishing the guardianship system.[17] Apess explicitly drew on the language of the US Constitution to assert native rights of self-government:

> *Resolved,* That we, as a tribe, will rule ourselves, and have the right to do so; for all men are born free and equal, says the Constitution of the country.
>
> *Resolved,* That we will not permit any white man to come upon our plantation, to cut or carry off wood or hay, or any other article, without our permission.
>
> *Resolved,* That we will put said resolutions in force after that date (July next), with the penalty of binding and throwing them from the plantation, if they will not stay away without.[18]

Immediately after the Mashpee voted on and approved the declaration, they began organizing as a self-governing body. In doing so, Apess wrote that the Mashpee formed a government "suited to the spirit and capacity of freeborn sons of the forest, after the pattern set us by our white brethren. There was but one exception, viz., that all who dwelt in our precincts were to be held free and equal, in truth, as well as in letter." In a basic sense, the resolutions read as an attempt to expose the hypocrisy of white settlers and encourage them to live up to the true meaning of their professed ideals. As the first resolution suggests, the Mashpee harnessed the authority of the "pattern" set before them to express their own claims for political independence. Yet by noting the "one exception" in which the Mashpee model of democracy deviated from the settler "pattern," Apess also zeroes in on the forms of colonial conquest that prevented the extension of liberal democratic ideals to natives.

All of this came to a head when the Mashpee resolutions went into effect on July 1, 1833. A few days later, two white brothers named Sampson defied the resolutions by taking wood away from the plantation. Catching the men in the act, Apess calmly explained the intentions of the tribe and the preceding resolutions declaring the plantation exclusive property of the Mashpee. After the men refused to cease loading their carts, Apess insisted that the Mashpee were intent on carrying their resolutions into effect, at which point a group of Indians arrived and began to unload the carts and return the wood. Although the brothers left without any violence, Apess was later arrested on charges of inciting a riot.[19] After he was released from jail in early August, the Mashpee continued their struggle. To further the cause, Apess and Blind Joe Amos mounted a publicity campaign and gained significant allies such as Benjamin Hallett, a prominent Massachusetts lawyer and editor of the *Boston Advocate* (who also served as a lawyer for the Mashpee tribe), and William Lloyd Garrison, whose newspaper the *Liberator* endorsed the Mashpee struggle. Such high-profile allies set off a storm of commentary in the political press debating the Mashpee incident in particular and the Indian question in general. Partially to clear his name of any wrongdoing and partially to further the cause of Indian rights, Apess composed a collection of documentary evidence surrounding the incident interspersed with his own commentary titled "Indian Nullification of the Unconstitutional Laws of Massachusetts Relative to the Marshpee Tribe; or, The Pretended Riot Explained."

The question of authorship in the text has presented considerable difficulties. As a documentary collection, "Indian Nullification" presents articles and arguments on all sides of the debate, including both defenders and opponents of the guardianship system, thus potentially preventing the single attribution of authorship. Following others, however, I will read Apess as the author. Maureen Konkle has argued that although he did not write every text in the collection, Apess did compose the documents in a way that demonstrates his assertion of authorial control over the text.[20] At the same time, however, it is important to remember, along with Barry O'Connell, that the Mashpee Revolt was not "simply a vehicle for [Apess's] ideas."[21] The Mashpee had a long legacy of opposition to settler rule, and while Apess may have given voice and theoretical coherence to that resistance he was not its originator.

One of the more compelling ways that Apess did this was to emphasize the parallels between the Mashpee struggle against settler domination and that of the American settlers against British imperial domination. Apess and others used comparisons between Mashpee dissidents and American revolutionaries to enforce their claims for equality and self-government. In justifying the actions of the Mashpee, Benjamin Hallett asserted that they "were as justifiable in what they did, as our fathers were, who threw the tea overboard."[22] In response to an editorial from the *Barnstable Journal*, the Mashpee collectively signed an open letter to the editors clarifying the causes of their discontent, which derived from subjection to the rule of guardians whose authority was "not constitutional." To further this point, the letter asked its settler audience to remember the days of their oppression under the yoke of the British Empire when they had "laid the foundation for their future independence:"

> We ask the good people of Massachusetts, the boasted cradle of independence, whom we have petitioned for a redress of wrongs, more grievous than what your fathers had to bear, and our petitioning was as fruitless as theirs, and there was no other alternative but like theirs to take our stand, and as we have on our plantation but one harbor, and no English ships of tea, for a substitute, we unloaded two wagons loaded with our wood.[23]

Like the colonial dissidents who resorted to other methods when their attempt to petition the Crown for redress failed, the Mashpee Indians symbolically likened themselves to American patriots to have their grievances heard by white settlers.

Yet rather than an unambiguous parallel between two modes of anticolonial struggle, Mashpee leaders emphasized differences by presenting the American colonists as invaders in their own right. In an opening letter of "Indian Nullification" addressed to "the white people of Massachusetts," three selectmen of the Mashpee Council House proclaimed, "The red children of the soil of America address themselves to the descendants of the pale men who came across the big waters to seek among them a refuge from tyranny and oppression."[24] Rather than simply ground the legitimacy of the Mashpee revolt in the authority of settler colonial revolt against the British Empire, the Mashpee exposed the contradictions and particularities of the American revolutionary experience. The address emphasized that the land belonged to "the red children of the soil" and thus illustrated that settler democracy was a foreign rather than native element of the political landscape. At once colonizer and colonized, American settlers developed a set of ideals that embraced dualistic legacies of democracy and dispossession.

Constituting Settler Democracy

To properly understand Apess's concept of Indian nullification, it is essential to locate it in the context of what I call "the paradox of settler sovereignty." To illustrate this paradox, I read Daniel Webster's "Plymouth Oration" for the dynamic interplay between democratic equality and settler sovereignty. Much like Tocqueville's *Democracy in America*, Webster's speech illustrates how the process of constitution making not only entails the founding act of establishing the formal political institutions that bind a community (i.e., the capital "C" Constitution), but also requires the ongoing cultivation of habits and norms that make those institutions and membership in them meaningful. It reveals how the underlying values of the North American social condition that sustain institutions of democratic self-rule are predicated on ideologies of native disavowal.

Settler colonialism necessarily relies on conquest as the primary means of land appropriation. In a simple sense, conquest is the coercive acquisition of territory. According to the right of conquest in early modern international law, superior strength confers just title to rule over newly acquired territories.[25] At a more complex level, conquest is the "paradigmatic form of founding violence." It enacts the erasure of a prior political order to make way for the constitution of a new regime. As a form of foundational violence, conquest institutes a "political and legal caesura" that ruptures and "interrupts political continuity," creating an empty space on which to impose a new political order.[26] In their notion of a "settler contract," Charles Mills and Carole Pateman argue that liberal democratic sovereignty in settler contexts arises from an "expropriation contract" in which consent and democratic government among white settlers necessitates coercive regimes of land appropriation.[27]

Insofar as it constitutes the foundation of popular sovereignty, settler conquest represents a foundational wrong of American democracy. As a constitutive exclusion that provides the condition of possibility for democratic sovereignty, settler conquest paradoxically unsettles the democratic foundations of the settler state. Any polity founded on conquest always risks subverting its own foundations because without ideologically masking its origins, it sanctions rebellion and sedition as a means of political change. In this way, the "paradox of conquest" closely mirrors the "paradox of sovereignty," both of which combine to form what I call "the paradox of settler sovereignty."[28] In this paradox, the constitutive exclusions of settler conquest that lay the basis of democratic order prevent the modern state from claiming full legitimacy and sovereignty. The concept of Indian nullification reveals the incomplete character of settler state sovereignty. Apess uses Indian nullification to create an antagonistic space of contestation in which indigenous claims for political and cultural autonomy might be articulated.

Webster's "Plymouth Oration" illustrates how American democracy was founded on and perpetuates settler conquest, further illuminating the paradox of settler sovereignty. The occasion of Webster's speech, delivered in December 1820, was to commemorate the Puritan foundations of the American republic. A generation apart from the founders, Webster intended his oration as both a celebration of their achievements and an account of the deep roots of their beliefs and principles in the American landscape. Webster's choice of location on the 200th anniversary of the founding of the Plymouth colony was not merely incidental to the praise showered upon the founding generation. Plymouth Rock symbolized more than a set of local attachments of interest only to the people of New England. Rather, it represented a founding moment of the US constitutional order. Webster traced a linear path from Plymouth Rock to the American Revolution and the Constitution. The "original character" of the colonies left an indelible impact on subsequent dynamics of US constitutional development.[29] Exemplifying the solid foundation of American ideals, Webster's glorification of the Plymouth colony casts a founding narrative that inadvertently articulates a settler colonial identity for the young republic.

Integrated into Webster's narrative of settler colonization was a comparative dimension that juxtaposed North American settlement to other projects of colonization. What made the North American colonies unique was that the primary aim of settlement was the constitution of a new socio-political order. In the Greco-Roman model of colonization "the owners of the soil and of the capital seldom consider themselves at home in the colony. . . . Nobody comes but to return." In the British colonies of North America, conversely, profits obtained from commercial ventures did not flow entirely back to the metropolis but were invested in the development of a new society. As a result, the "spirit of permanent improvement" prevailing in New England solidified an attachment to place and location that in turn fueled a drive for separation and independence.[30]

Another distinguishing feature of North American colonization was the specific form of government that settlers carried with them. Even before they had reached the shores of North America, Puritan settlers already developed an elaborate political system that was based on quasi-democratic models of congregational governance. Webster pronounced, "At the moment of their landing, therefore, they possessed institutions of government . . . framed by consent, founded on choice and preference." But Webster was clear that what makes the US system of government unique extends beyond its constitutional form. "A republican form of government," Webster proclaimed, rests on more than "political constitutions." The firmer foundation of a free state resides in those laws that regulate the inheritance and transmission of property, which through the abolition of primogeniture prevent the formation of a landed aristocracy. Presaging by a decade what Tocqueville called the "equality of conditions," Webster appreciated that a "condition of comparative equality in regard to wealth" enabled the form of government constructed in New England. Coupled with the plentitude of fertile soil "unreclaimed from barbarism" and open to anyone willing to cultivate it, the equality of conditions provided the foundation of democratic government by guarding against the resurgence of feudal land title.[31]

For Webster, republican self-government enshrined in the Constitution gained its energy and coherence from the virtue, customs, and habits of free citizens, which settlers cultivated on top of a land base marked by the absence of indigenous societies. In another well-known speech at Bunker Hill, Webster similarly pronounced, "The principle of free government adheres to the American soil. It is bedded in it, immovable as its mountains."[32] Webster's conceptions of self-rule and democratic equality rely on a conceptualization of land that disavows indigenous political presence. Native elimination operated in Webster's speech, however, not as the overt presence of colonial conquest but as the absence of indigenous sovereignties. Despite the fact that Puritan society suffered from continuous Indian wars in the seventeenth century and fundamentally defined settler identity, Webster purified the American founding by disavowing the colonial violence at its core.

In King Philip's War of 1676, for instance, the modes of violence inflicted on the physical landscape and settlers' property paralleled the interpretive violence that marred the mental landscape of settler identity. Like Locke, Puritan settlers closely equated the ownership of property with political and personal identity. The ownership of the physical products of one's labor required ownership of and mastery over the self. Property and the ability to claim property rights was integral to Puritan colonial identity. From this perspective, there was much more at stake in the destruction of King Philip's War than the loss of property. Because property placed settlers above natives in terms of civilization, the Indian destruction of property called into question the stability of the borders of Puritan colonial identity in the new world.[33] The erasure of indigenous sovereignties in North America thus conceptually grounded the positive valence of American democracy by masking the colonial violence that established the condition of democratic equality for white settlers in the first place.

Nullification and American Constitutionalism

The idea of nullification entered US constitutionalism with the Virginia and Kentucky Resolutions of 1798, which James Madison and Thomas Jefferson, respectively, drafted in response to the Alien and Sedition Acts. While Madison's notion of interposition only granted states the authority of constitutional interpretation and the right to make their complaints heard, Jefferson's theory of nullification went further by declaring the Alien and Sedition Acts "void and of no force," signaling that states had the right to prevent the enforcement of the law within their jurisdiction when the federal government unlawfully exercised power outside its proper limits.[34]

While it is unnecessary to rehash the debates about the legitimacy of nullification in the nineteenth century, there are three dimensions of the concept that Apess directly engaged in formulating the notion of "Indian nullification." First, who is the foundation of constitutional authority? Nullificationists generally held to a compact theory of government that viewed the separate and independent states as the basis of constitutional authority. Operating under the assumption that the Constitution should be interpreted as a compact among separate and independent political communities rather than a contract among free and equal individuals where "the people" rather than states form the basis of the federal union, the Virginia and Kentucky Resolutions carved out a role for state legislatures to challenge federal authority and call into question the constitutionality of the Alien and Sedition Acts. During political debate over the legitimacy of a tariff imposed on British imports in 1828, then Vice President John Calhoun asserted that individual states had the right to impede "unconstitutional oppression" by preventing the enforcement of laws that overstepped the proper boundaries of federal authority.[35]

Conversely, nationalists like President Andrew Jackson and Massachusetts Senator Daniel Webster adhered to a contract theory of government that located constitutional legitimacy in the protection of individual rights. In opposition to Calhoun, Webster asserted that the Constitution is not a compact among separate sovereigns but is the result of a contract establishing the basis of civil law for the new nation.[36] In his Proclamation declaring the illegality of nullification, Jackson elaborated a similar theory in maintaining that the Constitution forms a government based on the consent of "all the people" and not a loose confederation of distinct political communities formed by a "compact between the States."[37]

Second, what is the proper relationship between minority and majority rights? While Webster and Jackson steadfastly held to principles of majority rule, Jefferson and Calhoun posed nullification as a means of protecting minority rights from the tyranny of the majority. Presaging his theory of the "concurrent majority" later developed in *The Disquisition on Government* (1848), Calhoun asserted that the Constitution must provide a check to "prevent the major from oppressing the minor interests of society."[38] As a veto reserved to minorities, nullification was a negative power that granted states the authority to contain the encroaching power of the majority.

While nullificationists saw the doctrine as a means of protecting minority rights against majority tyranny, Jackson argued that it led to the fragmentation of popular sovereignty and consequently corruption and faction.[39] Webster also charged proponents of nullification with violating the "first great principle of all republican liberty; that is, that the majority must govern." He further stated, in "matters of common concern, the judgment of a majority must stand as the judgment of the whole."[40] If Calhoun rejected the notion that "the entire sovereignty of this country belongs to the American people," Webster maintained that majority rule was the only legitimate expression of popular sovereignty.[41] Although Jackson remained committed to states' rights in contrast to Webster's loose construction of federal authority, they agreed that the Constitution formed a liberal contract among free and equal individuals, not a compact among states, and that nullification violated democratic sovereignty and majority rule.[42]

Third, who has the right to invoke the powers of nullification? Jefferson and Calhoun asserted that you must be part of the original compact that established constitutional authority to claim the powers of nullification. For both, the federal government derived its authority from a compact among the individual states. As a result, "every State has a natural right in cases not within the compact, (*casus non foederis*), to nullify of their own authority all assumptions of power by others within their limits."[43] Indian nullification stood in a peculiar relation to the doctrine elaborated by Jefferson and Calhoun. Distinct from equal states that constituted the federal compact, native nations were never independent agents in the creation of the federal state.

This aspect of nullification must be understood in the context of US constitutional debates regarding the status of indigenous nations. In *Cherokee Nation v. Georgia* (1831), Chief Justice John Marshall famously declared that the Cherokee people and other native communities were "domestic dependent nations," neither full citizens nor foreign and fully sovereign nations. Reinforcing the basic logic of the Massachusetts guardianship laws, Marshall further decided that the relation of tribes to the federal government resembled that of a "ward to its guardian."[44] In casting indigenous communities as both separate nations and dependent wards, Marshall prevented natives from harnessing constitutional authority in making their own political and legal claims. Insofar as Indians were wards of the state and lacked standing to sue in court, as Marshall's decision in *Cherokee Nation* made clear, they did not count as legal and political subjects. If Indians were excluded from the federal compact based on their status as wards of the state, then they had no right to claim the rights of nullification.

Nullifying Settler Democracy

Although settlers often aspire to native elimination, the continued presence and contestation of indigenous peoples prevent the full replacement of native sovereignty with settler sovereignty. Vicki Hsueh has shown that the development of proprietary constitutions in British North America in the seventeenth century did not represent the stable and unidirectional transfer of sovereignty and law from metropolitan center to colonial periphery. Less a linear process in which authority radiated from center to periphery, the founding of the proprietary colonies proceeded in "hodgepodge fashion" in which settlers assembled constitutions out of disparate and contradictory legal elements such as civic humanism, common law, and feudal law.[45] Although Hsueh focuses on settler thought, a similar insight can be extended to native appropriations of US constitutionalism. Apess merged the concept of nullification with a defense of native land rights to contest dominant narratives of modern democracy and expose the founding violence of the American democratic order.

Keeping partially within the compact theory of government, Apess draws on the language of nullification to assert that the liberal contract is in fact a "settler contract" premised on the erasure of indigenous sovereignty and to interpose indigenous authority into the hegemonic space of constitutional discourse.[46] In the concept of Indian nullification, the basic constituent of government is not the abstract, unencumbered individual, but rather independent political communities with their distinct forms of culture and property. Indian nullification not only calls into question the legitimacy of settler democracy, it also asserts the cultural and political autonomy of indigenous communities whose distinct social systems have been subject to settler logics of indigenous erasure. As a counterpoint to the colonial tendencies of American democracy, Apess adopts the tradition of Jeffersonian republicanism in upholding the legitimacy of nullification. The concept of Indian nullification, however, is not a constitutional doctrine establishing institutional rules and procedures. It is a narrative mode of representing the constitutive exclusions of American democracy. By calling for Indian nullification, Apess stages a performative contradiction that exposes the complicities of democracy in settler colonialism.

At first glance, it appears that Apess draws on American founding documents to call on white settlers to extend their founding ideals to Indians. But one gets an immediate sense that much more is at work in the Indian Declaration when the Mashpee National Assembly announce to the white guardians their intention to "nullify the existing laws." They claim that in nullifying the authority of the guardians "we acted in accordance with the spirit of the Constitution, *unless that instrument be a device of utter deception.* And now we would say to our white friends, we are wanting nothing but our rights betwixt man and man."[47] Such a formulation provokes a paradox that unsettles the legitimacy and authority of the Constitution. When the proclamation invokes "our rights betwixt man and man," the previous point about the Constitution being an instrument of deception complicates any notion that constitutional ideals are themselves wholly sufficient to secure Mashpee rights. Apess goes on to say immediately after presenting the proclamation, "We then proceeded to discharge all the officers appointed by the governor . . . firmly believing that each and every one of the existing laws concerning the poor Israelites of Mashpee was founded on wrong and misconception." Such an assertion suggests that it was not only the Massachusetts laws but also the Constitution itself that "was founded on wrong and misconception."[48] As such, settler conquest and the exclusion of indigenous peoples from settler citizenship cannot be corrected through the universalization of constitutional ideals.

At the same time, Apess insists that the guardianship laws were unconstitutional. Drawing on the discourse of American independence he asserts, "We Mashpees account all who opposed our freedom, as Tories, hostile to the Constitution and the liberties of the country."[49] The question to arise from this peculiar composition of constitutional discourse is, how do Apess and the Mashpee both claim constitutional authority and maintain that the Constitution is a device of deception? My argument is that this is not an inconsistency or an oversight, but rather a deliberate rhetorical strategy that stages a contradiction by asserting that the Constitution is at once a source of liberty and equality and a device of conquest designed to dispossess Indians of their customary lands. As a rhetorical strategy, Indian nullification calls the attention of settlers not to the gap between their professed ideals and political practice, but to the contradictions that inhabit the very foundation of their polity. Furthermore, it is not simply a call for constitutional rights to be extended to Indians. Rather, it is a call for a refounding of the North American political order and the creation of a new arrangement of rights and obligations that would redefine relations between settlers and Indians.

In something of a paradoxical twist, Apess bases his rights claims on the authority of a constitution that he himself exposes as lacking authority. The effect of this is to ideologically unveil the modes of settler conquest that form the basis of American democracy. Although Apess harnesses the authority of the Constitution and Declaration in his argument for indigenous autonomy, he clearly understands that both documents rest on a conception of citizenship that fundamentally excludes indigenous practices of property. Immediately preceding Apess's arrest, a lawyer for the state requested a local judge "to explain to the Indians the laws, as they then stood, and the consequences of violating them." Paralleling ongoing debates about the validity of nullification in Congress, the judge explained to Apess that "merely declaring a law to be oppressive could not abrogate it" and that a surer remedy would be to act as "good citizens" and wait for suitable relief from the state legislature. Apess interjected into his report of the proceedings the assertion that the category of citizenship did not apply to the people of Mashpee: "Surely it was either insult or wrong to call the Mashpees citizens, for such they never were, from the Declaration of Independence up to the session of the Legislature in 1834."[50]

In American liberalism, settlers are citizens because they possess what Indians lack: the capacities for rational self-government and legal institutions of private property, both of which define legal personhood. Insofar as citizenship is legally "defined through the natural right to own property" and rests on the self-ownership of the possessive individual, Indians negatively define settler citizenship by representing the negation of the proprietary-self in the absence of dominant conceptions of private property.[51] To the extent that modern democracy depends on the propertied independence of citizens, the enclosure of land in private property mirrors the enclosure of settler sovereignty, both of which cast native dispossession as a precondition of settler citizenship. In illustrating these constitutive exclusions, Indian nullification operates less as an institutional feature of constitutional design than as a rhetorical mode of capturing the foundational division of settler democracy, i.e., the settler-indigene divide.

While the debate between nullificationists and nationalists revolved around the proper balance between majority rule and minority rights, Indian nullification fundamentally unsettles this distinction. Indian nullification cannot be taken as an assertion of minority rights because the debates between minority and majority rest on the exclusion of Indians from counting as part of either faction. Giving an entirely different cast to Tocqueville's thesis about the "tyranny of the majority," Apess shows how the rights of both majority and minority rest on the exclusion of Indians from the standards of American citizenship. Indian nullification is not a discourse asserting the validity of minority rights. Instead, it asserts that even the rights of the minority of white settlers depend for their coherence upon settler colonialism. As such, it must be understood not as an assertion of minority rights but as the "staging of a nonexistent right."[52]

It is important here to appreciate the very different conceptions of property rights at work in the two notions of nullification. While Jefferson's theory of nullification embraced a liberal understanding of individual rights, Apess directly challenged the hegemony of liberal property rights as the basis of an egalitarian constitutional order. Ostensibly reflecting a liberal understanding of property rights, Apess condemned white settlers for dispossessing "the red men of the woods" of their land and violating their "inherent rights."[53] Apess, however, meant by "inherent rights" something very different than individual property rights, a point adequately grasped by considering the complex practices of property at work in Mashpee, which consisted of a hybrid mix of proprietary rights operating in the English plantation system and aboriginal customary law. In 1685, the Plymouth Court stipulated that Mashpee land could not be purchased or taken by English settlers without consent. By 1723, the Mashpee developed their own practices of property rights and created a proprietary system where the tribe owned the land and was allocated to individual families. While children could inherit land, it reverted to tribal control in the absence of an heir. "Tribal membership assured the individual the right to land, and, conversely, having a right to land identified an individual as a member of the group." A standard practice among Algonquian tribes, aboriginal customary law had long provided for the allocation of "parcels of land for agricultural use by members of the extended family."[54]

It is in this context that the meaning of the second resolution of the Indian Declaration must be understood, which proclaimed that "we will not permit any white man to come upon our plantation" to expropriate land or resources without consent. Article Two thus tied the meaning of self-government to a hybrid conception of property that cast tribal land in individual terms but nevertheless restricted the liberal right of expropriating uncultivated waste land. These hybrid proprietary arrangements were central to the notion of independence expressed by the Mashpee. Apess's central problem with the guardianship laws, and paternalistic systems of governance more generally, was that they reinforced "the logic of native elimination," an impulse in settler colonial states aimed at the construction of a "new colonial society on the expropriated land base."[55] Apess wrote of federal and state laws, "The laws were calculated to drive the tribes from their possessions and annihilate them as a people. . . . It is a sorrowful truth that, heretofore, all legislation regarding the affairs of Indians has had a direct tendency to degrade them, to drive them from their homes and the graves of their fathers, to give their lands as a spoil to the general government."[56]

He thus exposed paternalist principles of the guardianship system as a means of land appropriation and eliminating native conceptions of political peoplehood. Rather than a method of civilizing and improving Indians, the guardianship system and paternalism of the federal government reinforced the political and historical erasure of indigenous peoples.

By calling attention to the foundational division of American democracy in regimes of land appropriation, nullification produced the "Indian" as a political subject. This directly challenged the "liberal paternalism" of President Jackson and the Massachusetts liberals, both of whom believed that Mashpee and Cherokee alike could not govern themselves because of their arrested capacities for rational improvement.[57] The assertion of indigenous self-determination first required the nullification of those laws of paternalism and elimination that deemed indigenous forms of polity and property incompatible with the settler social state. Indian nullification thus represents not a principle of constitutional design asserting minority rights over the tyranny of the majority, but a means of contesting the wardship status imposed on Indians.

In Rancière's terms, Indian nullification reconfigures civic space by introducing the Indian as political subject into a political order whose authority rests on the exclusion of that subject. The "partition of the perceptible," for Rancière, is a distinct configuration of political space, an ordering of subjects that determines who can be represented.[58] All constitutional orders are governed by regimes of representation. Certain bodies are rendered visible and legible and consequently able to speak and enunciate political claims as legitimate subjects. But the imputation of wardship status onto Mashpee and Cherokee alike prevents them from registering as legal and political subjects able to have their political claims heard as legitimate enunciations. Liberal paternalism politically neutralizes indigenous communities by rendering them as administrative populations subject to state protection rather than as political entities that relate to the settler state in terms of a friend-enemy distinction.[59]

One sees this configuration of settler society play out in Apess's ongoing concern about the representation of the Mashpee struggle in the New England liberal press. He wrote, "All the editors were very willing to speak on the favorite topic of Indian wrongs; but very few of them said anything about redress."[60] Although many liberal-minded editors presented sympathetic accounts of the oppression inflicted on Indians, Apess insisted that they were incapable of addressing colonial injustice precisely because they were incapable of hearing native claims for self-rule. In one example, the liberal-minded editors of the *Boston Advocate* published a sympathetic plea of support for the Mashpee. The article agreed that the Mashpee have been wronged by white settlers and encouraged whites to act with justice toward the Indians. Yet, as if to contain the gravity of the wrongs imposed upon Indians, the letter also accused the Mashpee of misrepresenting the severity of their grievances: "Undoubtedly some of their supposed grievances are imaginary and much exaggerated, but others are real, and tend greatly to depress them."[61] The article then exhorted the Mashpee to refrain from violence and place their hopes for redress fully in the state legislature.

To give their white audience a flavor of Indian grievances, the *Advocate* published two anonymous letters from the Mashpee Indians. As if to respond to Gayatri Spivak's famous question—"can the subaltern speak?"—the anonymous authors of the two letters, both of whom spoke in the name of the whole community, stated, "Mashpee Indians speak for themselves. It is not to be doubted that the public would like to hear the Indians speak for themselves. It has been represented that the Indians were troublesome, and war-like movements were among us. If to make an inquiry into our rights by us, is war-like, so it is."[62] The difficulty of hearing native rights claims stems from liberal discourses of civilization that cast native refusal of settler sovereignty as savagery and in turn depoliticize native articulations of oppression and injustice. As a result, the wrong the Mashpee voiced was an impossible enunciation that could not be heard within the hegemonic language of liberal-democratic discourse except as a radical mode of dissensus.

The letters thus depict the aporetic nature of articulating the foundational wrong of settler democracy within the linguistic terms of the colonizing discourse. In response to the accusations of exaggerated grievances, the anonymous authors assert, "It is impossible to give the details of the wrongs imposed upon the Indians."[63] The impossibility of representing Mashpee grievances in the language of liberal democracy points to the inadequacy of linguistic categories grounded in liberal constitutional discourse to represent the foundational wrong of settler democracy. But rather than remain within the space of paradox and agree with Spivak that the representation of colonized subjects only reinforces the power of the settler state, the Mashpee appropriated the language of the colonizer and articulated their rights claims in a language they were not entitled to use. The effect was to stage a polemical form of dissensus that reveals the constitutive divisions of political society.[64]

Counter-Narratives of the American Founding

Apess's "Indian Nullification" and his "Eulogy on King Philip" are clearly structured by different conventions of literary form and are driven by different political intentions. On the one hand, "Indian Nullification" was a collection of documents and legal commentary explaining the motivations of the Mashpee in nullifying the authority of the Massachusetts government. On the other hand, "Eulogy on King Philip" was a public speech that memorialized an indigenous leader and in turn mimicked similar genres of American speechmaking focused on the commemoration of patriotic events such as the founding of the Plymouth colony and the Declaration of Independence. Nonetheless, they share a similar set of questions concerning the foundations of the settler social state. Returning to the theme of Puritan society, Apess elaborates his contention that American political order was founded on the mutually constitutive relationship between democracy and colonial dispossession. If Puritan political culture and the equality of conditions prevailing in colonial society comprise "the Constitution-beneath-the-Constitution,"[65] then Apess's "Eulogy" reads as a further elaboration of Indian nullification insofar as it continues to reveal the dynamic interplay between settler colonialism and American democracy.

Indian nullification is not simply a doctrine of constitutional design, but is a narrative mode of contesting colonial dispossession.

Apess first delivered the "Eulogy" in Boston on January 8, 1836. On one level, his immediate concern was a commemoration of King Philip's War and a tribute to the Wampanoag sachem, Metacomet, or King Philip, who led an alliance of Algonquian nations against Puritan settlers in 1676. To revitalize King Philip's legacy for contemporary Indian struggles, Apess drew a direct comparison between King Philip and General George Washington as two great defenders of civil and political rights for whites and Indians alike. In his speech, Apess also deconstructed Anglo-centric histories of the United States by counterposing indigenous narratives of settler conquest to founding narratives of the sort offered by Webster. In doing so, he provided a counterpoint to liberal constitutional discourses that cast Indians as state wards unable to make political and legal claims. What was at stake in *Cherokee Nation v. Georgia* was less the prevention of Cherokee people from speaking up in court for their own rights than the narrative closure it enacted. Without standing to make political claims in court, the Cherokee people also lacked the ability to narrate their own stories, thus preventing counter-narratives of conquest from entering official legal discourse.[66] Against the narrative foreclosure of indigenous counter-narratives, Apess's "Eulogy" illustrates how colonial dispossession grounds the normative legitimacy of America democratic values.

To accomplish both tasks, Apess engaged a master-narrative of American civic identity that has also served as a powerful discourse authorizing the elimination of the native: the myth of the savage war. The savage war myth, which animated American literature from the seventeenth to twentieth centuries, characterized history as a clash between civilization and savagery, a dichotomy given moral valence with civilization positioned as the triumphant force. If civilized people rule over each other in a "civil government," then uncivilized people occupy an anarchical state of nature lacking the rule of law. Further underwriting this dichotomy was a distinction between "savage war" and "civilized war." While the latter was rational, honorable, and subject to the dictates of natural law and just war theory, the former was characterized by irrationality and the ferocity of unrestrained violence. Savage wars were irrational because they exceeded the moral boundaries of just conduct and were driven by uncontrollable passions such as revenge or the fulfillment of sadistic desires. Savage wars were wars of extermination because civilization could only triumph if the savage races were thoroughly eliminated.[67]

Instead of treating "savage war" as a natural category grounded in the conflict between savagery and civilization, Apess asserted that the state of war between settlers and Indians was itself produced by the foundations of Puritan society. As with "Indian Nullification," his primary aim in the "Eulogy" was to represent the foundational division of American democracy (i.e., the settler-indigene divide, which in this case is represented by the distinction between civilized and savage war). Toward this end, he began the "Eulogy" by rejecting the assumption that settler and Indian modes of warfare can be adequately captured through the distinction between civilized and uncivilized, insisting that "we cannot but see that one mode of warfare is as just as the other." Portraying it as a just war, Apess contended that King Philip's War was "no savage war of surprise . . . but one sorely provoked by the Pilgrims themselves."[68] Apess clearly understood that the political effect of the savage war myth was to depoliticize native forms of refusal of settler rule by conjuring specters of savage violence. In "Indian Nullification," he similarly noted that one of the reasons white settlers charged him with inciting a riot and open rebellion was that they believed "we had armed ourselves and were prepared to carry all before us with tomahawk and scalping knife; that death and destruction, and all the horrors of savage war, were impending."[69] In order to create a space in which native contestation might be heard, Apess had to counteract the depoliticization of native refusal engendered by the savage war myth.

In so doing, Apess challenged civilizational discourses of colonial injustice circulating in Jacksonian political culture found in the writings of Emerson and Boudinot (see Chapter 4). Against these civilizational discourses that re-inscribed the superiority of Anglo-American culture and masked the colonial foundation of modern democracy, Apess's counter-narrative reversed the image of the United States as a civilizing force.[70] He wrote, "O thou white Christians, look at acts that honored your countrymen, to the destruction of thousands, for much less insults than that. And who, my dear sires, were wanting of the name of savages—whites, or Indians? Let justice answer."[71] Throughout his speech, Apess initiated a set of rhetorical reversals by turning denigrating terms used to describe natives back on his white audience: civilized settlers become savage oppressors, the just become unjust, democrats become tyrants, and "lovers of liberty" become "conquerors and slaveholders."[72] Justice, for Apess, is not achieved through a civilizational process by which natives become more like white settlers, but through a deconstructive process in which categories of justice and civilization in settler political thought are recast as their opposite and exposed as false universals. Apess thus reversed the categories of savagery and civilization by showing how it was the Pilgrims rather than Indians who acted without regard for law, morality, and justice. Apess's de-naturalization of the savage war myth allowed him to cast King Philip as a defender of civil and political rights on par with founding figures like General Washington.

But Apess does not argue that the wrongs committed by Pilgrims are simply anomalous acts that stood outside the founding principles of colonial political traditions. Rather, he argues that colonial injustice stems from the foundations of settler democracy itself:

> Our groves and hunting grounds are gone . . . our council fires are put out, and a foundation was laid in the first Legislature to enslave our people, taking from them all rights, which has been strictly adhered to ever since. . . . Look at the treaties made by Congress, all broken. Look at the deep-rooted plans laid, when a territory becomes a state. . . . Yea, every charter that has been given was given with the view of driving the Indians out of the state.[73]

By connecting his criticism of the savage war myth with the "foundation" that destroyed indigenous rights, Apess posits that the Puritan foundations of colonial society instituted a state of war between settlers and Indians. In evoking new states and broken treaties, he also suggests that colonial dispossession is not a one-time event but is rather an ongoing process that continues with the further expansion of the settler state westward. In doing so, he confronts the common assumption that colonial assemblies and charters established the democratic legacy in America by conceiving of those founding documents as instruments of conquest. Damning the "foundation which destroyed our common fathers in their struggle together," he thus exposes the spirit of conquest as a foundational aspect of the American democratic tradition.[74]

To understand Apess's counter-narrative it is helpful to compare his story of Puritan society with other founding narratives. One example resides in Webster's Plymouth Oration, but another is in Tocqueville's account of colonial society as the "point of departure" for explaining American democracy. He wrote of the well-known symbol of Puritan society:

This Rock has become an object of veneration in the United States. I
have seen bits of it carefully preserved in several towns in the Union.
Does this not sufficiently show that all human power and greatness
is in the soul of man? Here is a stone which the feet of a few outcasts
pressed for an instant; and the stone becomes famous; it is treasured
by a great nation; its very dust is shared as a relic.[75]

Like Webster, Tocqueville cast Plymouth Rock as a symbol of democratic
foundations. Both held that the original process of colonization laid the basis
of democracy in America. What made America democratic was the way the
settlers founded the original colonies, which were lacking in the aristocratic
and feudal structures of European society. Plymouth Rock, for Tocqueville,
was a powerful symbol in American founding narratives. It represented the
aspiration the settlers had for freedom and equality and the hold this aspiration has on future generations.

Apess has a wildly different take on the symbol of Plymouth Rock. He
writes, "What, then, shall we do? Shall we cease crying and say it is all
wrong, or shall we bury the hatchet and those unjust laws and Plymouth
Rock together and become friends?"[76] Although it might seem here that
Apess is seeking consensus and reconciliation, and even friendship among
Indians and settlers, I propose to read this as a discursive strategy aimed at
contesting American sovereignty that draws on the logic of Indian nullification. In a single rhetorical sweep, he equates three things: the hatchet (a
symbol of division, conflict, and the state of war); injustice against Indians
(which derives from settler colonialism and dispossession); and Plymouth
Rock (which is a symbol of the foundations of modern American democracy).
Notice here that the familiar metaphor of burying the hatchet is extended
to all three elements, not just the hatchet itself. Instead of a celebration of
the founding of the Plymouth colony as the germ of American democracy,
Apess offers a condemnation by enjoining his audience to see this particular founding moment as an occasion for mourning rather than joy: "let
it be forgotten in your celebration, in your speeches, and by the burying
of the rock that your fathers first put their foot upon."[77] To bury injustice
along with Plymouth Rock and the hatchet is to nullify the foundations of
American democracy, which is also to call for a refounding in which natives
and settlers would be treated as equal participants in a shared democratic
polity. Burying the hatchet—which is a triple symbol of division, injustice,

and the American founding—is thus a precondition for peace and friendship among natives and settlers.

In this forceful passage, Apess provides an implicit critique of the treaty system which governed US-Indigenous relations. His counter-narrative challenges the narrative closure of *Cherokee Nation v. Georgia* by contesting the imposition of dependent status and speaking in a language of rights and liberties natives were not entitled to use. One of the questions that Marshall left untouched, however, was precisely how the status of "domestic dependent nations" was established. In his concurring opinion, Justice Johnson answered this question by pointing to the 1785 Treaty of Hopewell between the Cherokee Nation and the Confederation government. Noting the provisions that stipulated the US obligation to provide protection for the Cherokee people from encroaching settlers, Justice Johnson concluded that "this is certainly the language of sovereigns and conquerors, and not the address of equals to equals."[78] Accordingly, the dependent status of the Cherokee derived from asymmetries of power and the fact of colonial conquest institutionalized in the treaty system.

Despite this, the treaty promised perpetual peace between the Cherokee Nation and the settler state. Article 13 proclaimed, "The hatchet shall be forever buried, and the peace given by the United States, and friendship established between the said states on the one part, and all the Cherokees on the other, shall be universal."[79] Apess's brilliant appropriation of the language of the treaty in the passage cited above reverses the valences of justice and injustice embedded in the colonial discourse of peace and friendship. Where the treaty casts the US government as the acting agent in the provision of perpetual peace, Apess's imagery of burying the hatchet along with Plymouth Rock forcefully inverts this formula. Rather than a source of peace and friendship, he sees the foundational principles of the US democratic tradition as well as the treaty system itself as sources of injustice. Where the language of the treaty tends toward consensus and reconciliation, Indian nullification radically contests the colonial injustice embedded in the cultural and constitutional foundations of American democracy.

Like Tecumseh and Black Hawk, Apess exposed the treaty system not as a genuine expression of democratic principles but as an instrument of colonial conquest that ideologically repackaged the expropriation of land as a voluntary process of consensual agreement. But unlike Tecumseh and Black Hawk, Apess did not seek the restoration of a precolonial, indigenous past, but rather a refounding of the American democratic polity that would both acknowledge and account for the historically rooted colonial injustices inflicted on indigenous peoples. Apess proclaimed in closing the Eulogy, "What, then, is to be done? Let every friend of the Indians now seize the mantle of Liberty and throw it over those burning elements that spread with such fearful rapidity, and at once extinguish them forever. . . . Give the Indian his rights, and you may be assured that war will cease."[80] While Apess allows for the possibility of friendship among Indians and settlers, it first requires that settlers historically confront the colonial violence inherent in the foundations of American democracy. For Apess, war between settlers and natives is not an incidental feature of the colonial encounter; it stems from the foundational principles and institutions of settler democracy. To the extent that the renewal of American democracy is possible, it requires not the fulfillment of the inherent egalitarian logic of founding principles, but a reconstituted democratic polity and a redefinition of friendship based on indigenous counter-narratives.

Conclusion

Read in this light, Apess's version of the Puritan founding narrative sharply contrasts with Webster's Plymouth Rock oration. In disavowing the indigenous presence in North America, Webster retains a sense of American identity as derived from pure and progressive origins untouched by the founding violence of settler colonialism. While Apess asks us to bury Plymouth Rock because fidelity to it perpetuates a state of war between settlers and Indians (signified by the hatchet that Apess also wants to bury), Webster insulates the cultural foundations of constitutional democracy from complicity in settler conquest. Moreover, while Webster and Tocqueville imagine the Puritan foundations of the United States as instituting a democratic social state, Apess asserts that those foundations have enacted a process of native elimination that vitally sustains the equality of conditions among white settlers.

To the extent that it renders this process intelligible, Indian nullification operates as a mode of narrative representation that exposes the political, social, and ethical roots of American democracy in settler colonialism. Nevertheless, we should read Apess's deployment of Indian nullification not in teleological terms as the progressive extension of equal rights to previously marginalized groups, but as an attempt to represent that which is unrepresentable in the terms of republican and liberal discourses of democracy, those constitutive exclusions that have provided the foundation for American democracy yet have been systematically disavowed by liberal and republican democratic discourse. Because they are about providing a public justification for the American settler state, liberal and republican democracy are unable to represent the founding of American society as an instance of settler conquest and colonial dispossession. Yet in appropriating the categories of American democratic theory, Apess's counter-narrative exposes popular sovereignty as settler sovereignty. He thus develops the concept of Indian nullification not to challenge particular unjust laws, but to nullify, in general, the injustice of the settler colonial foundations of modern American democracy.

Afterword
Decolonizing the Democratic Tradition

Grappling with the foundational role of colonial dispossession in shaping modern democratic thought must lead to a reimagining of the democratic tradition and democratic identity. Unsettling democracy requires more than simply attaching more inclusionary frameworks of constitutional law to democratic institutions. It requires rethinking the theoretical and conceptual foundations of democratic practice in a way that critically confronts their ideological entwinement with colonial legacies of native dispossession. As Mahmood Mamdani puts it, "Engaging with the native question would require questioning the ethics and the politics of the very constitution of the United States of America. It would require rethinking and reconsidering the very political project called the USA."[1] Deep engagement with the history of settler colonialism necessitates revising the ethical and political basis of modern democracy. Through a conceptual and historical reconstruction of the relationship between settler expansion and American democracy, this book provides the basis for a decolonial theory of democracy that de-normalizes settler experiences as the unsurpassable horizon of democratic politics.

This effort must start, however, with recognizing and confronting democratic theory's implication in and dependence upon settler colonialism for its foundational values and logics. This entails more than simply recognizing the fact democratic theory has been deployed in the justification of settler colonization or that contexts of settler colonialism have historically informed the development of democratic theory. It requires that we grapple with the way that settler colonialism has in part constituted democratic theory as a field of knowledge production and a theoretical enterprise. Democratic theory has become increasingly concerned with the contradictions and dynamics of political foundings.[2] Yet for most of the modern world, the "founding of new societies," as Louis Hartz has put it, occurred through a process of settler colonization where European populations displaced and replaced native populations.³ To rethink political foundings through the lens of settler colonization would help foreground the colonial ideologies and practices that underpin foundational democratic ideals. As a result, democratic theory would need to more squarely deal with these legacies of settler colonialism if it is to appropriately rethink the prospects for the decolonization of democracy in the present.

The place of settler colonialism in the American democratic tradition has become an increasingly contentious issue among scholars of US political thought. Samuel Huntington has led the charge in reclaiming American national identity as a settler democracy, which he defines in terms of the American Creed, a relatively fixed and stable cluster of beliefs, customs, and habits that give substance to American citizenship. The targets of his scorn are the new Hispanic immigrants who, he believes, have failed to assimilate into the core American culture. Insistent on maintaining dual citizenship and hybrid identities, Hispanic immigrants have largely retained their traditional cultural values rooted in Hispano-phone culture and Catholic religion at the expense of forming deep attachments to American national identity characterized by the Protestant work ethic, individualism, the rule of law, egalitarianism, and popular sovereignty. Operating under the assumption that a stable democracy requires a common set of cultural values, Huntington draws on Tocquevillean insights to call for more restrictive immigration policies. Reversing the polarity of settler narratives of colonial invasion, he contests that restrictive immigration is necessary to protect settler democracy from la reconquista of North America by Hispanic immigrants.⁴

In this effort, Huntington criticizes a dominant trope of American national identity, the idea of a "nation of immigrants." He does not deny that immigration helped define American identity, but he asserts that it is a "partial truth" that obscures a more important aspect: the fact that the American founders were not immigrants but Anglo-Protestant setters. If immigrants leave an existing society to join a new one (thereby accepting an obligation to adopt the new norms and culture), settlers leave an existing society, often as a community rather than as individuals, to create a new political society, carrying their metropolitan culture and values with them and then implanting those values in a distant territory. While settlers constitute a new political order through the exercise of constituent sovereignty, immigrants join an existing society rather than create a new one. If settlers are founders with distinct social values rooted in Anglo-Protestant culture, then the process of settlement and founding are synonymous. Huntington asserts that the American Creed was "the product of the distinct Anglo-Protestant culture of the founding settlers," highlighting how settler colonization established durable cultural patterns that laid the basis of American democracy.[5] Thus, to protect America from immigrant invasion is to protect the sanctity of the founding of settler democracy.

Huntington offers his narrative of settler democracy not only as a defense of restrictive immigration policy but also as an active disavowal of indigenous sovereignty and settler conquest. He writes, "The seventeenth- and eighteenth-century settlers came to America because it was a *tabula rasa*. Apart from Indian tribes, which could be killed off or pushed westward, no society was there; and they came in order to create societies that embodied and would reinforce the culture and values they brought with them from their origin country."[6] Clearly evidenced in the Lockean assumptions concerning America as a state of nature, such an assertion self-consciously recapitulates the narrative trope and legal doctrine of *terra nullius*. For Huntington, native tribes were so sparse and weak that they did not constitute recognizable societies with legitimate claims over land that settlers appropriated. By presenting North America as empty land, he obscures the constitutive role of conquest in the founding of settler democracy.

In opposition to Huntington's enlistment of America's settler colonial legacy in a continued defense of nativist and exclusivist conceptions of democracy, Aziz Rana has recently proposed the reclamation of settler traditions of democracy to sever constitutional thought and practice from its colonial foundations. In this effort, Rana differs from the efforts of Rogers Smith and others to conceive of settler colonialism and republican political theory as separate and analytically distinct multiple traditions.[7] Specifically, Rana takes "the multiple traditions thesis" to task for neglecting how "democratic ideals themselves gained strength and meaning through frameworks of exclusion."[8] Instead, Rana seeks to uncover how republican liberty in the Americas both necessitated and was politically constituted through its deep connections to settler colonial ideology and practice. In response, Rana aims to "universalize settler freedom" by stripping it of its "colonial roots" and extending the promise of republican independence to colonized subjects through the creation of more inclusive structures of constitutional law.[9] Through engagement with the political thought of Orestes Brownson, Thomas Paine, and Randolph Bourne, Rana seeks to reclaim the settler democratic tradition in hope of creating a more inclusive and egalitarian project of popular self-rule that sheds its attachments to ascriptive traditions and practices.[10] Yet in his overwhelming focus on settler-republican political thought, Rana overlooks the productive role that indigenous political thought can play in the project of decolonizing democracy by transforming the theoretical, political, and cultural foundations of democratic thought and practice.

To meet this need, I close by drawing on indigenous critical theory and decolonial theory to highlight two aspects of *the decolonial theory of democracy*. The first key aspect of decolonial democratic theory entails elaborating a nonsovereign conception of democracy that sheds the desire to define self-rule in terms of control and mastery. Although critiques of sovereignty in contemporary political theory are plentiful, very few scholars have turned to indigenous political practices and ideas. Furthermore, most political theorists limit their critique of sovereignty to the command-and-control conception of state sovereignty, sparing the idea of popular sovereignty from the piercing gaze of their critical lens. To develop a nonsovereign conception of democracy, these limitations of contemporary democratic theory must be overcome.

In her recent work, *On Sovereignty and Other Political Delusions*, Joan Cocks provides a useful starting point in thinking about nonsovereign democracy and highlighting the colonial entanglements of popular sovereignty. In particular, Cocks argues that "the struggle to gain freedom through sovereign power is not only more delusional but also potentially more dangerous than the attempt to attain sovereign power *per se*."[11] While many political theorists might share this sentiment and direct their efforts toward a critique of state sovereignty, Cocks focuses on how modern ideals of freedom and self-rule expressed in notions of popular sovereignty also recapitulate colonial logics that not only exclude certain subjects from who belongs to "the people," but also rest on the erasure of prior indigenous orders as a precondition of freedom as self-rule. In other words, the dangers inherent in the logic of sovereignty are "exaggerated, not ameliorated, when the concept of sovereign power is democratized."[12]

Cocks points to three forms of domination inherent in the quest for democratic freedom as popular sovereignty. The first form entails an "impulse to self-domination." Whether as a political collectivity or as an individual, the search for freedom as sovereignty ends in the insulation of the self from the other so as to realize the illusion of mastery over the self, its appetites, instincts, and desires. The second form of domination concerns "the self's drive to dominate everything outside itself in the physical space that it inhabits." To provide the illusion of control, the collectivity that rules itself seeks the mastery not only of itself as a collective body but also the habitat, objects, other species, and other human beings whose presence complicates the search for sovereign power. The third form of domination resides in "the self's drive to dominate other objects (especially objects that are other subjects) outside its place of habitation." The desire for self-control does not stop at the borders of the self but extends outward in an attempt to achieve mastery by impressing its will on the outside world.[13]

In opposition to the logics of domination inherent in the quest for sovereignty, Cocks uncovers a form of "indigenous counter-sovereignty" in native traditions of political thought, particularly those of the Gitxsan people of the Pacific Northwest. Such a conception of anti-sovereign power surfaces in the Gitxsan oral tradition: "The ownership of territory is a marriage of the Chief and the land. Each Chief has an ancestor who encountered and acknowledged the life of the land. From such encounters came power. The land, the plants, the animals and the people all have spirit—they all must be shown respect. That is the basis of our law."[14] Importantly, the conception of democratic rule implicit in Gitxsan thought divorces democracy from territorial control. Power can never be over land because land itself is the source of power. If so, the idea of ruling oneself as a people over a given land breaks down because the line between land and the self that rules over it dissolves. If land is a source of power that generates the conditions of peoplehood in the first place, then the people who rule over the land cannot do so and continue to rule over themselves without contradiction. For when the line between land and collective self dissolves, the self is no longer an independent entity that stands over land but becomes subordinate to and dependent upon certain human and nonhuman relations that sustain a specific ecology of life. Understood in this way, democracy is not a relation of rule over others, land, and the self but a respectful cultivation of the relations that allow one to sustain a certain system of power premised upon a rich egalitarianism and the healthy acknowledgment of our interdependence upon an ecological system of relations.[15]

In this critique of democratic freedom qua popular sovereignty, Cocks draws on the work of indigenous critical theorist Taiaiake Alfred (Kahnawà:ke Mohawk), who also develops an idea of indigenous counter-sovereignty that conceives of democratic rule in terms of relationality and thick interdependence rather than self-mastery. Like Cocks, Alfred attributes the drive to domination in the Euro-American political tradition not to the inherent evil of white settlers but to "white society's understanding of its own power and relationship with nature."[16] Although he does not go this far, I would like to extend Alfred's critique of the coercive logic of sovereignty to the notion of popular sovereignty in democratic theory. To the extent that popular sovereignty requires a collective self that rules in its own name, it also requires a separation of self and other. If such notions of popular sovereignty also imply an insulated self untouched by the other that rules through the attainment of self-mastery, then there is little preventing the coercive logic of sovereignty from extending to the other that stands opposed to the democratic self.

In opposition to a notion of democracy oriented around popular sovereignty and collective self-mastery, a nonsovereign conception of democracy might draw from native political thought and styles of governance in order to rethink power on altogether different premises. Rejecting the desire for self-insulation and self-mastery, nonsovereign democracy is marked by a sense of justice involving the "restoration of harmony to the network of relationships" sustaining collective life. In nonsovereign democracy, justice might be "seen as a perpetual process of maintaining that crucial balance and demonstrating true respect for the power and dignity of each part of the circle of interdependency."[17] As long as democracy remains wedded to a notion of popular sovereignty conceived as a form of insulated self-control, it will be unable to fully extricate the tethered logics of democracy and dispossession.

The second aspect of the decolonial theory of democracy embraces a relational conception of democratic identity that avows the constitutive influence of indigenous political ideas on the Western democratic tradition as well as the productive role of relations of colonial domination in shaping democratic thought and culture. Rather than an insulated body of thought that originates in the West and then spreads to the colonial peripheries through Euro-American imperialism, modern democratic theory was the product of transcultural cross-pollination between both Western and non-Western traditions. Yet by relying on Eurocentric assumptions that treat modern democracy as the exclusive domain of North Atlantic cultures, dominant strains of democratic theory reject as illegitimate native political traditions while also masking "the West's role in subverting those traditions, particularly democratic ones."[18] Eurocentrism not only denies the productive influence of indigenous and non-European political traditions on modern

democratic thought; it also masks the destruction of those political traditions in the language of civilization, liberty, and progress.

In *The Invention of the Americas*, the Latin American philosopher Enrique
Dussel seeks to correct the Eurocentric stranglehold over political thought
by developing the notion of what he calls "transmodernity." The first step
in elaborating the idea of transmodernity involves cutting through colonial
myths of European modernity. Instead of seeing modernity as a political
and cultural configuration originating in Europe, Dussel introduces a
"world-encompassing paradigm that conceives modernity as the culture
incorporating Amerindia and managing a world-system." As such, Euro-
American democracy "does not exist as an independent, self-producing, or
self-referential entity, but as a part, as the center of the [colonial] system."[19]
The idea of transmodernity captures how modernity was a planetary phe-
nomenon rather than one that emerged solely out of Western Europe or
North America. For Dussel, modern political values are not to be rejected
(as in postmodernism), but should be understood as a global assemblage
composed of constitutive connections with Europe's colonial outskirts in
a center-periphery system. Put differently and more concretely, the legacies
of the conquest and colonization of the Americas are not ancillary to or
anomalous in the emergence of democratic modernity but are rather the
central productive process.

If the first step of transmodernity is negative and deconstructive, the second step involves a positive and reconstructive project centered on reclaiming
the traditions of colonized peoples that have been rendered invisible by the
interpretive colonization of meta-narratives of Euro-American modernity.
In transmodernity, Dussel writes, "the creative force does not come from
the interior of Modernity, but rather from its exteriority," from the colonial
peripheries of settlement and conquest. More than a negative and deconstructive form of critique, thinking from the perspective of transmodernity
involves the reconstructive task of reconceiving the ethical and political basis
of modernity. In thinking of modernity from a place other than Western
Europe and North America, transmodernity affirms that which is devalued
and rendered exterior to modernity.[20] Dussel's notion of transmodernity
forces us to fruitfully reread the history of modern democracy against the
enduring legacies of settler colonial domination. By attending to the constitutive role of settler colonialism in the creation of modern democratic norms
and values, we might open new interpretive spaces in which to rethink and
recover the productive influence of indigenous political thinking, the exterior

that has been cast outside the institutional and intellectual development of Euro-American settler democracy.

In this effort, Iris Marion Young has elaborated a similar idea of trans-modern democracy by rethinking the relational construction of democratic identity. Achieving justice in the present for indigenous peoples, according to Young, requires facing up to the task of undoing the historical legacies of colonialism by creating new systems of global and domestic democratic governance. Instead of a global system organized around state sovereignty, Young proposes a "model of governance based on decentered, diverse, democratic federalism."[21] Although correcting the historical injustice of settler colonialism is certainly an institutional project, it also has an interpretive aspect that requires rereading the history of modern democracy from the perspective of colonized actors whose agency has been disavowed in Eurocentric narratives. To the extent that democracy is seen not only as an institutional element of modern politics but also a facet of collective identity, decolonizing modern democratic identity requires rethinking the self in relation to the colonized other. In undertaking this rereading of democratic modernity, Young turns to transcultural narratives concerning the historical influence of the Iroquois Confederacy (Haudenosaunee) on American democratic republicanism.

In conventional Euro-American historical consciousness, history follows a linear pattern of progress where modern democracy emerges out of a savage, prehistorical state and eventually evolves into a flourishing political form that privileges political values of individual autonomy and popular sovereignty, as well as the destruction of aristocratic hierarchies. The concept of time in these narratives was universal and evolutionary, arraying all people and societies along the same process of linear, sequential development. To the extent that indigenous peoples figured into such an account, they existed merely as decaying civilizations that held onto North American territory "in the meantime," as Tocqueville put it. If American settlers are always-already modern, native peoples are de facto excluded as participants in the construction of modernity. Indigenous peoples are thus consigned to a premodern space and time outside modern democracy. While such stories include the complex histories of contact and conflict between natives and settlers, Euro-American thought and culture is understood as largely untouched by the influence of indigenous modes of governance.

Rather than a linear narrative of democratic modernity where modern values of liberty and equality originate in Europe and then emanate outward, the Iroquois "influence thesis" suggests that important elements of modern democracy found their most forceful expression not in the English colonies of Puritan New England, but in the political thinking of the Iroquois Confederacy. "Long before European settlers appeared at the shores of North America," Young writes, "five nations of the Iroquois—Mohawk, Oneida, Onondoga, Cayuga, and Seneca—formed a federation which espoused peace and brotherhood, unity, balance of power, the natural rights of all people . . . and the sharing of resources."[22] Insofar as it was based on principles of consent, noncoercion, public deliberation, federated decision-making, and the self-determination of constituent members of the nation, Iroquois governance was deeply democratic. Drawing on the work of Donald Grinde and Bruce Johansen, Young argues that Iroquois modes of federative governance had influenced the political thinking of the American founders and that American democracy can be considered a hybrid construction forged through intercultural contact.[23]

This influence of Iroquois ideas on the American founders was at times quite direct. At a treaty council in 1744, the Iroquois leader Canassatego advised English colonists to form themselves into a federative union modeled on the Iroquois confederation so as to ensure unity and strength. After reading the proceedings of the treaty council and other works on Iroquois government, Benjamin Franklin heeded this advice by designing the Albany Plan for colonial union, one of the first concerted attempts at fostering colonial unity among settlers.[24] In other instances, influence was more indirect. Enlightenment thinkers like Locke and Rousseau developed their notions of the state of nature and natural liberty through reading ethnographies and travel narratives about native peoples published by European explorers. Less a hypothetical stage of human development, the state of nature and the condition of freedom its inhabitants enjoyed was modeled on the political lives of Native Americans, who, as Locke wrote, lived in "a state of perfect freedom, to order their actions and dispose of their possession and persons as they see fit."[25] Drawing on these same images of native life in opposing British imperial authority, American settler thought was indirectly shaped through contact with native traditions, even as settlers expropriated indigenous land. Young writes, "The Enlightenment political philosophers that influenced the American founders to establish a democratic republic were themselves conditioned by real and imagined interaction with Native Americans."[26]

It is not my objective here to engage the debates among historians and political theorists about the interpretive validity of the influence thesis. Rather, my concern is how the influence thesis might contribute toward the decolonization of democratic theory by replacing modern meta-narratives of linear progress with more polyvocal narratives of transmodern democracy.[27] Young's reflections on the influence of Iroquois democracy—perhaps unbeknownst to her—have a long lineage in Iroquois political theory and oral histories. The influence thesis, for instance, centrally grounds the political thinking of Laura Cornelius Kellogg (Wisconsin Oneida), who was a pivotal and polemical intellectual figure (as well as founding member) of the Society of American Indians, a Pan-Indian movement that promoted transnational unity among Native Americans from 1911 to 1923. In her essay "Our Democracy and the American Indian" (1920), Kellogg promoted her own vision of democratic tribal governance and economic improvement for native peoples, which she called the "Lolomi Program of Self-Government."[28] The Lolomi Program drew on progressive principles to promote the restoration of economic self-sufficiency, native sovereignty, and traditional values to tribal communities.

Her transformative vision of indigenous democracy, however, started with an address to "the American people," which sought to foreground the vital dynamism of indigenous democratic traditions in North America. Kellogg began, "The idea of the League of Nations and Democracy originated on the American Continent about 600 years ago. It came from an American Indian."[29] Referencing the origins of the Iroquois Confederacy in the unifying actions of the Huron prophet Dekanawida (the Great Peacemaker), Kellogg then recounts the centrality of the League of Five Nations to the construction of modern American democracy. In this familiar story, upon hearing of the animating principles of the Iroquois Constitution, Franklin slammed his hand on the table, proclaiming it to be "the greatest wisdom I have heard among the nations of men." Based on this revisionist history, Kellogg confirms that the "great democratic principles" of the Iroquois Constitution laid the basis for the democratic commonwealth.

Yet more than simply a history lesson of intellectual curiosity, Kellogg's history represents a call for a renewal of democratic commitments and a reconstruction of American democratic peoplehood: "Without these bases for a commonwealth, Liberty is impossible. Without the spirit which promoted the first Awakener of the people to lay the foundations of American liberty, democracy is dead." The irony of ongoing forms of indigenous dispossession is not simply that white settlers have failed to extend their democratic principles equally to natives, but that those democratic principles were first developed by Native Americans themselves. Kellogg closes her address to the American people by asking, "Shall the American Indian who first conceived the democracy of this continent call for liberty in vain?"[30] To extend democratic principles to native peoples in the form of honoring treaty commitments and tribal self-government, Kellogg suggests, requires a fundamental historical revision of modern democratic thought.

In her history of the Iroquois Confederation, Kellogg divorces democratic time and space from Enlightenment meta-narratives where democratic norms and ideals originate in Europe and then emanate outward through international trade and imperial expansion. By foregrounding the positive contributions of the Iroquois and other indigenous peoples to modern democratic thought, both Kellogg and Young enlist the indigenous other as a constructive participant in the making of the modern world. Rather than as premodern societies that are vanishing with the further process of colonial settlement, indigenous democracies appear in transmodern narratives as disrupting the temporal flow of democratic development by placing the origins of American democracy not solely in European settlement but also in a pre-European, Native American modernity. Understanding democracy in light of transmodern rather than modern temporality forces us to rethink the very nature of democratic identity in relational terms. Young writes, "In this hybrid mode, when we think of American society and identity as a product of the interaction of Native and European cultures, the very meaning of being American becomes decentered and relational . . . such a relational and decentered notion of subjectivity and polity contributes to reconceptualizing self-determination and global governance."[31] In order to decolonize the democratic tradition, a nonsovereign and transmodern conception of democracy is essential to the reversal of legacies of colonial domination and the realization of native self-determination.

NOTES

Introduction: The Settler Colonial Foundations of Modern Democratic Thought

1. Scholarship on the colonial origins of American democracy focuses solely on one side of the colonial relationship. Although scholars readily acknowledge that colonial settlement had a profound impact on the subsequent development of democratic thought, they largely ignore that settlement also meant dispossession, displacement, and conquest. See Louis Hartz, The Liberal Tradition in America (Boston: Harcourt, 1955); Seymour Martin Lipset and Jason Lakin, The Democratic Century (Norman: University of Oklahoma Press, 2004); Daniel Elazar, Covenant and Constitutionalism: The Great Frontier and the Matrix of Federal Democracy (New Brunswick, NJ: Transaction Publishers, 1998); Gordon Wood, The Radicalism of the American Revolution (New York: Vintage, 1991); and J. S. Maloy, The Colonial American Origins of Modern Democratic Thought (New York: Cambridge University Press, 2008).

2. Michael Warner, "What's Colonial about Colonial America?," in Possible Pasts: Becoming Colonial in Early America, ed. Robert Blair St. George (Ithaca, NY: Cornell University Press, 2000), 49–50.

3. According to Ellen Meiksins Wood, it was Thomas More's Utopia (1516) that first brought the Roman concept of colonia back into English usage to refer to the settlement of foreign territories. More outlined the modern logic of colonialism in Utopia, in which the inhabitants of distant lands absorbed the surplus population of the metropole and send back their surplus profits to Utopia, making the arrangement beneficial for both settlers and the indigenous; Empire of Capital (New York: Verso, 2003), 74–75. Christopher Tomlins explains how More shifted discussions of empire from a focus on the conquest and discovery of unknown lands under the Spanish Empire to the creation of new English commonwealths on empty land; Freedom Bound: Law, Labor, and Civic Identity in Colonizing English America, 1580–1865 (New York: Cambridge University Press, 2010), 142. On the etymology of colonus, see Raymond Williams, Keywords: A Vocabulary of Culture and Society (New York: Oxford Press, 1985), 87.

4. Crèvecœur, Letters from an American Farmer (New York: Penguin, 1986), 43, 54.

5. Ibid., 108, 119.

6. Ibid., 42.

7. Jean-Jacques Rousseau, On the Social Contract (Indianapolis: Hackett, 1987), 40, 48.

8. William Connolly, Ethos of Pluralization (Minneapolis: University of Minnesota Press, 1995), 137–140.

9. Walter Benjamin, "Critique of Violence," in Reflections: Essays, Aphorisms, Autobiographical Writings (New York: Schocken Books, 1986), 277–300; Joan Cocks, "Foundational Violence and the Politics of Erasure," Radical Philosophy Review 15, no. 1 (2012): 103–126; and Cocks, On Sovereignty and Other Political Delusions (New York: Bloomsbury, 2014).

10. James Tully, Public Philosophy in a New Key: Volume 1, Democracy and Civic Freedom (New York: Cambridge University Press, 2008), 262.

11. Sheldon Wolin, for instance, argued that in liberal social contract theory the forgetting of past injustice serves as "a condition, perhaps even a precondition, of a certain form of society"; *The Presence of the Past: Essays on the State and the Constitution* (Baltimore: Johns Hopkins University Press, 1990), 36, 38; Ali Behdad, *A Forgetful Nation: On Immigration and Cultural Identity in the United States* (Durham, NC: Duke University Press, 2005).

12. Sibylle Fischer, *Modernity Disavowed: Haiti and the Cultures of Slavery in the Age of Revolution* (Durham, NC: Duke University Press, 2004), 37–38.

13. My focus on the politics of colonial disavowal distinguishes this work from others that have emphasized the formative influence of native conquest on American thought. In these accounts, settlers become American and construct their identity through conquest and frontier violence. For instance, Winthrop Jordan asserts, "Conquering the Indian symbolized and personified the conquest of the American difficulties, the surmounting of the wilderness. To push back the Indian was to prove the worth of one's own mission, to make straight in the desert a highway for civilization"; *The White Man's Burden: Historical Origins of Racism in the United States* (New York: Oxford University Press, 1974), 50. Also see Michael Paul Rogin, *Fathers and Children: Andrew Jackson and the Subjugation of the American Indian* (New York: Vintage, 1976); and Richard Slotkin, *Regeneration through Violence: The Mythology of the American Frontier, 1600–1680* (Norman: University of Oklahoma Press, 1973). Although I draw on these important works, I ultimately focus on a different set of ideological operations to uncover how the disavowal of indigenous peoplehood shaped democratic thought and culture. While Rogin and Slotkin emphasize the positive role of frontier violence in shaping American democratic identity, I focus on how narratives of native absence underpin democratic thought.

14. Edmund Morgan, "Slavery and Freedom: The American Paradox," *Journal of American History* 59, no. 1 (June 1972): 6; and *American Slavery, American Freedom: The Ordeal of Colonial Virginia* (New York: Norton, 1975).

15. Morgan, "Slavery and Freedom," 29. Morgan's analysis has given rise to an impressive and dynamic body of work in philosophy, political theory, and cultural studies. See David Roediger, *The Wages of Whiteness: Race and the Making of the American Working Class* (New York: Verso, 1999); Joel Olson, *The Abolition of White Democracy* (Minneapolis: University of Minnesota Press, 2004); Charles Mills, *The Racial Contract* (Ithaca, NY: Cornell University Press, 1997); and Alex Gourevitch, *From Slavery to the Cooperative Commonwealth: Labor and Republican Liberty in the Nineteenth Century* (New York: Cambridge University Press, 2015). Important precursors include C. L. R. James's *The Black Jacobins* (New York: Random House, 1963) and W. E. B. Du Bois's *Black Reconstruction in America* (New York: Free Press, 1992).

16. Jodi Byrd, *The Transit of Empire: Indigenous Critiques of Colonialism* (Minneapolis: University of Minnesota Press, 2011), xxiii. David Temin has also recently argued that narratives of civic/racial inclusion lead to the disavowal of the constitutive coloniality of the settler state, thereby casting indigenous peoples as needing incorporation into settler constitutional structures rather than as colonized subjects seeking decolonization;

"Custer's Sins: Vine Deloria Jr. and the Set-tler-Colonial Politics of Civic Inclusion," *Political Theory*, forthcoming and available at http://journals.sagepub.com/doi/abs/10.1177/0090591717712151.

17. Byrd, *Transit of Empire*, 135. Also see Kevin Bruyneel, *The Third Space of Sovereignty: The Postcolonial Politics of U.S.-Indigenous Relations* (Minneapolis: University of Minnesota Press, 2007).

18. Alyosha Goldstein, "Where the Nation Takes Place: Proprietary Regimes, Antistatism, and U.S. Settler Colonialism," *South Atlantic Quarterly* 107, no. 4 (Fall 2008): 833–861.

19. Uday Mehta, *Liberalism and Empire: A Study in Nineteenth-Century British Liberal Thought* (Chicago: University of Chicago, 1999); Jennifer Pitts, *A Turn to Empire: The Rise of Imperial Liberalism in Britain and France* (Princeton, NJ: Princeton University Press, 2005); Domenico Losurdo, *Liberalism: A Counter-History* (New York: Verso, 2011); Karuna Mantena, *Alibis of Empire: Henry Maine and the Ends of Liberal Imperialism* (Princeton, NJ: Princeton University Press, 2010); Richard Tuck, *The Rights of War and Peace: Political Thought and the International Order from Grotius to Kant* (New York: Oxford University Press, 1999); James Tully, *Public Philosophy in a New Key: Volume 2, Imperialism and Civic Freedom* (New York: Cambridge University Press, 2009); David Armitage, "John Locke, Carolina, and the Two Treatises of Government," *Political Theory* 32, no. 5 (October 2004): 602–627; and Barbara Arneil, *John Locke and America: The Defense of English Colonialism* (New York: Oxford University Press, 1996).

20. Mehta, *Liberalism and Empire*, 46; Dipesh Chakrabarty, *Provincializing Europe: Postcolonial Thought and Historical Difference* (Princeton, NJ: Princeton University Press, 2009), 8.

21. Jennifer Pitts, "Political Theory of Empire and Imperialism," *Annual Review of Political Science* 13 (2010): 217. A few notable exceptions here include a body of work exploring how settler colonization has shaped early American political development. See Tomlins, *Freedom Bound*; Daniel Hulsebosch, *Constituting Empire: New York and the Transformation of Constitutionalism in the Atlantic World, 1664–1830* (Chapel Hill: University of North Carolina Press, 2005); Paul Frymer, "Building an American Empire: Territorial Expansion in the Antebellum Era," *UC Irvine Law Review* 1 (2011): 913; Frymer, "A Rush and a Push and the Land Is Ours: Territorial Expansion, Land Policy, and U.S. State Formation," *Perspectives on Politics* 12, no. 1 (March 2014): 119–144; and Craig Yirush, *Settlers, Liberty, and Empire: The Roots of Early American Political Theory, 1675–1775* (New York: Cambridge University Press, 2011). The most powerful of these accounts is Aziz Rana's *The Two Faces of American Freedom* (Cambridge, MA: Harvard University Press, 2010).

22. For those who attempt to import the framework of liberal imperialism into the American context, see Maureen Konkle, "Indigenous Ownership and the Emergence of U.S. Liberal Imperialism," *American Indian Quarterly* 32, no. 3 (Summer 2008): 297–323; and Julian Go, *Patterns of Empire: The British and American Empires, 1688 to the Present* (New York: Cambridge University Press, 2011).

23. John Stuart Mill, "On Liberty," *On Liberty and Other Essays* (New York: Oxford University Press, 1991), 14–15.

24. John Stuart Mill, "Considerations on Representative Government," *On Liberty and Other Essays* (New York: Oxford University Press, 1991), 264–265, 454–455.

25. William Appleman Williams importantly distinguishes between

"settler colonialism" and "administrative colonialism" in which state officials are charged with ruling an indigenous society by formal or informal means rather than settling and populating a distant area; *Empire As Way of Life* (New York: Oxford University Press, 1980), 6–7.

26. Charles Maier, *Among Empires: American Ascendancy and Its Predecessors* (Cambridge, MA: Harvard University Press, 2009), 21. For this definition at work, also see Herfried Münkler, *Empires: The Logic of World Domination from Ancient Rome to the United States* (Cambridge, UK: Polity Press, 2007), 154–161.

27. Franklin Giddings, *Democracy and Empire* (New York: MacMillan, 1900), 3, 11. On Giddings, see Sandra Gustafson, "Histories of Democracy and Empire," *American Quarterly* 59, no. 1 (March 2007), 116–117.

28. Jason Frank, *Constituent Moments: Enacting the People in Postrevolutionary America* (Durham, NC: Duke University Press, 2009); Paulina Ochoa Espejo, "Paradoxes of Popular Sovereignty: A View from Spanish America," *Journal of Politics* 74, no. 4 (October 2012): 1053–1065; and Lisa Disch, "Democratic Representation and the Constituency Paradox," *Perspectives on Politics* 10, no. 3 (September 2012): 599–616.

29. Sheldon Wolin, Democracy Incorporated: *Managed Democracy and the Specter of Inverted Totalitarianism* (Princeton, NJ: Princeton University Press, 2008), 189.

30. Gerard Bouchard, *The Making of the Nations and Cultures of the New World* (Montreal: McGill-Queen's Press, 2008), 14; Louis Hartz, *The Founding of New Societies* (Boston: Houghton Mifflin, 1969).

31. Duncan Bell, "The Dream Machine: On Liberalism and Empire," in *Remaking the World: Essays on Liberalism and Empire* (Princeton, NJ: Princeton University Press, 2016), 47–48.

32. Mill, "Representative Government," 445. For a further exploration of this in Mill's writings, see Duncan Bell, "John Stuart Mill on Colonies," *Political Theory* 38, no. 1 (February 2010): 34–64. The distinction between these two types of colonies was a persistent feature of nineteenth-century British discourse on imperialism and colonialism. See Bell, *The Idea of Greater Britain: Empire and the Future of World Order, 1860–1900* (Princeton, NJ: Princeton University Press, 2009); and Tadhg Foley, "An Unknown and Feeble Body: How Settler Colonialism was Theorized in the Nineteenth Century," in *Studies in Settler Colonialism: Politics, Identity, and Culture*, eds. Fiona Bateman and Lionel Pilkington (New York: Palgrave MacMillan, 2011), 275.

33. This distinction first emerged in the work of D. K. Fieldhouse, *The Colonial Empires: A Comparative Study from the Eighteenth Century* (London: Weidenfeld and Nicolson, 1966). Also see George Fredrickson, "Colonialism and Racism: The United States and South Africa in Comparative Perspective," *The Arrogance of Race: Historical Perspectives on Slavery, Racism, and Social Inequality* (Middletown, CT: Wesleyan University Press, 1989).

34. Ian Tyrrell, "Beyond the View from Euro-America: Environment, Settler Societies, and the Internationalization of American History," in *Rethinking American History in a Global Age*, ed. Thomas Bender (Berkeley: University of California Press, 2002), 170; and James Belich, *Replenishing the Earth: The Settler Revolution and the Rise of the Anglo World, 1783–1939* (New York: Oxford University Press, 2011).

35. Mehta, in *Liberalism and Empire* (chapter 2), explains two strategies of

exclusion in liberal imperial ideologies. *Civilizational infantilism* portrays the anthropological capacities of colonial subjects as infantile and immature. *Historical inscrutability* involves a refusal to engage India in its own political, cultural, and social context.

36. Patrick Wolfe, *Settler Colonialism and the Transformation of Anthropology: The Politics and Poetics of an Ethnographic Event* (New York: Bloomsbury, 1999), 1–2.

37. Lorenzo Veracini, *Settler Colonialism: A Theoretical Overview* (New York: Palgrave MacMillan, 2010), 3.

38. Patrick Wolfe, "Settler Colonialism and the Elimination of the Native," *Journal of Genocide Research* 8, no. 4 (December 2006): 388.

39. Carole Pateman and Charles Mills, "The Settler Contract," in *Contract and Domination* (Cambridge, UK: Polity Press, 2007), 35–78; Jean O'Brien, *Dispossession by Degrees: Indian Land and Identity in Natick, Massachusetts, 1650–1790* (Lincoln: University of Nebraska Press, 2003).

40. Patrick Wolfe, "Race and the Trace of History," *Studies in Settler Colonialism*, 275; Jeffrey Ostler, *The Plains Sioux and U.S. Colonialism* (New York: Cambridge University Press, 2004), 15.

41. Quentin Skinner, "Meaning and Understanding in the History of Ideas," *Visions of Politics*, Vol. 1 (New York: Cambridge University Press, 2002).

42. Ellen Meiksins Wood, *Liberty and Property: A History of Western Political Thought from the Renaissance to the Enlightenment* (New York: Verso, 2012), 30.

43. It is necessary to clarify that despite this, my focus remains on dominant strains of democratic thought rather than the development of public policy. To be sure, US policy toward indigenous peoples embraced a broad range that at times exhibited modest support for native sovereignty through the treaty system to war and extermination. Nevertheless, my goal is not to make claims about the development of US policy but rather about how practices of colonization contextually shaped democratic thought. Richard Slotkin, *The Fatal Environment: The Myth of the Frontier in the Age of Industrialization, 1800–1890* (Norman: University of Oklahoma Press, 1985), 21.

44. Eric Foner, *Free Soil, Free Labor, Free Men: The Ideology of the Republican Party before the Civil War* (New York: Oxford University Press, 1971), 5; Alexander Saxton, *The Rise and Fall of the White Republic: Class Politics and Mass Culture in Nineteenth-Century America* (New York: Verso, 2003), 142. On the implications of this for political theory, see Richard Ashcraft, "Political Theory and the Problem of Ideology," *Journal of Politics* 42, no. 3 (August 1980): 687–705.

45. Joyce Appleby, *Liberalism and Republicanism in the Historical Imagination* (Cambridge, MA: Harvard University Press, 1992), 19.

46. Priscilla Wald, *Constituting Americans: Cultural Anxiety and Narrative Form* (Durham, NC: Duke University Press, 1995); Rogers Smith, *Stories of Peoplehood: The Politics and Morals of Political Membership* (New York: Cambridge University Press, 2003).

47. Mahmood Mamdani, "Settler Colonialism: Then and Now," *Critical Inquiry* 41 (Spring 2015): 608.

48. Marilyn Lake and Henry Reynolds, *Drawing the Global Color Line: White Men's Countries and the International Challenge of Racial Equality* (New York: Cambridge University Press, 2008).

49. Edward Said, *Culture and Imperialism* (New York: Alfred A. Knopf, 1993), 3.

50. For other possibilities, see Kennan Ferguson, "Why Does Political Science Hate American Indians?," *Perspectives on Politics* 14, no. 4 (December 2016): 1029–1038.

Chapter 1: From Colonial Dependence to Imperial Equality

1. On Arendt's neglected writings on federalism, see Samuel Moyn, "Fantasies of Federalism," *Dissent Magazine* (Winter 2015). Available at: http://www.dissent magazine.org/article/fantasies-of-fed eralism.

2. Hannah Arendt, *On Revolution* (New York: Penguin, 2006), 153. Also see Douglas Klusmeyer, "Hannah Arendt's Case for Federalism," *Publius: The Journal of Federalism* 40, no. 1 (Winter 2010): 35.

3. Hannah Arendt, *Origins of Totalitarianism* (Boston: Harcourt, 1976), 130–131. I am thankful to Michael Mosher for drawing my attention to this distinction.

4. Hannah Arendt, "Reflections on Little Rock," in *The Portable Hannah Arendt*, ed. Peter Baehr (New York: Penguin, 2003), 233.

5. Arendt, *On Revolution*, 168.

6. Ibid., 167, 194. Cocks, *On Sovereignty and Other Political Delusions*, 58–59.

7. Anders Stephanson, "An American Story? Second Thoughts on Manifest Destiny," in *Manifest Destinies and Indigenous Peoples*, eds. David Maybury-Lewis et al. (Cambridge, MA: Harvard University Press, 2009), 31.

8. There is now a growing literature examining the role of empire in the politics and thought of the American Revolution. The present work stands out among these works by using the framework of settler colonialism to clarify imperial discourses and self-conceptions of the revolutionary generation. Other important works include Karl Friedrich-Walling, *Republican Empire: Alexander Hamilton on War and Free Government* (Lawrence: University Press of Kansas, 1999); Mark Egnal, *Mighty Empire: The Origins of the American Revolution* (Ithaca, NY: Cornell University Press, 1988); Francis Jennings, *The Creation of America: Through Revolution to Empire* (New York: Cambridge University Press, 2000); Fred Anderson and Andrew Cayton, *The Dominion of War: Empire and Liberty in North America, 1500–2000* (New York: Penguin, 2005); Robert Kagan, *Dangerous Nation: America's Foreign Policy from Its Earliest Days to the Dawn of the Twentieth Century* (New York: Alfred A. Knopf, 2006); Patrick Griffin, *American Leviathan: Empire, Nation, and Revolutionary Frontier* (New York: MacMillan, 2008); David Hendrickson, *Union, Nation, or Empire: The American Debate over International Relations* (Lawrence: University Press of Kansas, 2009); and Eric Hinderaker, *Elusive Empires: Constructing Colonialism in the Ohio Valley, 1673–1800* (New York: Cambridge University Press, 1999).

9. Benjamin Franklin, "Observations Concerning the Increase of Mankind," *Autobiography and Other Writings* (New York: Cambridge University Press, 2004), 220.

10. John Adams to James Sullivan, *Works of John Adams*, vol. 9 (Boston: Little, Brown, 1850), 376–377.

11. Franklin, "Observations," 218, 220.

12. Benjamin Franklin to Lord Kames, January 3, 1760; *The Works of Benjamin Franklin*, vol. 3 (New York: G. P. Putnam's Sons, 1904), 248.

13. John Adams, "The Education of Mr. Adams" (1755), *Works of John Adams*, vol. 1, 23. See the final stanza of "Verses on the Prospect of Planting Arts and Learning in America" in George Berkeley, *The Works of George Berkeley*, vol. 2 (Boston: John

Exshaw, 1784): "Westward the course of empire takes its way / The four first acts already past / A fifth shall close the drama with the day / Time's noblest offspring is the last" (444).

14. G. W. F. Hegel, The Philosophy of History (New York: Colonial Press, 1899 [1837]), 86; Anders Stephanson, Manifest Destiny: American Expansionism and the Empire of Right (New York: Hill and Wang, 1995), 18.

15. Joel Barlow, Vision of Columbus (London: J. Stockdale, 1787), 169. Also see Jedediah Morse's The American Geography, 2nd ed. (London: J. Stockdale, 1792): "Besides, it is well known that empire has been traveling from east to west. Probably her last and broadest seat will be America" (469).

16. Benjamin Franklin, "Reasons and Motives for the Albany Plan of Union," in Autobiography and Other Writings, 238–241; Walter Lafeber, The American Age: United States Foreign Policy at Home and Abroad (New York: Norton, 1989), 14.

17. Thomas Pownall, The Administration of the Colonies, 3rd ed. (London: J. Dodsley, 1766), 3–10.

18. Ibid., 27–28, 202.

19. Jack Greene, Peripheries and Center: Constitutional Development in the Extended Polities of the British Empire and the United States, 1607–1788 (Athens: University of Georgia Press, 1986), 131. Blackstone asserted the supremacy of Parliament: "There is and must be a supreme, irresistible, absolute, uncontrollable authority, in which . . . the rights of sovereignty reside," Commentaries on the Laws of England, vol. 1 (Philadelphia: J. B. Lippincott, 1893), 48.

20. Pownall, Administration of the Colonies, 36.

21. Stephen Hopkins, "Rights of Colonies," in Pamphlets of the American Revolution, 1750–1776, ed. Bernard Bailyn

(Cambridge, MA: Belknap Press, 1965), 510–512, 519; Wolin, Presence of the Past, 129–130.

22. Max Savelle has noted that many colonial writers during the Imperial Crisis expressed a form of "imperial federalism" that integrated the political autonomy and internal sovereignty of the colonies into an imperial state by placing the colonies on a plane of equality with metropolitan legislatures; Empires to Nations: Expansion in America, 1713–1824 (Minneapolis: University of Minnesota Press, 1974), 28.

23. Pownall, Administration of the Colonies, 30–33, 54–55.

24. King George III, "Proclamation of 1763," in Documents of American History, vol. 1 (New York: F. S. Crofts, 1946), 47–50.

25. Robert Williams, The American Indian in Western Legal Thought: The Discourse of Conquest (New York: Oxford University Press, 1990), 234; Fred Anderson, The Crucible of War: The Seven Years' War and the Fate of Empire in British North America (New York: Random House, 2007), 535, 545; and Gary Nash, The Unknown American Revolution: The Unruly Birth of Democracy and the Struggle to Create America (New York: Penguin, 2006), 67–70.

26. Williams, The American Indian in Western Legal Thought, 238–241, 248–249.

27. Samuel Johnson, "Taxation No Tyranny," in Political Writings (Indianapolis: Liberty Fund, 2000), 419.

28. Blackstone, Commentaries on the Laws of England, vol. 1, 107–108.

29. Blackstone further wrote, "if an uninhabited country be discovered and planted by English subjects, all the English laws are immediately there in force. For the law is the birthright of every subject, so where they go they carry their laws with them;" quoted in Yirush, Settlers, Liberty, and Empire, 47. The implication is

that because conquest figured into the settlement of the colonies, settlers did not carry the rights ensured by the English constitution with them in the process of colonization.

30. In a related line of analysis, Yirush argues that the universalism of natural rights emerged in American thought not through abstract notions of humanity but in reference to settler colonization. By rejecting the geographic particularity of the common law and asserting a universal understanding of natural rights, Anglo settlers fit their ideas of natural rights into a framework of "transnational legal norms to justify European expansion into the New World"; "The Idea of Rights in the Imperial Crisis," *Social Philosophy and Policy* 29, no. 2 (July 2012): 101.

31. Yirush, *Settlers, Liberty, and Empire*, 16–18; Alison L. LaCroix, "The Labor Theory of Empire," *Common-Place* 12, no. 3 (April 2012). Available at: http://www.common-place.org/vol-12/no-03/reviews/lacroix.shtml.

32. Richard Bland, "The Colonel Dismounted," in *Pamphlets of the American Revolution*, vol. 1, 320; Michael Kammen, "The Meaning of Colonization in American Revolutionary Thought," *Journal of the History of Ideas* 31, no. 3 (July–September 1970): 344–345.

33. Bland, "The Colonel Dismounted," 174–175.

34. This understanding of transposable rights schemes rests on an understanding of new territory as *terra nullius*—land belonging to no one. *Terra nullius* does not mean that nobody is present in newly discovered lands, but more precisely that there were no political institutions analogous to modern European sovereignty. The assumption that European rights schemes are automatically

valid in newly settled territory implies a refusal to acknowledge the prior forms of governance existing in that space. On *terra nullius* see Robert Miller et al., *Discovering Indigenous Lands: The Doctrine of Discovery in the English Colonies* (New York: Oxford University Press, 2010).

35. Bland, "The Colonel Dismounted," 319. Anthony Pagden, *Lords of All the World: Ideologies of Empire in Spain, Britain, and France c. 1500–c. 1800* (New Haven, CT: Yale University Press, 1995), 77, 87.

36. Richard Bland, "An Inquiry into the Rights of the British Colonies," in *American Political Writings during the Founding Era: 1760–1805*, vol. 1, eds. Charles Hyneman and Donald Lutz (Indianapolis: Liberty Fund, 1983), 79.

37. Thomas Jefferson, "Summary View," in *The Works of Thomas Jefferson*, vol. 2 (New York: G. P. Putnam's Sons, 1904–1905), 84.

38. Williams, *The American Indian in Western Legal Thought*, 268–269.

39. Jefferson, "Summary View," 64–65.

40. Ibid., 64.

41. Kagan, *Dangerous Nation*, 32.

42. George Washington, *A Collection* (Indianapolis: Liberty Fund, 1988), 326. The centrality of settler ideology to the drive for separation can be better understood by comparing the thought of North American settlers to that of their West Indian counterparts. British colonists in the West Indies thought of themselves as being in "a land of exile, never as a place where they plan to live, prosper, and die." While West Indian colonists understood their position in plantation society as a transient state, North American settlers were "permanent, born in the country and attached to it; they have no motherland save the one they live in." The lack of a desire to create permanent settlements

prevented the revolutionary ethos from taking root in the British Caribbean; Andrew Jackson O'Shaughnessy, *An Empire Divided: The American Revolution and the British Caribbean* (Philadelphia: University of Pennsylvania Press, 2000), 3.

43. Edward Gibbon, *The History of the Decline and Fall of the Roman Empire*, vol. 1 (Dublin: William Hallhead, 1776), 13.

44. Thomas Paine, "Public Good," *The Writings of Thomas Paine*, vol. 2 (New York: G. P. Putnam's Sons, 1908), 34–35, 61.

45. US Congress, "Resolution on Public Lands" (October 10, 1780), *Journals of the Continental Congress*, vol. 18 (Washington, DC: Government Printing Office, 1980), 915.

46. James Tully, *Strange Multiplicity: Constitutionalism in an Age of Diversity* (New York: Cambridge University Press, 1995), 92.

47. James Madison, "Federalist #38," in James Madison, Alexander Hamilton, and John Jay, *The Federalist Papers*, ed. Isaac Kramnick (New York: Penguin, 1987), 253. Several land speculators accused Paine of having shares in the Indiana Company, suggesting that he wrote the pamphlet for self-interested reasons to open western territory to further speculation; Frederick Jackson Turner, "Western State-Making in the Revolutionary Era," *American Historical Review* 1, no. 1 (October 1895): 84–85. But as Philip Foner points out, the evidence for this claim is dubious because Paine's arguments would have equally undermined the claims of the Indiana Company; *The Complete Writings of Thomas Paine*, vol. 2 (Westport: Greenwood Press, 1945), 303.

48. Richard Young and Jeffrey Meiser, "Race and the Dual State in the Early American Republic," in *Race and American Political Development*, eds. Joe Lowndes,

Julie Novkov, and Dorian Warren (New York: Routledge, 2012), 40.

49. US Congress, "Resolution on Public Lands," 915.

50. Jefferson to Archibald Stuart (January 25, 1786), *Works*, vol. 5, 75.

51. "Ordinance for the Government of the Western Territory" (April 23, 1784), *The Documentary History of the Ratification of the Constitution*, ed. Merrill Jensen, vol. 1 (Madison: State Historical Society of Wisconsin, 1976), 151–153.

52. Quoted in Peter Onuf, *The Origins of the Federal Republic: Jurisdictional Controversies in the United States, 1775–1787* (Philadelphia: University of Pennsylvania Press, 1983), 44.

53. Stefan Heumann, "The Tutelary Empire: State- and Nation-Building in the 19th Century United States" (PhD dissertation, University of Pennsylvania, 2009).

54. US Congress, "Resolution on Public Lands," 915.

55. Paine also argued that bringing western land title under the Confederation government was necessary because settlers, as mere extensions of Virginia, would feel as though they were "aliens to the commonwealth" and thus dependent colonial entities lacking in national representation; Paine, "Public Good," 59, 65.

56. "Ordinance for the Government of the Territory of the United States Northwest of the River Ohio" (July 13, 1787), *Documentary History*, vol. 1, 172; Jack P. Greene, "The Imperial Roots of American Federalism," *This Constitution* 6 (1985), 4–11.

57. Gordon Wood, *Empire of Liberty: A History of the Early Republic, 1789–1815* (New York: Oxford University Press, 2009), 122. Robert Hill also aptly put the point when he argued that the "colonies were to be self-governing states in embryo";

"Federalism, Republicanism, and the Northwest Ordinance," *Publius* 18, no. 4 (Autumn 1988): 43.

58. Madison continues: "The denial of these principles by Great Britain, and the assertion of them by America, produced the revolution," *Writings of James Madison*, vol. 7 (New York: G. P. Putnam's Sons, 1900–1910), 373.

59. William Riker, *The Development of American Federalism* (Boston: Kluwer, 1987), 131.

60. "Northwest Ordinance," *Documentary History*, vol. 1, 174; Paul Finkelman, *Slavery and the Founders: Race and Liberty in the Age of Jefferson* (Armonk, NY: M. E. Sharpe, 2001), 37–38.

61. Tomlins, *Freedom Bound*, 516.

62. "Northwest Ordinance," *Documentary History*, vol. 1, 173.

63. Henry Knox, "Report on the Northwestern Indians" (June 15, 1789), *American State Papers: Documents, Legislative and Executive, of the Congress of the United States*, vol. 4, eds. Walter Lowrie and Matthew Clarke (Washington, DC: Gales and Seaton, 1832), 14.

64. Ibid., 13–14. Francis Paul Prucha, *The Great Father: The United States Government and the American Indians* (Lincoln: University of Nebraska Press, 1984), 31. On the use of law and purchase to dispossess natives of their land, see Stuart Banner's *How the Indians Lost Their Land: Law and Power on the Frontier* (Cambridge, MA: Harvard University Press, 2007); and Dorothy Jones, *License for Empire: Colonialism by Treaty in Early America* (Chicago: University of Chicago Press, 1982).

65. Henry Knox, "Report on Indian Affairs" (August 1787), *Journals of the Continental Congress*, vol. 33 (Washington, DC: Government Printing Office, 1904), 479–480; Kagan, *Dangerous Nation*, 88.

66. Knox, *American State Papers*, vol. 4, 257, 543–544; Reginald Horsman, *Race and Manifest Destiny: The Origins of American Racial Anglo-Saxonism* (Cambridge, MA: Harvard University Press, 1986), 106–107.

67. Washington, Letter to James Duane (September 7, 1783), *A Collection*, 265–266.

68. Ibid., 261.

69. Edward Gibbon Wakefield, *England and America: A Comparison of the Social and Political State of Both Nations* (New York: Harper & Brothers, 1834), 238.

70. The idea of "systematic colonization" was first developed by Hegel, which he contrasted with "sporadic colonization." While sporadic colonization was driven by the uncoordinated efforts of civil society, systematic colonization was coordinated by the state as a means of public relief. By colonizing unpeopled lands, industrial society might escape class conflict, leading to a higher ethical unity; *Elements of the Philosophy of Right* (New York: Cambridge University Press, 1991), 269; Gabriel Paquette, "Colonies and Empire in the Political Thought of Hegel and Marx," in *Empire and Modern Political Thought*, ed. Sankar Muthu (New York: Cambridge University Press, 2012).

71. Wakefield, *England and America*, 242.

72. Ibid., 248–254.

73. Foley, "An Unknown and Feeble Body," 15–16.

74. Wakefield, *England and America*, 254–255.

75. One notable point here is that Wakefield almost willfully neglects another important means of colonization: land appropriation. By depicting the land as empty, Wakefield relegates processes of conquest, dispossession, and expropriation to the margins of systematic colonization.

76. For the sake of brevity, I will focus here only on the process of disposing colonial land. Regarding the removal of people, Wakefield advocated for a program by which a national fund would help partially subsidize the emigration of settlers to the colony; *England and America*, 260–261, 294.

77. Ibid., 261–264.

78. Ibid., 269–270.

79. Ibid., 275.

80. Ibid., 266–267.

81. US Constitution, Article IV, Section 3; in *The Federalist Papers*, 498.

82. Wakefield, *England and America*, 195.

83. Wakefield, *A Statement of the Principles and Objects of a Proposed National Society, for the Cure and Prevention of Pauperism, by Means of Systematic Colonization* (London: James Ridgway, 1830), 4.

84. Wakefield, *England and America*, 322.

85. Ibid., 232–233.

86. Mill, "Considerations on Representative Government," 448–449. Although he placed questions concerning the government of colonies in a separate chapter from federal forms of government, Mill still understood the union of the colonies with Great Britain as "the slightest kind of federal union; but not a strictly equal federation."

87. Richard Garnett, *Edward Gibbon Wakefield: The Colonization of South Australia and New Zealand* (London: T. Fisher Unwin, 1898), 159.

88. John Arthur Roebuck, *The Colonies of England: A Plan for the Government of Some Portion of Our Colonial Possessions* (London: John W. Parker, 1849), 190–191, 194, 196.

89. Ibid., 14, 76.

90. Ibid., 90–91.

91. John Manning Ward, *Colonial Self-Government: The British Experience,*

1759–1856 (Toronto: University of Toronto Press, 1976), 211, 218. Duncan Bell has also shown that later architects of British colonial expansion in the late nineteenth century (e.g., John Seeley) turned to the United States for a model of "imperial federation" that linked autonomous settler states in a global federated system; *The Idea of Greater Britain*.

92. As Aziz Rana rightly argues, "Americans rarely think of themselves as part of an imperial family of settler polities and instead generally conceive of the country as quintessentially anti-imperial"; "Colonialism and Constitutional Memory," *UC Irvine Law Review* 5 (2015): 263–288.

93. Riker, *The Development of American Federalism*, 131. David Hendrickson similarly poses what he calls a "unionist paradigm" based on federalist principles to imperial frameworks; *Peace Pact: The Lost World of the American Founding* (Lawrence: University Press of Kansas, 2003).

Chapter 2: The Coloniality of Constituent Power

1. Arendt, *On Revolution*, 35.

2. Arendt, *Origins of Totalitarianism*, 126, 128, 137–138.

3. Arendt, *On Revolution*, 45–46.

4. My definition here draws on Edmund Morgan, *Inventing the People: The Rise of Popular Sovereignty in England and America* (New York: Norton, 1989), 81. Andreas Kalyvas helpfully distinguishes between two senses of sovereignty: the power to command, which is associated with constituted power; and the power of the people to constitute a new order, which is associated with popular sovereignty and constituent power; "Popular Sovereignty, Democracy, and the Constituent Power," *Constellations* 12, no. 2

(June 2005): 223–244. Also see Antonio Negri, *Insurgencies: Constituent Power and the Modern State* (Minneapolis: University of Minnesota Press, 1999).

5. Andreas Kalyvas, "Constituent Power," *Political Concepts: A Critical Lexicon* 3, no. 1 (Fall 2013). Available at: http://www.politicalconcepts.org/constituent power/.

6. I draw here on the work of Anibal Quijano, who develops the concept of "the coloniality of power" to clarify how interlinked systems of modern political and economic power rest on colonial logics: (1) the capitalist world-system; (2) the modern inter-state system; and (3) western philosophy and epistemology. Quijano focuses on how these distinct configurations of power rely on racial classifications for their basic material operation. I adapt this basic idea to focus on how the modern form of power known as constituent sovereignty similarly relies on geographic representations that deny the validity of native forms of governance. Quijano, "Coloniality of Power, Eurocentrism, and Social Classification," in *Coloniality at Large: Latin America and the Postcolonial Debate*, eds. Mabel Moraña, Enrique Dussel, and Carlos Jáuregui (Durham, NC: Duke University Press, 2008), 181–224.

7. Veracini, *Settler Colonialism*, 53.

8. Negri, *Insurgencies*, 2.

9. Willi Paul Adams, *The First American Constitutions: Republican Ideology and the Making of the State Constitutions in the Revolutionary Era* (Chapel Hill: University of North Carolina Press, 1980), 65.

10. Quoted in ibid., 65. Thomas Young, "To the Inhabitants of Vermont, a Free and Independent State, Bounding on the River Connecticut and Lake Champlain," reprinted in Zadock Thompson, *A History*

of Vermont, Natural, Civil, and Statistical (Burlington, VT: Chauncey Goodrich, 1842), 106.

11. Adams, *The First American Constitutions*, 93–94. For a brief history of Vermont's path to sovereign statehood, see Peter Onuf, "State-Making in Revolutionary America: Independent Vermont as a Case Study," *Journal of American History*, 67, no. 4 (March 1981): 797–815. Onuf explains that the Articles of Confederation exacerbated the problem for two reasons. First, they provided no mechanism by which new states and territories were to be admitted to the confederation. Second, the focus on the protection of territorial integrity in the Articles made it so that a recognition of Vermont's sovereignty would be a violation of New York's sovereignty.

12. Onuf, "State-Making in Revolutionary America," 802, 804.

13. Virginia Declaration of Rights, Article I (June 12, 1776), *The Avalon Project: Documents in Law, History, and Diplomacy*, Yale Law School. Available at: http://avalon.law.yale.edu/18th_century/virginia.asp.

14. Vermont Constitution, Article V, Chapter 1 (July 8, 1777), *The Avalon Project*. Available at: http://avalon.law.yale.edu/18th_century/vt01.asp. Pennsylvania Constitution, Article IV (September 28, 1776), *The Avalon Project*. Available at: http://avalon.law.yale.edu/18th_century/pa08.asp.

15. The following discussion builds off Adams, *The First American Constitutions*, 137–144.

16. Article VI, Chapter 1 of the Constitution of Vermont.

17. Preamble of the Constitution of Vermont.

18. Section XLIV, Chapter 2 of the Constitution of Vermont.

19. Article XVII, Chapter 1 of the Constitution of Vermont.

20. William Hill, *The Vermont State Constitution* (New York: Oxford University Press, 2011), 103.

21. In this regard, the emigration clause operates in a similar manner to the settler contract, which as Robert Nichols argues serves as an ideological fiction, rather than as a set of justificatory legal precepts that guide political practice, for imagining the foundations of modern society and concealing the foundational antinomies of liberal democratic societies founded in conquest, colonization, and usurpation; see "Realizing the Social Contract: The Case of Colonialism and Indigenous Peoples," *Contemporary Political Theory* 4, no. 1 (February 2005): 42–62.

22. Negri, *Insurgencies*, vi–vii.

23. Preamble of the Constitution of Vermont, *The Avalon Project*.

24. Locke, *Second Treatise of Government* (Indianapolis: Hackett, 1980), 55.

25. Ibid., 63–64.

26. Jimmy Casas Klausen, "Room Enough: America, Natural Liberty, and Consent in Locke's *Second Treatise*," *Journal of Politics* 69, no. 3 (August 2007): 760–769.

27. Locke, *Second Treatise*, 64–65.

28. Klausen, "Room Enough," 762.

29. Thomas Paine, "Common Sense," *Writings*, vol. 1, 69–70.

30. Ibid., 70–71.

31. Onuf, *The Origins of the Federal Republic*, 65–66.

32. Veracini, *Settler Colonialism*, 62.

33. Turner, "Western State-Making in the Revolutionary Era," 71.

34. Frederick Merk, *Manifest Destiny and Mission in American History* (Cambridge, MA: Harvard University Press, 1963), 4. Theodore Roosevelt, *The Winning of the West*, vol. 1: *From the Alleghenies to the*

Mississippi, 1769–1776 (New York: G. P. Putnam's Sons, 1889), 193.

35. Roosevelt, *The Winning of the West*, 166. Rogin, *Fathers and Children*, 87.

36. Roosevelt, *The Winning of the West*, vol. 1, 171.

37. Ibid., 183.

38. Ibid., 185.

39. There are no surviving copies of the Watauga Compact. The best source of information about the Watauga colony is the "Pioneer Petition to North Carolina" (August 22, 1776), S. G. Heiskell, *Andrew Jackson and Early Tennessee History* (Nashville: Ambrose Printing Company, 1920), 35.

40. Jean O'Brien, *Firsting and Lasting: Writing Indians Out of Existence in New England* (Minneapolis: University of Minnesota Press, 2010), xv.

41. "Pioneer Petition to North Carolina," 37.

42. Roosevelt, *The Winning of the West*, vol. 2: *From the Alleghenies to the Mississippi, 1776–1783* (New York: G. P. Putnam's Sons, 1896), 214, 342.

43. "The Cumberland Compact," *Andrew Jackson and Early Tennessee History*, 179.

44. Ibid., 180, 182, 183–184.

45. Ibid., 183.

46. Locke, *Second Treatise of Government*, 23, 52. Rogin, *Fathers and Children*, 87.

47. Declaration of Independence of the State of Franklin, in Samuel Cole Williams, *History of the Lost State of Franklin* (Boone: Watauga Press, 1924), 65.

48. Petition of the Inhabitants of the Western Country, in Williams, *History of the Lost State of Franklin*, 348.

49. North Carolina Constitution (December 18, 1776), *The Avalon Project*. Available at: http://avalon.law.yale.edu/18th_century/nc07.asp.

50. The Constitution of the State of

Franklin, in Williams, *History of the Lost State of Franklin*, 339.

51. Declaration of Independence of the State of Franklin, 65.

52. Frederick Jackson Turner, "Western State-Making in the Revolutionary Era, II," *American Historical Review* 1, no. 2 (January 1896): 267.

53. Quoted in Wood, *Empire of Liberty*, 120.

54. Washington Country Democratic Society, "Remonstrance to the President and Congress on Opening Navigation of the Mississippi River," *The Democratic-Republican Societies, 1790–1800: A Documentary Sourcebook of Constitutions, Declarations, Addresses, Resolutions, and Toasts*, ed. Phillip Foner (Westport: Greenwood Press, 1976), 127.

55. "Northwest Ordinance," 174. It is important to note here that although the Northwest Ordinance expressly dealt only with the disposal of land in the Northwest Territory, it immediately signaled to participants in the Constitutional Convention and settlers along the southern frontier a method for expanding the incipient constitutional republic. In 1790, Congress enacted the Southwest Ordinance, which replicated the features of the original land ordinance except for the provision banning slavery.

56. "Northwest Ordinance," 172.

57. Belich, *Replenishing the Earth*, 167–168.

58. Negri, *Insurgencies*, 156–157.

59. On the centrality of the Northwest Ordinance to eighteenth- and nineteenth-century state building, see Bethel Saler, *The Settlers' Empire: Colonialism and State Formation in America's Old Northwest* (Philadelphia: University of Pennsylvania Press, 2015); and Peter Onuf, *Statehood and Union: A History of the Northwest Ordinance* (Bloomington: Indiana University Press, 1987).

60. For Rufus King, the idea of "equal footing" was a "fundamental article of compact." Madison agreed, "If the Western States hereafter arising should be admitted into the Union, they ought to be considered as equals & as brethren"; *Records of the Federal Convention*, vol. 1, ed. Max Farrand (New Haven, CT: Yale University Press, 1911), 373, 541. Also see James Madison in "Federalist #14," *The Federalist Papers*, 143.

61. Madison, *Records of the Federal Convention*, vol. 2, 452.

62. Alexander Hamilton, "Federalist #1," *The Federalist Papers*, 87.

63. John Jay, "Federalist #2," *The Federalist Papers*, 91. In contrast, Arthur Schlesinger Jr. argues that the term "empire" in early American thought meant only sovereignty or rule and was lacking in expansionist connotations; *Cycles of American History* (New York: Houghton Mifflin, 1998), 137–138. For a thorough refutation of this position, see William Appleman Williams, "The Age of Mercantilism: An Interpretation of the American Political Economy, 1763–1828," *William and Mary Quarterly* 15, no. 4 (October 1958): 425–426.

64. Madison, Letter to Jefferson (August 20, 1784), *Writings*, vol. 2, 72.

65. Madison, Letter to Lafayette (March 20, 1785), *Writings*, vol. 2, 120.

66. Another important aspect of Madisonian and Jeffersonian visions of settler expansion was a republican political economy in which capitalist expansion posed an alternative to classical republican temporality marked by cyclical rise and decline. The ethical benefits of territorial expansion and colonization—i.e., individual independence and social equality—would accrue only if settlers

were linked in to larger commercial networks. In republican political economy, a system of agrarian capitalism in which farmers sold their surplus crops on market was the surest method of providing social equality and individual liberty, and hence, political stability. In this "hybrid republican vision," the American republic was to be virtuous and self-governing as well as commercial and free of external restraint, both of which were essential to forestalling corruption and instability; Drew McCoy, Elusive Republic: Political Economy in Jeffersonian America (Chapel Hill: University of North Carolina Press, 1980), 9–10, 237. Joyce Appleby has also shown that republican ideology in the Revolutionary era promoted a political economy of agrarian capitalism rather than one based on subsistence farming; "Commercial Farming and the 'Agrarian Myth' in the Early Republic," Journal of American History 68, no. 4 (March 1982): 833–849.

67. Quoted in Walter Nugent's Habits of Empire: A History of American Expansion (New York: Vintage, 2009).

68. Donald Pease, "American Studies After American Exceptionalism? Toward a Comparative Analysis of Imperial State Exceptionalisms," Globalizing American Studies, eds. Brian T. Edwards and Dilip Parameshwar Gaonkar (Chicago: University of Chicago Press, 2010), 64; Peter Onuf, Jefferson's Empire: The Language of American Nationhood (Charlottesville: University Press of Virginia, 2000).

69. This point was repeatedly made in Senate debates on the Louisiana Purchase, US Congress, "Objection to the Louisiana Purchase," in Issues of Westward Expansion, ed. Mitchel Roth (Westport, CT: Greenwood Press, 2002), 25.

70. Jefferson, Second Inaugural Address (March 4, 1806), Works of Thomas Jefferson, vol. 10, 131. Jedidiah Morse also drew on Jeffersonian logic in responding to fears that settlers moving west will be lost to the United States by either establishing their own independent republics or subsuming themselves into the Spanish, French, or British empires. He argued, in contrast, that there is very little substance to this risk if the western settlements are governed with the same principles of representation, liberty, and federalism as the eastern states. "The emigrants will be made up of citizens of the United States. They will carry along with them their manners and customs, their habits of government, religion and education." Morse made these assertions in the context of discussing the Northwest Ordinance, The American Geography, 467–468.

71. Jefferson, Letter to William Ludlow (September 6, 1824), Political Writings (New York: Cambridge University Press, 1999), 590–591.

72. Michael Shapiro, Deforming American Political Thought: Ethnicity, Facticity, and Genre (Lexington: University Press of Kentucky, 2006), 8.

73. Ibid., 10.

74. Tecumseh, Speech to W. H. Harrison, The Portable North American Indian Reader, ed. Frederick Turner (New York: Viking Press, 1977), 246.

75. Anthony Hall, American Empire and the Fourth World (Montreal: McGill-Queens Press, 2005), 423–424.

76. Black Hawk, Life of Black Hawk, or Ma-ka-tai-me-she-kia-kiak (New York: Penguin, 2008), 56.

77. Shapiro, Deforming American Political Thought, 10–11.

78. Black Hawk, Life of Black Hawk, 62.

79. Mark Rifkin, "Documenting

Tradition: Territoriality and Textuality in Black Hawk's Narrative," *American Literature* 80, no. 4 (2008): 684.

80. Jefferson to Kercheval (July 12, 1816), *Works*, vol. 12, 3.

81. Richard Drinnon, *Facing West: The Metaphysics of Indian-Hating and Empire-Building* (Norman: University of Oklahoma Press, 1997), 93–94.

82. Ibid., 92.

83. Jefferson, First Inaugural Address; *Works*, vol. 9, 194. Second Inaugural Address; *Works*, vol. 10, 133.

84. O'Brien, *Firsting and Lasting*, xxi–xxii, 52–53, 105.

85. Jefferson to Harrison (February 27, 1803); *Political Writings*, 525.

86. Jefferson, "Notes on the State of Virginia," *Political Writings*, 503.

87. Ibid., 475.

88. Catherine Holland, *The Body Politic: Foundings, Citizenship, and Difference in the American Political Imagination* (New York: Routledge, 2001), 39.

89. James Tully, *Public Philosophy in a New Key: Volume II, Imperialism and Civic Freedom*, 210–212.

90. Ibid., 37.

91. Ibid., 144–145.

Chapter 3: Colonial Dispossession and the Settler Social State

1. Alexis de Tocqueville, *Democracy in America* (Chicago: University of Chicago Press, 2000); Lipset and Lakin, *The Democratic Century*; Hartz, *The Liberal Tradition in America*.

2. For a similar set of reflections, see Kevin Bruyneel, "The American Liberal Colonial Tradition," *Settler Colonial Studies* 3, no. 3-04 (2013): 311–321.

3. Rana, *Two Faces of American Freedom*, 7.

4. Ibid., 14, 23.

5. Rogers Smith, "Beyond Tocqueville,

Myrdal and Hartz: The Multiple Traditions in America," *American Political Science Review* 87, no. 3 (September 1993): 549–566; and *Civic Ideals: Conflicting Visions of Citizenship in US History* (New Haven, CT: Yale University Press, 1999).

6. William Connolly, *Ethos of Pluralization*; Karena Shaw, *Indigeneity and Political Theory* (New York: Routledge, 2008).

7. Jennifer Pitts, *A Turn to Empire*, chapter 7.

8. Tocqueville, *Democracy*, 19.

9. Ibid., 23.

10. Ibid., 25–26.

11. Ibid., 26.

12. Ibid., 27.

13. Wolfe, *Settler Colonialism and the Transformation of Anthropology*, 165.

14. Henri Lefebvre, *The Production of Space* (Malden: Blackwell Publishing, 1991), 42.

15. Wolfe, "Settler Colonialism and the Elimination of the Native," 388.

16. Sherene Razack, *Race, Space, and the Law: Unmapping a White Settler Society* (Toronto: Between the Lines, 2002).

17. Mark Reinhardt, *The Art of Being Free: Taking Liberties with Tocqueville, Marx, and Arendt* (Ithaca, NY: Cornell University Press, 1997), 23. Also see Mark Rifkin, *Manifesting America: The Imperial Construction of U.S. National Space* (New York: Oxford University Press, 2009).

18. Alexis de Tocqueville, "Two Weeks in the Wilderness," *Democracy in America and Two Essays on America* (New York: Penguin, 2003), 887–888.

19. Ibid., 876.

20. In a few important instances, Tocqueville was mildly critical of the policy of Indian removal pursued by President Andrew Jackson. While the Spanish "pillaged the New World . . . without pity," the "conduct of the Americans of the United

States toward the natives . . . breathes the purest love of forms of legality." Rather than expropriating land directly by force and conquest, Americans "do not permit themselves to occupy their lands without have duly acquired them by means of a contract." If the Spanish have committed the most "monstrous deeds" in settling the new world, Anglo-Americans have achieved the same results "without spilling blood" and "without violating . . . the laws of humanity." Thus, even where he saw practices of removal at work, he asserted that they operated within the scope of legality rather than through a right of conquest; Tocqueville, *Democracy*, 325.

21. Ibid., 264, 267.

22. Pekka Hämäläinen, *Comanche Empire* (New Haven, CT: Yale University Press, 2009).

23. Tocqueville, *Democracy*, 392.

24. At the time of Tocqueville's writing, Russia under Nicholas I had possession of Alaska as well as other islands in the Pacific Northwest, and they had just recently rescinded claims to the Oregon Territory in 1824; Tocqueville, *Democracy*, 395–396. For a comparison of American and Russian expansion, see Jane Burbank and Frederick Cooper, *Empires in World History: Power and the Politics of Difference* (Princeton, NJ: Princeton University Press, 2011).

25. Tocqueville, "Two Weeks in the Wilderness," 880.

26. Tocqueville argued that democratic culture ran directly counter to the "spirit of conquest" and "warlike passions." Because the democratic social state diffuses property ownership, democratic citizens will be more "friendly to peace" so as to preserve political stability and their own material interests; *Democracy*, 617.

27. Ibid., 46.

28. Wolfe, *Settler Colonialism and the Transformation of Anthropology*, 1.

29. Tocqueville, *Democracy*, 53.

30. Ibid., 30, 43.

31. Ibid., 40.

32. Ibid., 32.

33. Ibid., 36–37.

34. Ibid., 30.

35. Ibid., 36.

36. Pateman and Mills, "The Settler Contract"; and Miller et al., *Discovering Indigenous Lands*.

37. Tocqueville, *Democracy*, 24–27.

38. Ibid., 267, 379.

39. Tocqueville quoted in Chad Goldberg, "Social Citizenship and a Reconstructed Tocqueville," *American Sociological Review* 66, no. 2 (April 2001): 294. Tocqueville, *Democracy*, 201, 607. On Tocqueville's place in the republican tradition regarding the relationship between property and liberty, see Eric Nelson, *The Greek Tradition in Republican Thought* (New York: Cambridge University Press, 2006), 239–244.

40. Tocqueville, *Democracy*, 223.

41. Sheldon Wolin, *Politics and Vision* (Princeton, NJ: Princeton University Press, 2004).

42. Williams, *Empire As Way of Life*, 4.

43. For example, see Smith, "Beyond Tocqueville, Myrdal and Hartz"; Stephen Frederick Schneck, "Habits of the Head: Tocqueville's America and Jazz," *Political Theory* 17, no. 4 (November 1989): 643–647; and Margaret Kohn, "The Other America: Tocqueville and Beaumont on Race and Slavery," *Polity* 35, no. 2 (Winter 2002): 169–193. One exception to this trend is Laura Janara, "Brothers and Others: Tocqueville and Beaumont, U.S. Genealogy, Democracy, and Racism," *Political Theory* 32, no. 6 (December 2004): 773–800. For Janara, Tocqueville and Beaumont treat Native Americans in

familial terms as inhabiting a different social state and African slaves as inhabiting the same social state as Anglo-Americans but in a subordinated position. My account here differs in emphasizing that these two distinct modes of racialization are rooted in different material regimes of domination.

44. Alexander Saxton, *The Rise and Fall of the White Republic.*

45. Joel Olson, *The Abolition of White Democracy.*

46. Charles Mills, *The Racial Contract.*

47. Tocqueville, *Democracy*, 303.

48. Ibid., 304.

49. Ibid., 305–306.

50. Patrick Wolfe, "Land, Labor, and Difference: Elementary Structures of Race," *American Historical Review* 106, no. 3 (June 2001): 866–905.

51. Tocqueville, *Democracy*, 305, 327.

52. Wolfe, "Settler Colonialism and the Elimination of the Native," 388.

53. Tocqueville, *Democracy*, 312–313.

54. Ibid., 321.

55. Ibid., 313, 26–27. Tocqueville drew on deep-seated liberal assumptions about the necessity of private property for democratic civilization and the inadequacy of customary land use and collective forms of property for modern forms of governance. A Lockean conception of labor is at the center of Tocqueville's views here: "The Indians occupied it [the land], but they did not possess it. It is by agriculture that man appropriates the soil, and the first inhabitants of North America lived from products of the hunt." On Locke's conception of property in relation to Indian forms of property, see James Tully, *An Approach to Political Philosophy: Locke in Contexts* (New York: Cambridge University Press, 1993). On the role that liberal conceptions of property played in the dispossession of Indians, see Rogin, *Fathers and Children*; and "Liberal Society and the Indian Question" in *Ronald Reagan, the Movie: And Other Episodes in Political Demonology* (Berkeley: University of California Press, 1987), 134–168.

56. Tocqueville, "Two Weeks in the Wilderness," 876.

57. Ibid., 876–877.

58. George Pierson, *Tocqueville and Beaumont in America* (New York: Oxford University Press, 1938), 231; Tocqueville, *Democracy*, 7.

59. Tocqueville, *Democracy*, 314.

60. On Tocqueville's positions on French colonialism, see Cheryl Welch, "Colonial Violence and the Rhetoric of Evasion: Tocqueville on Algeria," *Political Theory* 31, no. 2 (April 2003): 235–264; Roger Boesche, "The Dark Side of Tocqueville: On War and Emoire," *Review of Politics* 67, no. 4 (Autumn 2005): 737–752; and Richard Boyd, "Imperial Fathers and Favorite Sons: J. S. Mill, Alexis de Tocqueville, and Nineteenth-Century Visions of Empire," in *Feminist Interpretations of Alexis de Tocqueville*, eds. Jill Locke and Eileen Hunt Botting (State College, PA: Penn State Press, 2009), 225–252.

61. Jennifer Pitts, "Empire and Democracy: Tocqueville and the Algeria Question," *Journal of Political Philosophy* 8, no. 3 (September 2000): 311, 314; and *A Turn to Empire*, 247–250. Tocqueville to J. S. Mill; March 18, 1841, in *Selected Letters on Politics and Society* (Berkeley: University of California Press, 1985), 150–151.

62. For a full collection of these writings, see Tocqueville, *Writings on Empire and Slavery*, ed. Jennifer Pitts (Baltimore: Johns Hopkins University Press, 2001).

63. On Lieber's early influence on Tocqueville, see the latter's interview notes